THE NEW CLARENDON BIBLE

(NEW TESTAMENT)

General Editor: THE REVD. H. F. D. SPARKS, D.D., F.B.A.

PAUL'S LETTERS FROM PRISON

(EPHESIANS, PHILIPPIANS, COLOSSIANS, PHILEMON)

IN THE
REVISED STANDARD VERSION

Introduction and commentary

by

G. B. CAIRD, D.PHIL., D.D., F.B.A.

PRINCIPAL OF MANSFIELD COLLEGE, OXFORD

OXFORD
UNIVERSITY
PRESS
1976

Oxford University Press, Ely House, London W.1

OXFORD LONDON GLASGOW NEW YORK
TORONTO MELBOURNE WELLINGTON CAPE TOWN
IBADAN NAIROBI DAR ES SALAAM LUSAKA ADDIS ABABA
KUALA LUMPUR SINGAPORE JAKARTA HONG KONG TOKYO
DELHI BOMBAY CALCUTTA MADRAS KARACHI

PRINTED IN GREAT BRITAIN
BY BUTLER AND TANNER LTD
FROME AND LONDON

CONTENTS

INTRODUCTION   1
LITERATURE   7

THE LETTER TO THE EPHESIANS
Introduction   9
Analysis   29
Commentary   30

THE LETTER TO THE PHILIPPIANS
Introduction   95
Analysis   105
Commentary   105

THE LETTER TO THE COLOSSIANS
Introduction   155
Analysis   164
Commentary   165

THE LETTER TO PHILEMON
Introduction   213
Analysis   218
Commentary   218

INDEX   224

PUBLISHER'S NOTE

THE design of this volume follows that of the series, except that it has been decided to omit the biblical text, partly in the interests of economy, and partly in order to tie the notes less closely to the RSV and facilitate reference to other versions.

INTRODUCTION

I. THE PRISONER

The four letters, Ephesians, Philippians, Colossians and Philemon, have one feature in common which distinguishes them from the other letters of Paul. Their author calls himself a prisoner (Eph. 3^1; 4^1; Philemon. 1, 9) and refers to his bonds (Phil. $1^{7,13,14,17}$; Col. 4^{18}; Philemon. 10, 13; cp. Col. 4^3) or to his chains (Eph. 6^{20}). But are these words being used literally or metaphorically? Paul was fond of vigorous metaphor. He could call himself and others slaves of Jesus Christ (Rom. 1^1; 1 Cor. 7^{22}; Gal. 1^{10}; Eph. 6^6; Phil. 1^1; Col. 4^{12}) and refer to his colleagues as fellow slaves (Col. 1^4; 4^7), although we know that he was proud of being a free man and a Roman citizen (Acts 22^{28}). We have no reason to suppose that he had ever borne arms, yet he can speak of the Christian warfare (Eph. 6^{12}) and of his colleagues as fellow soldiers (Phil. 2^{23}; Philem. 2), or even as fellow prisoners-of-war (Rom. 16^7; Col. 4^{10}; Philem. 23). Thus, when he describes himself as 'prisoner of Christ Jesus', and tells Philemon that he would have liked Onesimus to stay and look after him 'in the bonds of the gospel' (Philem. 9, 13), he is clearly using a similar metaphor; and, if these passages stood alone, there would be nothing to suggest that they involved a literal imprisonment. On the other hand, the meta-phorical nature of these phrases does not exclude the literal. Whenever Paul was in prison, as he often was, it was because he was Christ's man; and he could be putting the best con-struction on his shackles by seeing in them the symbols of his captivity to Christ, just as elsewhere he regards the scars left by many floggings as 'the marks of Jesus branded on my body' (Gal. 6[17]; cp. 2 Cor. 11[24-25]). He can also tell slaves to transform their menial status by looking on themselves as 'slaves of Christ' (Eph. 6[6]).

There are convincing reasons for believing that Paul was actually in prison at the time of writing each of these letters. (1) He describes Onesimus as his 'child, begotten in my bonds' (Philem. 10). If the bonds were merely figurative, these words could apply to any of his converts, since he had been in captivity to Christ ever since his own conversion (cp. Gal. 4[19]). But Paul clearly has a special affection for Onesimus because of the peculiar circumstances in which he had become a Christian. (2) Paul tells Philemon and his family that he hopes to be granted to them in answer to their prayers (v. 22). This is hardly the way he would speak if he were in control of his own movements. (3) He asks the church at Colossae to remember his bonds (4[18]). He can scarcely be asking them not to forget that he is in the service of Christ. (4) He tells the church at Philippi that it is common knowledge to the *praetorium* and other pagan neighbours that his bonds are for the cause of Christ (1[13]). This can only mean that, while his bonds themselves are obvious to all, the reason for them has but gradually come to be recognized. (5) 'An ambassador in chains' would be a harsh, almost unintelligible, mixed metaphor unless the chains were intended to be literal (Eph. 6[20]).

For these reasons there is general agreement that Paul was in prison when he wrote these letters, and that he was using the word 'prisoner' on two levels at the same time.

2. THE PRISON

From what prison or prisons, then, were the letters written? On the evidence of the personal names they have in common Colossians and Philemon certainly belong together, and Ephesians (if Paul wrote it) is as decisively linked to Colossians by similarities of content and style; but Philippians could have been written from a different prison. What we are looking for in each case is a period of imprisonment long enough to allow for visits of friends from a considerable distance and later (in the case of Philippians much later) than the foundation of the churches addressed. We know from Acts that Paul was in prison for two years in Caesarea (24[27]) and for a further two years in Rome (28[30]). In a letter written before either of these imprisonments Paul himself mentions numerous other occasions when he had been in prison (2 Cor. 11[23]), but none of these is likely to meet both our requirements, unless we suppose that he had a long spell in prison during his three year stay in Ephesus (Acts 20[31]). He tells us that he had fought with wild beasts in Ephesus (1 Cor. 15[32]), and, although this cannot be taken literally, since Roman citizens were not exposed to mortal danger in a provincial arena, it must be taken seriously. He also refers to a time near the end of his stay in the province of Asia when he nearly lost his life (2 Cor. 1[8]). This is not strong evidence for an Ephesian imprisonment, but we must at least add Ephesus to the list of possibilities.

The traditional assumption was that all four letters were written from Rome, and this is still the opinion of the majority of scholars. Among recent writers only Lohmeyer has argued for Caesarea. Of those who believe in an Ephesian imprisonment, some have thought that all the letters were written from there (with or without Ephesians), some that Philippians was written from Ephesus and the others from Rome, some that Philippians was written from Rome and the others from Ephesus; and this very divergence of opinion has done much to undermine their case. The verdict depends on the weight we give to the following points.

(a) In Philippians Paul mentions the *praetorium*, which means either the Praetorian Guard or a palace (1[13]), and Caesar's household (4[22]). Both are most naturally located in Rome. But it cannot be denied that detachments of the Praetorian Guard and members of the imperial household were sometimes stationed in provincial centres of administration, or that *praetorium* was the name given to Government House, the official residence of a provincial governor (cp. John 18[28]; Acts 23[35]).

(b) The distance from Rome to Philippi was over 800 miles, including at least two days on a boat crossing from Brundisium to either Dyrrachium or Aulona; and to Colossae it was a further 400 miles, including at least three days on a boat from Neapolis to Troas. On the other hand, from Ephesus the journey by sea to Philippi could be done in under a week; and to Colossae the distance was very little over 100 miles. The travelling implied in the imprisonment epistles would have been simpler if Paul was at Ephesus than if he was at Rome. Epaphroditus had come from Philippi to Paul's place of imprisonment, word had reached home that he was ill, and he had heard that they were worried (Phil. 2[25-26]); and now Paul proposed to send him home. Epaphras and Onesimus had come from Colossae quite independently of one another, Onesimus was to be sent back with Tychicus, and Paul himself intended to follow as soon as he could (Col. 1[8]; 4[7-12]; Philem. 12). But this argument is not as impressive as it at first seems. The affair of Epaphroditus involved less travel than is commonly supposed (see notes). A runaway slave might well be expected to put as much distance between himself and his master as he could. And in any case there was a vast amount of travel along the Roman roads, undeterred by distance or delay.

(c) It has been argued that these letters cannot have been written after Romans, since Paul's own plans (Phil. 2[24]; Philem. 22) conflict with his intention, declared in Romans 15[23-24], of going on from Rome to Spain. But after four and a half years in custody it would scarcely be surprising if Paul abandoned all hope of opening up an entirely new mission field. Besides, his proposals to return to Philippi or Colossae look as though they were made more to bolster his readers' morale than with any real confidence in his acquittal.

(d) 1 and 2 Corinthians, Galatians and Romans were written during or shortly after Paul's long stay in Ephesus. Colossians and Ephesians are different from these letters of the central period both in style and in theology; and these differences could be accounted for in part at least by a gap of over four years. Philippians, on the other hand, seems in some respects closer to the central period letters than to Colossians and Ephesians. This consideration, however, is balanced by another. Phil. 2^{17} is echoed in 2 Tim. 4^6. If, as seems probable, 2 Tim. 4$^{6-8}$ is a genuine fragment of Paul's farewell letter to Timothy, then Philippians must be regarded as Paul's last complete letter to survive. The death sentence half expected in Philippians has in 2 Timothy become an accepted fact.

(e) Three of the letters of the central period show a deep pre-occupation with the collection Paul was organizing for the church of Jerusalem (1 Cor. 16$^{1-4}$; 2 Cor. 8–9; Rom. 15$^{25-28}$). It is almost incredible that during this period he would have accepted a private gift of money for his own needs from Philippi; and it is unlikely that he would have failed to mention the collection in any letter he then wrote, unless it was, like Galatians, written under the stress of overpowering emotion.

(f) We do not actually know that Paul was ever in prison at Ephesus, or, if he was, that he would have been allowed to receive visitors, as at Rome. The letters envisage something more serious than protective custody (Phil. 1$^{20-24}$; Philem. 22). Luke, who was with Paul when he wrote Colossians and Philemon (Col. 4^{14}; Philem. 24), records no Ephesian imprisonment in Acts. He probably was not with Paul in Ephesus. If he had known of an imprisonment in Ephesus, especially one on a capital charge, which ended in acquittal, he would surely have recorded it in the interests of his apologetic purpose.

(g) In Phil. 1$^{20-24}$ Paul is facing a possible death sentence, and declares that, if he had the choice, he does not know which way he would wish the verdict to go. But against any verdict of a provincial governor in Ephesus or Caesarea he knew that he could as a last resort appeal to the Emperor (Acts 25:11).

Whatever choice we make, there will be outstanding problems. But the view which still commands the most widespread support is that all the references to imprisonment are most satisfactorily interpreted as references to a single prison, and that the balance of probability rests with Rome.

LITERATURE

T. K. ABBOTT, *A Critical and Exegetical Commentary on the Epistles to the Ephesians and to the Colossians*, International Critical Commentary, 1897.

K. BARTH, *The Epistle to the Philippians*, 1962.

F. W. BEARE, *The Epistle to the Ephesians*, Interpreter's Bible, 1953.

F. W. BEARE, *The Epistle to the Philippians*, Black's New Testament Commentaries, 1959.

F. W. BEARE, *The Epistle to the Colossians*, Interpreter's Bible, 1955.

M. DIBELIUS, *An die Kolosser, Epheser. An Philemon*, Handbuch zum Neuen Testament, 1927.

J. L. HOULDEN, *Paul's Letters from Prison*, Pelican New Testament Commentaries, 1970.

G. JOHNSTON, *Ephesians, Philippians, Colossians, and Philemon*, Century Bible, 1967.

J. C. KIRBY, *Ephesians, Baptism, and Pentecost*, 1968.

J. KNOX, *The Epistle to Philemon*, Interpreter's Bible, 1955.

J. B. LIGHTFOOT, *Saint Paul's Epistle to the Philippians*, 1868.

J. B. LIGHTFOOT, *Saint Paul's Epistles to the Colossians and to Philemon*, 1875.

E. LOHMEYER, *Kyrios Jesus: eine Untersuchung zu Phil. 2, 5–11*, 1928.

E. LOHMEYER, *Die Briefe an die Philipper, an die Kolosser und an Philemon* (revised ed.), 1964.

R. P. MARTIN, *Carmen Christi: Philippians ii, 5–11*, Society for New Testament Studies, Monograph Series 4, 1967.

C. MASSON, *L'Epitre de Saint Paul aux Ephesians*, 1953.

8

J. H. MICHAEL, *The Epistle of Paul to the Philippians*, Moffat New Testament Commentary, 1928.

C. L. MITTON, *The Epistle to the Ephesians*, 1951.

C. F. D. MOULE, *The Epistles to the Colossians and to Philemon*, Cambridge Greek Testament, 1957.

E. PERCY, *Die Probleme der Kolosser- und Epheser-briefe*, 1946.

J. A. ROBINSON, *St. Paul's Epistle to the Ephesians*, 1903.

H. SCHLIER, *Der Brief an der Epheser*, 1962.

E. F. SCOTT, *The Epistles of Paul to the Colossians, to Philemon, and to the Ephesians*, Moffatt New Testament Commentary, 1930.

E. F. SCOTT, *The Epistle to the Philippians*, Interpreter's Bible 1955.

E. K. SIMPSON and F. F. BRUCE, *The Epistles of Paul to the Ephesians and to the Colossians*, New London Commentary, 1957.

M. R. VINCENT, *A Critical and Exegetical Commentary on the Epistles to the Philippians and to Philemon*, International Critical Commentary, 1897.

THE LETTER TO

THE EPHESIANS

INTRODUCTION

I . DESTINATION

In the Greek manuscripts which have come down to us from
the third and fourth centuries (p⁴⁶, B and ℵ) the Pauline
epistles have been supplied with titles: 'to the Romans', 'to the
Galatians', 'to the Ephesians' etc. The uniformity of the titles
shows that they must have been added by second century
scribes after the letters had been collected into a corpus. The
only letter which contains nothing to justify its title is Ephesians. For the words 'in Ephesus', which are found at 1^1 in all
later manuscripts, are missing from these early ones, and also
from early patristic quotations of the verse; and we have from
Basil (*Adv. Eunom.* ii. 19) an explicit statement, written about
A.D. 370, that they were omitted by the oldest authorities
known to him. It is in any case incredible that this letter should
have been written to the church at Ephesus, for it is wholly
devoid of personal greeting and reference, and Paul spent longer
at Ephesus than at any other place he visited on his missionary
travels. If, as seems likely, Romans 16 was originally a separate
note, written not to Rome but to Ephesus, as a letter of introduction for the deacon Phoebe, its long list of affectionate greetings shows us what might be expected in a letter from Paul to a
church he knew better than any other. The traditional title was

probably an uncritical guess, based on the combination of Eph. 6²¹⁻² with 2 Tim. 4¹² ('Tychicus I have sent to Ephesus').

To whom then was this letter written? Could it possibly be the letter to Laodicea mentioned in Col. 4¹⁶? This was the opinion of Marcion (see Tertullian, *Adv. Marc.* v. 17), and his early date (*c.* A.D. 140) gives some weight to his evidence. It has been conjectured that it was the ill repute of Laodicea, reflected in Rev. 3¹⁴⁻²², that caused later scribes to supply the epistle with a more respectable name. On the other hand, Marcion could simply have been drawing conclusions from Col. 4¹⁶ and from the obviously close relationship between Colossians and Ephesians. But the decisive point again is that, although Paul was not personally known to the church in Laodicea, he had at least one close friend there to whom he might have been expected to send a greeting (Col. 4¹⁵).

Another possibility is that Ephesians was a circular letter, addressed to many churches, perhaps with a blank space left in the address to be filled in by the courier. If we retain the tradition of Pauline authorship (see below), we shall certainly have to argue that the letter was some sort of encyclical, in order to explain the absence of personalia. But the theory of a blank space has little to commend it. There is scanty evidence for the use of such a device in ancient times[1] and much evidence to the contrary (Galatians and 1 Peter, for example, are circular letters). There is no manuscript evidence that any other name ever stood in any textual tradition. A more important point is the awkwardness of the syntax if any place-name is included. For τοῖς οὖσιν ἐν Ἐφέσῳ καὶ πιστοῖς ('who are in Ephesus and faithful') is a syllepsis or zeugma (a linking by a single word of two words or phrases which are differently related to it), and this is a solecism which neither Paul nor a disciple of Paul was likely to make. It has been argued that the harshness remains even in the shorter text adopted by the RSV, but I have suggested in the notes a way in which this shorter, and undoubtedly correct, text may be idiomatically construed.

[1] But see G. Zuntz, *The Text of the Epistles*, p. 228.

For those who think that the letter was not by Paul the problem of destination hardly arises, since a pseudonymous letter need not have been sent to anyone, and any address it contained would be merely part of its cloak of pseudonymity. But those who consider the case against Pauline authorship unproven are under a pressing necessity of discovering a historical setting in which such a letter could conceivably have been written. It was clearly written to Gentile Christians (2^{11}; 3^1), in churches not founded by Paul (3^{2-3}; cp. Col. 2^1), in order to impress upon them their unity with all other Christians, Jewish Christians included, in the one church, and to make them acquainted with Paul's special insight into the scope of the redemptive purpose of God and the place of special privilege he held within the Gentile mission as a whole. H. Chadwick[2] has made the interesting suggestion that the purpose of the encyclical letter was to bring the whole Gentile mission under the aegis of Paul's sole apostleship. For, though there were many missionaries to the Gentiles, working independently of Paul (1 Cor. 9^5), there was only one apostle of the Gentiles. Paul believed that by the direct commission of Christ and by the agreement of the Jerusalem 'pillars' he held the same unique position in the mission to the Gentiles as Peter held in the mission to the Jews (Gal. 2^{7-9}; cp. 1 Cor. 3^{10}; Rom. 1^5; 12^3; 15^{15-16}). Others might carry on the work of evangelism, and Paul was scrupulously careful not to trespass in another man's territory (2 Cor. 10^{13-16}; Rom. 15^{20}). but he alone held the quasi-priestly responsibility of offering the faith of the Gentile world to God, adding if need be the libation of his own surrendered life (Rom. 15^{16}; Phil. 2^{17}; 2 Tim. 4^6).

2. AUTHORSHIP

Ephesians claims to be by Paul, not only in the two verses which mention his name (1^1; 3^1), but in the whole tenor of its composition. Until the beginning of the nineteenth century

[2]'Die Absicht des Epheserbriefes', *Zeitschrift für die Neutestamentliche Wissenschaft* li (1960), pp. 145–153.

this claim went unchallenged. The epistle was certainly known to Ignatius (*c.* A.D. 115), Polycarp, and Hermas, and probably known to Clement of Rome (*c.* A.D. 97), though the inexact manner of his allusions to New Testament writings makes it hard to be certain.[3] It was accepted as Pauline by Marcion, Irenaeus (*Adv. Haer.* V. ii. 3; cp. I. viii. 5), the Muratorian Canon, and Clement of Alexandria (*Strom.* iv. 65; *Paed.* i. 18). The internal evidence appears on the face of it to support this unanimous external attestation. No one has ever questioned that the fundamental ideas of the epistle are Pauline, or that the grandeur and originality of its thought are fully worthy of Paul at the highest stretch of his genius. J. A. Robinson (p. vii) went so far as to call it 'the crown of St. Paul's writings'.

Yet for the past 150 years Ephesians has come more and more to be regarded as a problem. It is unlike any of the other letters of Paul, in spite of its superficial resemblance to Colossians. It is a general letter, not addressed to the particular circumstances and affairs of communities known either through personal contact or by the report of friends. In addition to this a great variety of reasons have been advanced to show that it cannot be accepted as an authentic letter of Paul: its language and style are not Pauline, it reflects a period of history later than the lifetime of Paul, it lacks many distinctively Pauline ideas and includes others not paralleled in the genuine letters, and, above all, it has literary relationships with the other letters, and particularly with Colossians, which betray the hand of the imitator. These arguments are neither so trivial that they can be disregarded nor so conclusive as to command general assent. Scholarly opinion still remains deeply divided. It is impossible here to do more than sum up the debate, and

[3]For the most thorough and careful assessment of the evidence see *The New Testament in the Apostolic Fathers* by a committee of the Oxford Society of Historical Theology. On Ignatius see also H. Rathke, *Ignatius von Antiochien und die Paulusbriefe*, which strongly implies that Ignatius regarded Ephesians as Pauline, though Rathke himself does not draw this inference.

for further study reference should be made to the protagonists on either side.[4]

There are five types of evidence which have been thought fatal to the tradition of Pauline authorship, and we must examine each of them briefly in turn.

Vocabulary

(a) Ephesians contains 42 words which are not found elsewhere in the New Testament and 52 others which are not used in other Pauline epistles. These figures, however, like most bare statistics, are misleading. Seven of the words occur in Old Testament quotations or references, so that they are only indirectly a part of the author's vocabulary; six are compounds of $\sigma\upsilon\nu$-, of which Paul was very fond, even to the point of coining new ones (he uses 64 in his other letters, of which 43 occur in one letter only); and 14 are cognates of words which Paul does use elsewhere. But even if we were to take the whole list as it stands, it is no argument against Pauline authorship. The average per page of words occuring in one letter only is: Galatians—10·3; Ephesians—10·6; 1 Corinthians—11·1; 2 Corinthians—12; Philippians—12·7.[5]

(b) Among these unusual words or phrases two have been thought particularly significant: the phrase 'in the heavenlies' (($\dot{\epsilon}\nu$ $\tau o \hat{\imath} s$ $\dot{\epsilon}\pi o\upsilon\rho\alpha\nu\acute{\iota}o\iota s$), which Ephesians uses five times; and

[4]For the arguments against Pauline authorship see J. Moffatt, *Introduction to the Literature of the New Testament*, 3rd edition (1918) pp. 375ff.; E. J. Goodspeed, *The Key to Ephesians*, (1956); C. L. Mitton, *The Epistle to the Ephesians* (1951); C. Masson, *L'Épitre de saint Paul aux Ephesians* (1953); G. Johnston in *The Interpreter's Dictionary of the Bible*, Vol. II, pp. 108–114 (1962); P. N. Harrison, *Paulines and Pastorals* (1964). The best defence of Pauline authorship is E. Percy's *Die Probleme der Kolosser- und Epheser-briefe* (1946). There is no full-scale defence in English to meet the case presented by Goodspeed and Mitton, but a good short one can be found in D. Guthrie's *The Pauline Epistles* (1961), pp. 99–128. An excellent survey of the whole debate is provided by J. C. Kirby, *Ephesians, Baptism and Pentecost*. pp. 3–56.

[5]P. N. Harrison's figures. See *The Problem of the Pastoral Epistles*, p. 23.

the double mention of the devil ($\delta\iota\acute{a}\beta o\lambda os$)), whom Paul else-where always calls Satan. But it is characteristic of Paul to get a word or phrase on the brain and to use it repeatedly in one letter only. In Romans he six times asks the question, 'What then shall we say?' In 1 Corinthians he uses $\dot{a}\nu a\kappa\rho\acute{\iota}\nu\epsilon\iota\nu$ ten times in three different senses. The repeated reference to the heavenlies in Ephesians is part of a more general preoccupation of the epistle with the exaltation of Christ and his gift of the Spirit and ought not to be treated in isolation (see below). As for the devil, it is hardly fair to say, as Johnston does, that $\delta\iota\acute{a}\beta o\lambda os$ is post-Pauline. It is the regular translation of the Hebrew *Satan* in the Septuagint (the Greek Old Testament), and would therefore be the natural word for Paul to use in a letter directed mainly, if not wholly, to Gentile Christians. Moreover, the injunction to resist the devil (Eph. 4[27]; 6[11]; cp. Jas. 4[7] 1 Pet. 5[8]) was one of the themes of the common catechetical tradition of hellenistic Christianity, which under-lies the whole pattern of ethical teaching in Ephesians;[6] and this influence of oral tradition is in itself a sufficient explanation of Paul's change of vocabulary.

(c) Some words regularly used by Paul are used in Ephesians, so we are told, in a non-Pauline sense.

(i) *Μυστήριον* (mystery). In Colossians (1[26-27]) the mystery is God's secret plan to incorporate all men into Christ, whereas in Ephesians (1[10]; 3[3,4,9]) it is God's secret plan to break down the barrier between Jew and Gentile and ultimately all other barriers which stand in the way of world unity. There is a discrepancy here only if we commit the elementary linguistic error of confusing a word's meaning with its reference or con-textual application. In each case the word means 'secret', and it is the content of the secret that is different. (1 Cor. 15[51] tells of a third, quite different, secret). But even the difference between the two secrets has been exaggerated. In Colossians it is God's secret plan to incorporate Gentiles as well as Jews into Christ, and in Ephesians it is God's secret plan to unite Jew and Gentile by their common incorporation into Christ.

[6] See P. Carrington, *The Primitive Christian Catechism*, pp. 31–44.

(ii) *Κεφαλή* (head). In Colossians Christ is said to be head of the cosmos (2^{19}) and in Ephesians head of the church (4^{16}). This point, repeated by one writer after another, not only involves the same confusion between sense and reference but is a simple mis-statement of fact. In Colossians Christ is said to be both head of the church (1^{18}) and head of all cosmic power (2^{10}), and the thought of Col. 2^{19} harks back to 1^{18}, not to 2^{10}.

(iii) *Πλήρωμα* (fulness). In Colossians the fulness of Godhead is said to dwell in Christ (1^{19}; 2^{9}), whereas in Ephesians the church is described as the fulness of Christ (1^{23}). Here again the argument depends on a confusion of meaning and reference. There is no reason why Paul should not use a word to say two different things in two different contexts. In fact, as the notes on Eph. 1^{23} explain, it is likely that in this instance the two epistles are in very close agreement. The belief that the ideas expressed by this word in the two epistles are incompatible rests largely on the ill-founded assumption that in Colossians *pleroma* is a technical term of Gnostic origin taken over by Paul from the heresy he was attacking.[7]

(iv) *Οἰκονομία*. In Colossians and 1 Corinthians this word is used to denote a commission given to Paul by God, and in Ephesians it means the putting into operation of a divine plan. Here at last there is a genuine difference. But both meanings are well attested in secular Greek. We should produce some queer interpretations of the letters of Paul if we were to insist that, having once used a word in one sense, he was thereby precluded from ever using it in another. In Rom. 5^{7}, for example, he uses *δίκαιος* (just) in a sense quite out of keeping with that required for the same word in the preceding argument on justification.

Style

(a) That the style of Ephesians is not that of Romans or 1 Corinthians is obvious, even to those who read the epistles in an English translation, and even more so to those who read them

[7] See Moule's commentary, pp. 164–169 and his article on 'Pleroma' in *The Interpreter's Dictionary of the Bible*, Vol. II, pp. 826–828.

in Greek. Goodspeed describes it as 'reverberating and liturgical, not at all the direct, rapid Pauline give-and-take'. (*Key*, p. vi). Its long sentences are loosely constructed with a profusion of purpose clauses, relatives and participles, with a piling up of prepositional phrases, with strings of genitives, often with pairs of synonyms held together in seeming tautology. About all this there is no dispute. But Percy has demonstrated that every stylistic feature of Ephesians can be paralleled in the other Pauline letters. There are long sentences in Rom. $1^{1-7,28-32}$; Phil. 3^{8-11}; 1 Thess. 1^{2-5}; 2^{14-16}; 2 Thess. 1^{3-10}, and above all in Col. 1^{9-20}. Rom. 1^{2-5} and 3^{25-26} provide examples of the piling up of prepositional phrases to a degree unequalled in Ephesians. There are strings of genitives in Rom. 2^5 and 2 Cor. 4^6. There are tautologies in 2 Cor. 5^1; 9^{12}; Phil. 2^2. In all his letters Paul has isolated passages in the style of Ephesians. The question is not whether he could write in this style, but whether he would be likely to write a whole letter in it.

(b) Harrison has claimed that what really distinguishes the style of Ephesians from that of the earlier letters of Paul is not the tricks of style it uses, but those it does not use. In $8\frac{3}{4}$ pages Ephesians has only one question; but in 26 pages Romans has 82 and in $16\frac{3}{4}$ pages 2 Corinthians has 27. Harrison also drew up a list of small words—particles, pronouns, conjunctions, and the like—which he believed to be typical of Paul's style, and gave a table of frequencies which apparently proved that Ephesians had an incidence of these words well below the average. Such statistics look impressive, whatever doubts we may have about the value of a statistical approach to documents as short as these. But when we probe beneath the surface, the serious limitations of this method are exposed. The questions in Romans and 2 Corinthians turn out to be concentrated in the argumentative parts of those letters, whereas other parts, approximately equal in length to Ephesians, have very few. As for Harrison's list of particles, it was originally drawn up as part of his work on the authorship of the Pastoral Epistles, and contains only those Pauline words which are not found in the Pastorals. An emended list yields a new table of frequencies with Ephesians almost in the middle.

(c) The explanation of the changes of style which occur even within Romans is that the rapid-fire rhetorical questions, together with many of the particles on Harrison's list, belong to Paul's debating style. But even Paul did not spend all his time in argument. He spent some of it, for example, in prayer, and he did not try to argue with God or ask him rhetorical questions. Since the first three chapters of Ephesians are almost continuous prayer, it is hardly surprising that their style is more liturgical than controversial. The argument from style has a certain limited validity, but we must not push it to the fatuous point of assuming that a man can have only one style, whether he is debating, joking, praying, telling a story, or writing a love letter.

(d) The most important contribution that Harrison made to this discussion was to show that the arguments from style which are supposed to tell against the Pauline authorship of Ephesians tell equally against the Pauline authorship of Colossians. The longest sentence in the Pauline corpus is not in Ephesians but in Colossians. Harrison therefore revived in a modified form a theory, first put forward by H. J. Holtzmann,[8] that the disciple of Paul who wrote Ephesians was also responsible for the insertion of two long passages into Colossians (1^{9b-25}; 2^{8-23}). The same line of argument led Harrison to conclude that Rom. 1^{19}—2^1 was a later interpolation. These proposals have not met with much enthusiasm. Yet Harrison has forced us to choose between three possibilities: we may say that Paul did not write Colossians and a fortiori that he did not write Ephesians; we may accept Harrison's theory of interpolation; or we must admit that the style of Ephesians is no argument against Pauline authorship (not even as part of a supposedly cumulative argument).

---

[8] *Kritik der Epheser- und Kolosser-briefe* (1872). C. Masson has advanced a different version of the same hypothesis.

Historical Setting

There are several reasons why Ephesians has been thought to imply a historical setting considerably later than the lifetime of Paul.

(a) According to Goodspeed (*Key*, p. v), 'the whole body of Christians addressed . . . were once physically heathen . . . there is no room for any Jewish Christianity in the picture . . . The writer himself has been in the same condition (2^3) and is therefore a Gentile Christian.' The first statement is true, but the second and third are demonstrably false. The writer contrasts his Gentile readers with himself and other Jewish Christians (1^{11-13}; $2^{1-3,11-22}$), and his belief that God intends to unite the whole cosmos in Christ is grounded in the fact of experience that in the church of his day Jew and Gentile have been united in the one body. His reference to his own Jewish origins is borne out by the thoroughly Semitic cast of his language and thought and by his acquaintance with Rabbinic methods of Old Testament exegesis.

Mitton follows Goodspeed, though with more scholarly moderation. 'So far as we know from Paul's other epistles and from other sources, this Gentile controversy could not be regarded as settled during Paul's lifetime. But in Ephesians it has been settled. . . . It is a closed question to which an acknowledged solution has been found' (op. cit., p. 16). But Paul's view of the Gentile question was that theologically it had been settled by the crucifixion (Rom. 3^{29-30}; Gal. 3^{28}; Col. 3^{11}), and ecclesiastically at his second visit to Jerusalem (Gal. 2^{1-10}). It is difficult to see why the treatment of this theme in Ephesians has to be read in a totally different light, unless we have already made up our minds on other grounds that it is un-Pauline.

b) Across the outer court of the Jerusalem temple ran a low barrier, on which were posted notices in Greek and Latin warning any Gentile caught attempting to penetrate further that he would have only himself to thank for his ensuing death. It has been argued that the reference to the breaking down of the dividing wall between Jew and Gentile in Eph. 2^{14} would have been unrealistic before the destruction of that barrier by the armies of Titus in A.D. 70. Two copies of the inscription have been recovered, in which the barrier is called τρύφακτος καὶ περίβολος, and Josephus uses the first of these words in his description of it (*Ant.* XV. xi. 5). If the writer of Ephesians had intended an allusion to it, he would surely have used the technical term instead of an obscure circumlocution. But in fact he makes it abundantly clear that he is speaking of a metaphorical barrier of hostility (the Iron Curtain rather than the Berlin Wall), a barrier broken down by the annulling of the Jewish law, and broken down not in A.D. 70, but in A.D. 30, at the moment when Jesus died on the Cross. We may indeed turn the tables by asking whether the destruction of Jerusalem by Titus could be thought to have broken down any barrier of hostility, and whether anyone in his senses could have written Ephesians after A.D. 70. For the author derives his confidence in God's intention and ability to bring all parts of the discordant universe to unity in Christ from the fact, which he expects to be self-evident to his readers, that Jews and Gentiles are meeting as fellow-citizens of the one new commonwealth and as members of the one body. But after A.D. 70 the synagogue broke off relations with the church, and Jewish converts must have been exceedingly rare.

(c) The writer of Ephesians has been thought to evince a veneration for Paul and the other apostles which places him firmly in the second generation. But his claims to have received a unique commission have many parallels in the other letters of Paul (Rom. 1⁵; 12³; 15¹⁵⁻¹⁶; 1 Cor. 3¹⁰; Phil. 2¹⁷; Col. 1²⁵). Moreover, the description of Paul as 'the very least of all the saints' (3⁸) may seem to modern ears 'a spurious humility', going far beyond that of 1 Cor. 15⁹⁻¹⁰; but it is easier to believe that it came from the pen of Paul than from a disciple who looked back on Paul with veneration.

(d) Finally, we are told that Ephesians reflects an ecclesiastical structure which never existed in Paul's day. It is difficult to know what to make of such an argument as this. Let us grant Mitton's assertion that, if Paul wrote the epistle, the functions ascribed to the church in Ephesians 'are far in advance of what he wrote elsewhere' (p. 18). But 1 Cor. 15 is also far in advance of anything Paul wrote elsewhere about life after death, and Col. 1^{15-20} is far in advance of anything he wrote elsewhere about Christology. Should we not expect that, when Paul devoted himself systematically to a fresh theme he would go beyond what he had said in passing reference elsewhere? If 'far in advance' was intended chronologically rather than qualitatively, it is by no means clear what criteria are being used. The only works from the sub-apostolic age which show any interest in ecclesiastical structure are the Pastoral Epistles and the letters of Ignatius; and Ephesians is theologically far in advance of either, without displaying a trace of their interest in offices and organization.

Theology

Nobody has ever denied that the theology of Ephesians is substantially Pauline, but there are one or two places where alien ideas have been thought to intrude.

(a) Eph. 2^{20} speaks of apostles and prophets as the foundation of the church, whereas Paul declares that no man can lay any other foundation than Jesus Christ (1 Cor. 3^{11}). But the two passages are not strictly comparable. The Corinthians have been playing off one preacher against another, and Paul reminds them that all preachers must build on the one foundation. Their building materials, some more valuable and durable than others, are not human lives but the instruction in faith and conduct with which they build up the community; otherwise we should be ascribing to Paul the outrageous opinion than an unsuccessful preacher will survive the last judgement, even though his congregation should be a total loss. But in Ephesians believers are the living stones who are built into the structure of God's house, and the apostles and prophets, the two sources of revelation, are not unnaturally treated as the beginning of the process. We are confronted, then, not with an incompatibility of doctrine, but with two radically different applications of a metaphor. But it is not hard to show that Paul habitually used his small store of favourite metaphors in new ways. The

Spirit, Epaenetus, Christ, and Stephanas are in three different senses first-fruits (Rom. 8²³; 16⁵; 1 Cor. 15²³; 16¹⁵). Christ celebrates a conqueror's triumph now over Christians (2 Cor. 2¹⁴), now over the principalities and powers (Col. 2¹⁵). The Corinthians are told: you (corporately) are the temple of God, and your (individual) body is the temple of God (1 Cor. 3¹⁶; 6¹⁹); and, if one of those passages had stood in Colossians and the other in Ephesians, what capital would have been made of the discrepancy!

(b) It has been held that Ephesians is shown to be post-Pauline by its reference to the descent of Christ into Hades, which is mentioned also in 1 Peter, but not in the undisputed letters of Paul. Even if we accept the interpretation of Eph. 4⁷⁻¹¹ on which this argument is based, the conclusion does not necessarily follow. We do not regard 1 Corinthians as post-Pauline because it contains the only explicit reference to the Lord's Supper in the New Testament. But in the notes it will be shown that there is a more probable interpretation: the descent of Christ, which in that passage is said to be entailed in his ascent to heaven, is his descent at Pentecost to give the gifts of the Spirit to the church.

(c) The teaching of Ephesians on the atonement has been thought to diverge from that of Paul at three points. Christians are told that they must continue to wrestle with the powers of evil (6¹²), whereas in Col. 2¹⁵ those powers are said to be defeated. The two mentions of salvation by grace (2⁵,⁸) use the verb σώζειν in the perfect tense, which Paul does not use else-where. And Christians are described as already seated with Christ in heaven (2⁶), a view which Paul on another occasion seems to repudiate with some vigour (1 Cor. 4⁸). All three objections betray a superficial understanding of Paul's theology. For him (as for other New Testament writers) salvation is always a past fact, a present experience, and a future hope, and it requires all three tenses for its adequate expression, although naturally in dealing with specific problems he will emphasize one rather than another. Salvation is a past fact because it has been achieved once for all in the representative and inclusive death and resurrection of Christ, but it still needs to be appropriated by his followers and to come to its consummation at his Advent. It is true that for the past fact Paul more often uses the aorist tense than the perfect, but perfects do occur when he wishes to emphasize the continuing effect of the historic event (Rom. 5^2; 6^7; Gal. 3^{18}). In the person of Christ Christians are already raised and seated in heaven, but that does not mean that they have no need of faith to make this status more and more their own. Christ has defeated the powers of evil, but his victory must be repeated in the lives of Christians until all resistance is crushed (1 Cor. 15^{24-8}).

(d) Apart from one mention of the age to come and one of the day of redemption (1^{21}; 4^{30}), Ephesians has nothing to say about the Parousia, but instead alludes somewhat vaguely to 'the coming ages' (2^7). But how consistent was Paul's eschatology? And was he under any obligation to include all he believed in every letter? In Romans his statement that the night is almost over and day is breaking follows hard on a vast missionary programme which involves the conversion of the whole Gentile world and of all Israel. In Galatians the only hint of eschatology is 'we wait for the hope of righteousness' (5^3).

Literary Relationships

Ephesians has an obvious kinship with Colossians. The general structure of the two letters is remarkably similar, and one third of the content of Ephesians and a quarter of the actual words used have their counterpart in Colossians. We have therefore to choose between three possibilities.

(a) Paul wrote Ephesians at the same time as Colossians and dispatched it by the same courier (Eph. 6^{21-2}; Col. 4^{7-9}). The letters are similar because both draw on the same stock of ideas that were running in Paul's mind at the time, but dissimilar because one is addressed to the particular problems of a single church and the other is an encyclical letter on a different, though allied, subject.

(b) Ephesians was written by a disciple of Paul who knew

Colossians thoroughly and used it as the model for his own work.

(c) The author of Ephesians interpolated some considerable passages into an originally much shorter letter of Paul to Colossae. This cumbersome theory of Holtzmann has had only two modern advocates, Masson and Harrison. But it is important because it shows that some acute observers have felt the one-way dependence of Ephesians on Colossians to be inadequate to account for the evidence.[9]

Goodspeed and Mitton have further claimed that Ephesians has a literary relationship with all the other letters of Paul. 'Not only are all nine letters used in Ephesians, but, except for a few lines of Luke and Acts and some Septuagint texts, they fully supply all that it contains. Ephesians is almost completely a cento of the known letters of Paul' (Goodspeed, *Key*, p. vii). Anyone who works through Goodspeed's table of parallels will be likely to conclude that more than half of them are fanciful, and even Mitton has shown that on three separate counts it needs to be drastically pruned. He has nevertheless argued that there is a sufficient residue of genuine evidence to prove that Ephesians is the work of an imitator, not of Paul. He admits that Paul might be expected to retain some memory of what he had written on other occasions, but thinks that in the case of a genuine Pauline letter the resemblances would have been more evenly spaced and would not have shown any predominance of striking phrases (pp. 111–14).

Those who reject the Pauline authorship of Ephesians all regard its literary associations with Colossians and the other letters as the weightiest part of their case. They dismiss the idea that Paul could have written in this way largely on the ground that words and phrases from the other letters appear in Ephesians in different combinations and with different meanings, and

[9]Cp. W. Michaelis, *Einleitung in das Neue Testament* (1946), p. 200: 'The relation between Colossians and Ephesians—the principal objection urged against their authenticity—is of such a kind that the hypothesis of the authenticity of the two letters is still the best solution.'

that the other letters do not display such self-quotation to the same degree.[10] Others on the contrary have thought that the repetition and variation of phraseology we find in Ephesians is exactly what is to be expected of an author subconsciously half-remembering his earlier works, but the last thing to be expected from an imitator. Abbott (p. xxi) quotes an impressive passage from Paley to this effect, and Guthrie refers to an article by A. B. Cook, which provides illuminating parallels from classical writers.[11] In addition to this, however, must we not question whether it is sound procedure to discuss these resemblances in purely literary terms? Paul was a speaker as well as a writer, and much of the material in his letters gives the impression of having been worked over many times in the more fluid configurations of the spoken word before it ever came to be written down.

The theory of an imitator is not without difficulties of its own. The most formidable of these arises if we attempt to resort to what has been called cumulative evidence. Are we to attempt to frame a cumulative case by adding to the argument from literary relationships the other arguments from language and style? We have already seen that these militate as much against the authenticity of Colossians as of Ephesians. Along this line of reasoning then we find ourselves dealing with two imitators instead of one. First the author of Colossians produces his imitation of Paul. Then the author of Ephesians, thinking to write a Pauline letter, models his own work on all the collected letters of Paul, but giving pride of place to the one member of the corpus which is not genuine. It is worth while spelling out this hypothesis in detail in order to expose its improbability. Yet the only honest alternative to it is to dismiss once and for all the arguments from language and style and admit that the other arguments look somewhat thinner without their support.

[10]It is not difficult, however, to find examples. A comparison of Philem. 4–5 with Phil. 1^{3-4} and Col. 1^{3-4} shows how easy it was for Paul to use familiar words in new combinations.

[11]'Unconscious Iteration, with special reference to Classical Literature', *Classical Review*, XVI (1902), pp. 146–158, 256–267.

But there are more conundrums to come. If the imitator had the whole Pauline corpus at his disposal, why pick on Colossians as his special exemplar? If he was intending to reproduce the substance of the other letters, which he had in front of him to guide him, why did he do the job so badly, since by hypothesis he used Pauline words and phrases in un-Pauline ways? If on the other hand he relied merely on a somewhat blurred memory, why out of the whole corpus should he have chosen to reproduce verbatim only the sentence about Tychicus (Col. 4^{7-9}; Eph. 6^{21-2})? What purpose did he intend his pseudonymous letter to serve? And how, if even as an imitator he proved incompetent, did he succeed in producing what subsequent generations have rightly hailed as a work of brilliant creative genius? Can we believe in an author who was at one and the same time slavishly and undiscerningly dependent and profound in his originality?

Goodspeed's theory owes much of its popularity to his recognition that these questions demand an answer if the imitator is to be a person in whose existence we can believe. He accordingly argued that, since the author knew the whole Pauline corpus of letters written to widely separated churches, he must have been its collector, who designed his own work to be an introduction to the series; that his choice of Colossians as a model showed that he must have known it longer than the rest, that he was in fact a member of the church at Colossae; and that his great veneration for Paul and intimate knowledge of his mind strongly suggested Onesimus. This attractive theory appears at first sight to tie all the evidence together in a neat and coherent solution, but it is open to several damaging criticisms.

(a) There is no evidence that Ephesians ever stood at the head of the Pauline corpus.

(b) The author of Ephesians was quite certainly a Jew. This is conclusively shown by the general Semitic quality of his style, by the frequence of Hebraisms, by his acquaintance with rabbinic exegesis, and by the way he refers to the Gentiles in 2^{11-12}.[12]

[12]This point is put beyond doubt by Kirby, op. cit., pp. 59–172.

(c) Ephesians is not a summary of Pauline theology, but a new and original treatise on a subject not systematically treated elsewhere in the Pauline writings. Indeed, a large part of the case against Pauline authorship has rested on the absence of many of the central themes of Pauline theology and the presence of ideas which have been thought foreign to Paul.

(d) P. Carrington has argued very convincingly in *The Primitive Christian Catechism* (1941) that resemblances between the ethical sections of the New Testament epistles are to be explained not as literary borrowings from one document by the author of another, but as the independent development by a number of authors of a common stock of catechetical ideas and formulae in use throughout the hellenistic mission of the church. In particular, he has suggested that, underlying the ethical instruction of Ephesians, Colossians, 1 Peter, and James there was a fourfold catechetical form:

(i) Put off the old life and put on the new

(ii) Be subject to all legitimate authority

(iii) Watch and pray

(iv) Resist the devil and stand firm.

The fourth of these headings is found in Eph. 6[11]; 1 Pet. 5[9]; Jas. 4[7], but not in Colossians. Since at this point Ephesians is demonstrably not dependent on Colossians, there is a strong presumption that this holds for the ethical teaching of the letter as a whole. We do not need to accept the details of Carrington's theory to appreciate the point he is making. Goodspeed's theory was formulated at a time when New Testament scholarship was still dominated by literary criticism, which tended to explain all similarities as the product of literary borrowing, and had not yet come to terms with the new insights of Form Criticism with its emphasis on oral tradition. The newer approach to the epistles exemplified by Carrington does not of itself establish the Pauline authorship of Ephesians; but it is compatible with Pauline authorship and incompatible with what has been up to now the only attractive alternative. To this C. H. Dodd has added the important corollary that

Eph. 6^{10-17} is closer to the eschatological pattern of the primitive teaching than its counterpart in Col. 4^{2-3}.[13]

(e) G. Bornkamm, in a brief study of the origin of 2 Corinthians, has made a strong case for the thesis that that epistle was not included in any collection of Paul's letters which may have existed prior to A.D. 115.[14] If this view is accepted, then the theory of Goodspeed and Mitton is demolished at a blow. For many of the most striking parallels between Ephesians and the other Pauline letters are parallels with 2 Corinthians. It is not integral to their case that the author was Onesimus, or that he was the collector of the corpus, or that he wrote Ephesians as an introduction to Pauline theology. But it is integral to their case that he should have been able to borrow from a complete corpus. We cannot believe in an imitator who shows knowledge of a document which in the nature of things was inaccessible to him.

Thus far we have been concerned simply to test the strength of the case against Pauline authorship. Now that it has proved brittle, we may add one or two small pieces of evidence which seem to point in a more positive way to Paul as the author.

(a) The author was not only a Jew who was familiar with rabbinic exegesis of the Old Testament; he himself used rabbinic methods in a thoroughly Pauline way. In 4^{7-11} he quotes a psalm which was appointed in the Jewish lectionary for use at Pentecost, and in which the rabbis had discovered an allusion to Moses's ascent of Sinai and subsequent gift of the Law to Israel; and he argues that this psalm is properly interpreted as a Christian Pentecostal psalm, describing Christ's ascension to heaven and his subsequent bestowal of spiritual gifts on the church. There is a close parallel between this and Paul's use of rabbinic exegesis in 1 Cor. 10^{1-4} and in Col. 1^{15-20}: for in the one case Paul takes the story of Moses's well (Num. 21^{17-18}), which according to the Rabbis became both a

---

[13]'The Primitive Catechism and the Sayings of Jesus' in *New Testament Essays*, ed. A. J. B. Higgins, p. 113.

[14]'The History of the Origin of the So-called Second Letter to the Corinthians', *New Testament Studies*, viii (1962), pp. 258–264.

rock that followed Israel on their desert wanderings and a symbol for the law, and transfers the allegory to Christ; and in the other case he takes a rabbinic combination of Gen. 1^1 with Prov. 8^{22} and adapts it in such a way that it is Christ and not Wisdom (= Law) who is declared to be the agent and goal of creation. It is difficult to see how an imitator of Paul could have produced an original example of this characteristically Pauline practice of adapting rabbinic interpretations to Christian purposes, especially if he had only the nine other letters to draw on for his material.[15]

(b) The elaborate use of a Pentecostal psalm suggests the possibility that the letter may have been written at the season of the festival. We know from both Acts and epistles that Paul continued to observe the Jewish festivals (Acts $20^{6,16}$; 1 Cor. 16^8), giving to them no doubt a distinctively Christian interpretation. His first letter to Corinth must have been written at about the time of the Passover, and it is a plausible theory that the proximity of the festival put into his mind some of the imagery he uses in it (1 Cor. 5^{7-8}; 15^{20}). If the proximity of Pentecost, interpreted as the season of Christ's exaltation and gift of the Spirit, had a similar influence on Ephesians, this would explain some of its peculiarities which have been thought un-Pauline: its repeated reference to 'the heavenlies', the statement that Christians share not only Christ's resurrection but his heavenly session at the right hand of God (2^6), and, since the Jewish Pentecost was a celebration of the Sinai covenant and of the betrothal of Israel to Yahweh, the description of the church as the bride of Christ (5^{22-32}). [16]

(c) Harrison, as part of his case for the interpolation of passages into Colossians by the author of Ephesians, points to a mixed metaphor which he thinks to be typical of that author's style, but impossible for Paul (Col. 2^7; cp. Eph. 3^{17}). The fact is, however, that the use of metaphor in Ephesians is one of its

[15]For a fuller statement of the evidence see G. B. Caird, 'The Descent of Christ in Ephesians 4, 7–11', *Texte und Untersuchungen*, lxxxvii (1964), pp. 535–45.

[16]See Kirby, op. cit., 59—121.

most conspicuously Pauline features. In all his letters Paul will go for long stretches without using any but the most common-place metaphors, and then will come a short passage in which colourful metaphors trip over one another in a fashion which a modern author, warned against mixing his metaphors, would avoid. See for example 1 Cor. 3^{6-15}, where farming imagery gives place to building imagery and to the curious picture of a house that is to be tested by fire; 2 Cor. 2^{14-16}, with its juxta-position of military and sacrificial language; and above all Phil. 2^{15-17}, where the readers are to be faultless children, shining like stars, and Paul himself has so run his race as to become the libation that crowns the sacrifice of their faith. This seems to me an aspect of Paul's style which would have been difficult for an imitator to copy.

When all this has been said, the problem of Ephesians remains. It is curiously unlike the other Pauline letters. There are difficulties in attributing it to Paul. But these are insignifi-cant in comparison with the difficulties of attributing it to an imitator. We shall therefore provisionally accept the traditional ascription. The real test will be whether, in the commentary, we can make sense of it as a genuine letter of Paul.

ANALYSIS

1	**1:1–2**	Address.
2	**1: 3–14**	Benediction.
3	**1: 15–23**	Intercession.
4	**2: 1–10**	God's Power in Redemption.
5	**2: 11–22**	The New Humanity.
6	**3: 1–13**	The Apostle of the Gentiles.
7	**3: 14–21**	Second Intercession.
8	**4: 1–16**	Diversity in Unity.
9	**4: 17–24**	The Old Life and the New.
10	**4: 25–5: 2**	General Rules for Christian Conduct.

11	**5: 3–20**	From Darkness into Light.
12	**5: 21–6: 9**	The Christian Family.
13	**6: 10–20**	The Christian Soldier.
14	**6: 21–4**	Closing Greetings.

COMMENTARY

1: 1–2 *Address*

Paul begins all his letters with the conventional salutation of the Greek letter-writer, A to B greeting (cp. Acts 15[23]; 23[26]); but he amplified each of the three terms, the names of sender and addressee and the greeting itself, in a variety of ways, always giving the address a specifically Christian character.

1. *Paul, an apostle of Christ Jesus.* It would be better, with the NEB, to omit the article, since Paul does not call himself *apostle* in order to place himself in a class, as the holder of an ecclesiastical office. His claim to apostleship is that he has seen the risen Christ (1 Cor. 9[1]; cp. Acts 1[22]) and has received directly from him, 'not from men or through men' (Gal. 1[1]), a commission to speak and act in his name. He was Christ's ambassador (2 Cor. 5[20]), and as proof of his claim he could point to 'the signs of a true apostle' (2 Cor. 12[12]), i.e. the results of his work in healing, conversion, and the establishment of churches, from which it should be clear that his whole success as a missionary was due to the power of God working in and through him. It was on this ground that the leaders of the Jerusalem church had accepted him as a colleague, recognizing that he had received a commission on a par with that of Peter (Gal. 2[7–9]). In one sense Paul's position was unique, for though there were many apostles, and many who claimed apostolic status (2 Cor. 11[5,13]; 12[11]; cp. Rev. 2[2]), there was only one Apostle of the Gentiles; and it is in this capacity that Paul now writes. *by the will of God.* Elsewhere Paul makes it clear that, though his conversion was a drastic upheaval in his own thinking and experience, it represented no break in the purpose of God. Like Jeremiah, he came to recognize the operation of a divine plan in his life, effectively at work long before he himself was able to respond to it (Gal. 1[15]; cp. Jer. 1[5]). But in the present letter this conviction takes on a deeper significance. The divine purpose which has shaped his life is now seen to be a part of a larger purpose, embracing not only all humanity but the whole creation.

Paul commonly refers to his fellow Christians as *saints*, not because they are distinguished from others by their moral or spiritual qualities, but because they are set apart from others by belonging to Christ. They are 'saints in virtue of God's call' (1 Cor. 1²). The term had been used in the Old Testament to denote Israel as a people dedicated to God by covenant (Deut. 7⁶; 33³; Ps. 31²³; 37²⁸; 50⁵). It is noteworthy that Paul never uses the word in the singular. Christians are saints only as members of the holy community. The word is therefore correctly translated 'God's people' (NEB).

The word πιστός regularly means *faithful* or 'trustworthy', and it is just possible that this is its meaning here. But it is also used in an active sense to denote those who have faith, i.e. believers (2 Cor. 6¹⁵; Gal. 3⁹; cp. John 20²⁷; Acts 10⁴⁵; 1 Pet. 1²¹), and this meaning makes better sense in the present context. We must not however construe it directly with the following phrase, as though it meant 'those who believe in Christ Jesus'. The phrase *in Christ* in the Pauline epistles always refers to the union of believers with their Lord, their incorporation into his new manhood. They are 'believers incorporate in Christ Jesus' (NEB). At first sight this description might seem tautologous, adding nothing to the designation *saints*. But in Paul's usage ἅγιος is never quite synonymous with Christian. He sometimes uses it to denote a special group of Christians, the members of the Jerusalem church, the original, metropolitan church of the whole Christian mission (Rom. 15²⁵⁻³¹ etc.,). In this letter, for all its emphasis on the unity of Jew and Gentile, he uses 'saints' to denote Jewish Christians, those who have their roots in the Old Testament people of God (see 2¹⁹); and so he qualifies his greeting to 'God's people' by adding 'who are also believers incorporate in Christ Jesus'. Herein is the justification for rendering πιστός as 'believer'. He is not addressing a group within the church which deserves to be called trustworthy, but those who have been admitted to membership in the historic people of God through faith in Christ and union with him.

On the omission of the words 'in Ephesus' from the authentic text, see Introduction, pp. 9–11.

2. For the verb χαίρειν used in the common epistolary greeting Paul substitutes the cognate noun χάρις (*grace*) and adds the Hebrew salutation *shalom* (*peace*). Both words are intended to carry rich overtones of Christian meaning, and it would be a mistake to attempt to give them precise definition.

1: 3–14 *Benediction.*

The first three chapters are an almost continuous prayer, in which Paul expounds for the benefit of readers who have never heard him in the flesh a great new thesis, hinted at but never fully developed in his earlier letters: that the union of Jew and Gentile in the fellowship of the one church is not only integral to God's comprehensive plan for the universe, but is the key to the understanding of that plan as a whole.

The opening benediction is dominated, as is the rest of the prayer, by the thought of Christ's exaltation to the right hand of God, the signal that he has fulfilled, at least in representative fashion, God's purpose for man and therefore for the whole creation. For the whole process of creation was designed to produce men like Christ, men fitted for God's own presence, not by their own achievement but by God's gracious gift of a share in the sonship of Christ (vv. 3-6). Through their association with Christ Christians have already received forgiveness and a new insight into the mysterious ways of God. For it is God's intention that his purpose for them and for the world should reach its goal only through their co-operation, and for this reason he has waited until the time was ripe to implement his purpose of bringing the whole universe to unity and harmony in Christ (vv. 7-10). This purpose has been at work in the past, particularly in the history of the Jews, so that it was natural that they should be the first to respond to its full manifestation in Christ. But as soon as the gospel reached the Gentiles,they too began to enter the new people of God through their union with Christ and to have their faith sealed with the stamp of God's approval by his gift of the Spirit, which is the anticipation and guarantee of fuller blessings to come when God's universal purpose reaches its consummation (vv. 11-14).

3. *Blessed . . . Jesus Christ.* The same opening clause is found word for word in 2 Cor. 1[3] and 1 Pet. 1[3]. Such similarities used to be explained as borrowing by one author from another, but they are now thought to be due rather to the independent use of a common liturgical tradition.[17] Blessing God for his gifts and benefits was a very common form of prayer in the Old Testament, and it was further developed in the worship of the synagogue, where the Eighteen Benedictions

[17]See J. P. Audet, 'Literary Forms and Contents of a Normal Εὐχαριστία in the First Century', *The Gospels Reconsidered*, ed. F. L. Cross, pp. 16–35.

formed, together with the Shema (Deut. 6^{4-9}), the nucleus of the liturgy. In Christian worship the Jewish practice was continued (Luke 1^{68}; Jas. 3^9), but the Jewish formulae would quickly have been adapted in a Christian sense. The liturgical character of the opening paragraph of Ephesians is seen in the rhythmical balance of the clauses and in the refrain-like repetition of phrases, *according to his purpose* (vv. 5, 9), *to the praise of his glory* (vv. 6, 12, 14).

the God and Father. Paul believed in the pre-existence of Christ (2 Cor. 8^9; Phil. 2^6), but this enters into the present theme only in so far as the inclusive and representative manhood of Christ pre-existed in the determining plan of God. His concern here is with the man Jesus, who lived in dependence on God and by faith in him and obedience to him, and who also experienced to the full what it means for man to have God as *Father*. Christ does not owe his position as lord of the cosmos to his divinity, but to his humanity; for it is God's design that man should be his agent in making his sovereignty effective over the rest of creation. Christ's knowledge of God and his human, filial relationship with God are the chief of the *spiritual blessings* which he is able to share with his followers.

The blessings are called *spiritual*, not because they are the work of the Holy Spirit, but because they belong to the inner, hidden life of men, in the realm of what is unseen and eternal (2 Cor. 4^{16-18}; Col. 3^3). Apart from 1 Cor. 12–14, Paul always uses πνευματικός in this second sense. Later in this paragraph he speaks of the function of the Holy Spirit in Christian experience, but then the point is that the Spirit is the seal and guarantee of future blessings precisely because his operations are visible and verifiable. But here the *blessing* is bestowed *in the heavenly places*.

Paul shared with his contemporaries an imaginative picture of a two or three-storeyed universe. But the pictures by which we make our beliefs real to the imagination are not to be confused with the beliefs themselves. Quite simple people are capable of drawing this distinction, and it is only the semi-sophisticated pedants who find it difficult, for themselves or for others. (Today everybody knows that the sun does not actually rise, but we all talk as though we believed it did, and it would be intolerable pedantry to speak otherwise.) We do Paul an injustice if we suppose that in any literal sense he believed in a three-storey house, with man inhabiting the ground floor, God in the upstairs flat, and less desirable tenants in the basement. Indeed, in this epistle he explicitly tells us that the powers of evil have their operation *in the heavenly places* (1^{20-1}; 6^{12}). There is, to be sure, an ambiguity in the biblical use of the word 'heaven'. Sometimes it is used to denote the dwelling-place of God, though even in early times there were those who knew better than to take this symbol literally (1 Kings $8^{13,27}$). Sometimes, particularly in Matthew's Gospel 'heaven' is simply a reverent way of speaking about God. But more often, as here, heaven is part of the created universe, part of man's world: God created the heavens as well as the earth (Gen. 1^1; Ps. 8^3), and the old heaven must ultimately go the way of the old earth (Isa. 65^{17}; 2 Pet. 3^{13}; Rev. 21^1). Paul has little of our modern interest in the physical universe as an object of study in its own right, though he has a deep sympathy with nature's bondage to decay and death (Rom. 8^{20-3}). For him 'heaven' is a term of human topography, standing for man's invisible, spiritual environment, as contrasted with the visible, tangible environment we call earth. It is the realm of all the unseen forces, good and evil, which struggle to dominate the individual and corporate life of man, through his politics, his religion, his social ideals and mores, and all the other influences that affect his beliefs and conduct. And it is in this realm that Christ has attained supremacy and become a source of blessing.

The heart of Paul's theology is contained in the phrase *in Christ.* Man is born into the natural solidarity of the human race, sharing the common manhood which is under the tyranny of sin and death, unable to free himself from the dominion of the dark powers; and this is what it means to be 'in Adam' (1 Cor. 15^{22}; Rom. 5^{12-14}). But on the fact of this solidarity of nature, which men share with one another whether they like it or not, rests the possibility of a new solidarity of choice, in which the voluntary offer of Christ meets the voluntary response of faith. Christ chose not only to become man (Phil. 2^{6-7}; cp. 2 Cor. 8^9), but as man to identify himself with his fellow men in their weakness and sin (Rom. 8^3; 2 Cor. 5^{21}), even to the point of dying a criminal death under the sentence of a human court and under the curse of the Jewish law (Phil. 2^8; Gal. 3^{13}). He thus made it possible for any man to be identified with him in his new, risen manhood, and so to be transferred out of the old environment of failure and defeat into a new environment of spiritual and moral victory (Col. 1^{13}).

4. *He chose us in him.* The biblical doctrine of election is compounded of three convictions: that man's salvation is from first to last the act of God's free choice, and not of man's own achievement; that it is not merely the repairing of the damage done by sin, but the fulfilment of God's original purpose for man; and that it involves appointment to a role in which the responsibilities bulk at least as large as the privileges. In securing agents for the working out of his purpose, God does not put the vacancies up to public competition and wait for applications. He does indeed summon all men to a life of holiness and moral goodness, but he lays upon some the burden of being in the vanguard of human progress. Whatever sting the idea of election may have for us is drawn by the words *in him.* To be the elect people of God cost the Jews so much in tragic suffering that no other nation would lightly

envy their calling, and to be God's Elect meant for Jesus carrying the whole burden of the world's sin, shame, and sorrow.

All references in Jewish and Christian literature to what happened *before the foundation of the world* are ways of pointing to the teleological character of the world, to the purpose inherent in the natural order. For the rabbis used to discuss which of the things that existed before the world began were really brought into being by God and which existed only in his predestining intention (*Bereshith Rabba*, 1). When they said that the Torah (the law of Moses) existed before the world began, they meant that the world was created for the Torah, i.e. to produce men capable of obeying the Torah. Similarly, to say that Christians were chosen *before the foundation of the world* is to say that the goal of the whole cosmic process was the coming of Christ and the emergence of a new race of men like him.

Paul's teaching that God expects men to be *holy and blameless before him*, not as a condition of acceptance into his presence, but as a consequence of undeserved forgiveness, freely offered by God's grace and accepted by faith, is no second best, necessitated by man's failure to live up to the demands of God's law. From the beginning God designed that man, in attaining to a holiness which mirrored that of God, should be dependent on divine grace and not on his own efforts. The idea that man must earn his way into God's favour is a distortion of God's intention, degrading man into the position of a slave in God's household where he ought to be a son.

5. The phrase *in love* may be taken as the beginning of v. 5 or as the end of v. 4. Either punctuation gives excellent sense. If with the RSV we take it with v. 5, then the motive behind the plan of God to produce men capable of becoming his sons is being defined as love. If with the AV, RV, and NEB we take the words with v. 4, then love is the essential quality of the holy, unblemished life to which the Christian has been destined by God. One good reason for preferring the second alternative is that throughout this passage the verb in every clause precedes the phrases which qualify it. This is one of the many Semitic characteristic which mark the style of the epistle.

The words translated *to be his sons* (εἰς υἰοθεσίαν) literally mean 'for adoption'. Paul can use the same word to denote one of the privileges of Israel, the status conferred upon the chosen people at the Exodus (Rom. 9⁴). But Israel's sonship was only a shadowy anticipation of what God had in store for them and for others in the coming of Christ. To be a son of God is not a matter of descent or legal rights but of a status established by God's proclamation and of the intimate relationship of trust and understanding which that status makes possible. For the Christian it is further defined as admission to a share in the filial relationship of Christ with his Father. But there is nothing automatic about it; it needs to be realized by a positive act of acceptance and in the style of life which follows as a result.

Purpose is too colourless a word for εὐδοκία, which signifies the delight or pleasure that God takes in his plans. Paul uses the word once of the most passionate concern of his own heart (Rom. 10[1]), and once of the generous good motives that have prompted some Christians in Rome to carry on his preaching (Phil. 1[15]). The NEB strikes the right note: 'such was his will and pleasure'.

6. *to the praise of his glorious grace.* The essence of sonship is the ability to appreciate and reflect the splendours of the Father. A utilitarian spirit prompts us to ask of everything, 'What use is it?' But the best things in the world are there not to be used but to be enjoyed, and to provide a propaedeutic to the worship of their Maker. As the Shorter Scottish Catechism tells us: 'Man's chief end is to glorify God and to enjoy him for ever.

freely bestowed stands for the Greek ἐχαρίτωσεν, which is derived from χάρις, *grace*. It is tempting to say with Beare: 'it is as if the writer were so enraptured with the word that he can hardly let it go'. But this picking up of a noun with a cognate verb is one of the stylistic tricks of this epistle (cp. 1[19-20]; 2[4]; 4[1]); and Percy is able to adduce ample evidence of its use in other Pauline letters (e.g. 1 Cor. 7[20]; 15[1]; 2 Cor. 1[3-4]; 8[24]; Gal. 5[1]; Col. 1[11,29]; 1 Thess. 2[8]).

Beloved (ἠγαπημένος) appears to be used here as if it were a recognized Messianic title, though in the rest of the New Testament, in the accounts of the Baptism and Transfiguration, it always appears in the adjectival form ἀγαπητός. The participial form is found in the Septuagint as a designation for Israel, where the Hebrew has Jeshurun (Deut. 32[15]; 33[5,26]; Isa. 44[2]) or *yahid*, 'darling' (Deut. 33[15]; Isa. 5[1]), and in Bar. 3[37], where no Hebrew text survives. In the Epistles of Barnabas and Ignatius and other early Christian literature it is undoubtedly a Messianic title, and it is unlikely that all these are dependent on Ephesians. For the full evidence, see J. A. Robinson, p. 229-53. But the title is used here to indicate that the bounty God lavishes on men consists in their being caught up into the love which subsists between Father and Son (cp. John 17[23,26]).

7. *Redemption* (ἀπολύτρωσις) is in origin a metaphor from the release of a slave or of alienated land by the payment of a ransom (Lev. 25[25-55]), and there are places in the New Testament where this metaphor is still vividly alive (Mark 10[45]; 1 Tim. 2[6]; 1 Pet. 1[18-19]). But the metaphor had been regularly used in the Old Testament to denote Israel's release from Egyptian bondage, and in Second Isaiah to denote the coming release from Babylonian exile. In these two settings, apart from one instance of hyperbole (Isa. 43[3]), there was no question of a ransom price (cp. Isa. 52[3]). Israel is set free by the sheer act of God's sovereign power. The same is true of the word in Pauline usuage; it is

Exodus language, without any attempt to hark back to the original metaphor. When Paul wishes to speak of a ransom price, he uses the verb ἀγοράζειν, 'to buy' (1 Cor. 6²⁰; 7²³). It follows that *his blood* is not a continuation of the ransom metaphor, but a new metaphor from sacrifice. Paul makes little use of the language of sacrifice and never makes it the centre of any theological argument, so that when he does use it it is hard to define exactly what he means by it. Sacrifice in the Old Testament never had any clear rationale, and by Paul's time the Jews continued to offer it simply because it was commanded in the Torah (Ecclus. 35⁵). When New Testament writers use the language of sacrifice, it is not so much because it helped them to understand the death of Christ as that the Cross helped them to see the reality for which men had been groping in the past (Heb. 10¹). Round the institution of sacrifice had gathered many powerful associations, whose blurred edges tended to fade into one another: the gift of tribute to the majesty of God, the establishment of communion or covenant, the commemoration of past redemption (Passover), and the release of power through the surrender of life. It is this last idea which seems to be uppermost here and in Col. 1²⁰ (cp. Heb. 7¹⁶).

Metaphor speaks more eloquently than literal language and with a stronger appeal to the imagination, but not always as clearly. There was a danger that Paul's Gentile readers, accustomed to the vague but florid spirituality of paganism, might overlook the true nature of the Egyptian bondage from which they had been rescued. So Paul explains that he is talking about *the forgiveness of our trespasses*, the cancellation by God of those offences against his law, his purpose, and his love which had disqualified men from entry into his presence and from knowing him as he really is. In Rom. 1 Paul gives a grim picture of the retribution that overtakes man when he wilfully flouts God's design for him: his mind becomes darkened, so that he is progressively less and less able to understand God's truth and his own nature or to make sound moral judgments, until he sinks in a morass of moral corruption. The first and most important result of forgiveness is that man's spiritual vision is so restored that he can know and respond to God *in all wisdom and insight*. The two words are roughly synonymous, and if there is any difference between them it is that the first refers to intellectual knowledge and the second to the understanding of its practical application.

9. It is sometimes said that the hidden truth of God is called a *mystery* by Paul because, even when it has been revealed, it remains mysterious, beyond the comprehension of man. Whatever justification there is for this must lie in the word 'God', not in the word μυστήριον,, which simply means 'a secret'. It can be used of the secret plans which a king shares with his confidential advisers (Judith 2²). According to Amos (3⁷), God never puts any of his secret plans into effect without

first taking the prophets into his confidence; and we shall see later (3⁵) that Christian prophets have had a part in making known to their fellow Christians the particular secret with which this epistle is concerned. The point on which Paul is here insisting is that it is no more theological innovation, no bright idea of his own, that Christians are called upon to understand and participate in God's plan for the whole creation; it is part of what God intended from the beginning, part of what it means to be a son of God. According to the RSV, this plan has been *set forth in Christ*, i.e. disclosed in his earthly life, death, and resurrection. This is a possible meaning of the verb προτίθημι (cp. Rom. 3²³) and squares with Paul's belief that Christ is the full and final revelation of God. But the verb can also mean 'to purpose or intend' (cp. Rom. 1¹³), and the relation of this verse to the following one requires that we take it in that sense here: God's *purpose* was 'determined beforehand in Christ' (NEB).

10. *as a plan for the fulness of time.* Οἰκονομία can mean 'the office of steward' (e.g. 1 Cor. 9¹⁷; Col. 1²⁵), 'household management', and in the most general sense 'administration' or 'arrangements'; but J. A. Robinson also cites many passages in which it means 'the actual working out of a policy or project'. This is the meaning which best fits all three passages where it occurs in Ephesians (cp. 3²·⁹). Here the correct translation is: 'to be put into effect when the time was ripe' (NEB). It is this that determines the way we must take the last clause in the previous verse. The point is not that God's plan had been set forth in Christ and was still to be put into operation at some future date, but rather that God had from all eternity formulated a plan for the cosmos which had Christ as its centre, intending to put it into operation when the right time came, as come it did with the advent of Jesus (cp. Gal. 4⁴).

This verse is of the greatest possible significance for our understanding of Paul's theology and for its relevance to modern thought. It is commonly assumed that in biblical theology God is supposed to have made a perfect world, which was subsequently spoiled by man's sin and needed to be restored by Christ to its primal goodness. This is certainly not Paul's view. He believed that God had made the world good but incomplete, to be completed in due course by man, acting as the agent of God's creative sovereignty; and that the precosmic design for man had begun to come into effect in the person of Jesus.

The ultimate goal of this cosmic process is *to unite all things in him*. The verb (ἀνακεφαλαιοῦν) is derived from κεφάλαιον, which means 'the total' of an arithmetical sum, or 'the summary' of an argument, i.e. the gathering together of diverse parts into one coherent whole. Paul uses the same verb when he declares that the whole Torah is comprehended in the command to love one's neighbour (Rom. 13⁹). Here he means that the universe is to find in Christ its principle of cohesion, which is to bring all its discrepant and conflicting forces to reconciliation with God's purpose and so with one another.

Christ's reconciling work is to have as its object *things in heaven and things on earth*. The second of these phrases presents no problems. In so far as Paul had an interest in the sub-human creation, he believed that it owed its bondage to futility and decay to its involvement in the fall of man, and that it depended for its liberation on man's attaining to his destined place in God's universal plan (Rom. 8^{20-3}). On the earthly scene, then, his primary concern was that the reconciliation of individual men to God in Christ should be seen to have social consequences in the removal of all those divisions of religion, nationality, class, and sex by which human society was so deeply ruptured. He believed that in Christ the divisive tendency of the old, sinful order had been transcended, and that Christians had been given the task of living out the implications of that conviction, so as to transform their world (Gal. 3^{27}; Col. 3^{11}). But what are we to make of the establishment of unity *in heaven*?

Paul's *heaven* is neither the eternal abode of God, nor yet a Platonic realm of perfect reality of which earth is but an imperfect copy. It is the spiritual and unseen aspect of man's environment, in which invisible forces, beneficent or sinister, compete for man's allegiance and the control of his destiny (cp. v. 3). It is the arena where function those principalities and powers of which we are to hear more as the epistle progresses (cp. 1^{21}; 2^2; 3^{10}; 6^{12}). Paul's notion of principalities and powers was compounded of three main elements.

(a) Faced with the fact of pagan religion and its close bond with pagan political power, the Jews denied the deity of the pagan gods, but could not deny their existence and influence; nor did they wish to deny some measure of divine authority even to the pagan state (Dan. 4^{17}; cp. Rom. 13^1). They declared that God had delegated his authority over the nations to angelic rulers (Deut. 32^8), whose power had become corrupted by their acceptance of men's idolatrous worship (Wisd. 14^{12}). The earthly king and the angelic ruler were thus the two symbols of national life, and what happened in the earthly sphere was thought to have its counterpart in the heavenly (Isa. 14^{12}; 24^{21}; Dan. $10^{13,20}$).

(b) Paul extended this Jewish idea to include the angelic mediators and guardians of the Jewish Torah, because the Jews had made the same mistake as the Gentiles in ascribing absolute authority to that which God intended to be derivative and provisional. He therefore draws no clear distinction between man's bondage to the angelic mediators of the Torah and to the pagan gods, but argues on the contrary that for a Gentile Christian to put himself under the Jewish Torah is to retreat into the very bondage to elemental spirits from which he was emancipated when he became a Christian (Gal. $3^{19}-4^{21}$; cp. Col. 2^{8-23}).

(c) The Jews also shared with other ancient peoples the belief that the forces of nature, and especially the heavenly bodies, were spiritual beings with an authority that could affect human life. In a world in which astrology was rife and the planets bore the names of the Olympian gods, these Jewish ideas would be readily understood, even if they were not readily accepted. Whether the Jews in general, and Paul in particular, believed literally in the existence of these angelic beings is hard to say. What is clear is that the powers stood for something real in human experience, as real today as it was then, viz. those structures of power, political, economic, social, and religious which interpenetrate the whole corporate life of man and decisively affect the fortunes of the individual. These are the *things in heaven* which Paul now asserts must be brought within the unifying purpose of God in Christ.

All this is of the utmost importance for our understanding of Paul's doctrine of redemption. The salvation of man is not to be conceived as the rescue of favoured individuals out of a doomed world to participate in an otherworldly existence totally unrelated to life on earth. Man's personality is so intimately linked with his environment that he must be saved in the context of all the corporate relationships and loyalties, achievements and aspirations, which constitute a genuinely human existence.

11–12. In these two verses the RSV has so drastically departed from the order of the Greek as to obscure the drift of the argument. Note first that, whereas Paul has so far used the pronoun 'we' to cover all Christians, he now begins to restrict it to Jewish Christians in contrast to 'you', the Gentile Christians. Up to this point he has been telling how Christ himself has fulfilled and made it possible for others to fulfil the precosmic plan of God, the plan that through the emergence of men fitted by holiness, innocence, and love to be God's sons, to reflect his glory, and to co-operate in his purpose, the universe should be brought to coherence and harmony. Now he affirms that, although God *accomplishes all things according to the counsel of his will*, i.e. although the whole of history is under the same providential ordering, nevertheless within this wider purpose the special part played by the Jewish people in preparing for the coming of Christ was also fore-ordained (*destined*). *Appointed* is an inadequate rendering of ἐκληρώθημεν, especially when the word is restored to its proper place at the beginning of the sentence. The verb is derived from κλῆρος, 'lot', and means either 'we were assigned a role' or 'we were taken (sc. by God) to be his special possession'. A small point in favour of the second sense is that the very passage which we cited above as the key text for the Jewish belief in national angels goes on in the next verse to declare that God kept Israel under his own direct rule as his special people (Deut. 32^{8-9}). But there is little to choose between the two interpretations, and both in any case amount to much the same thing. The clause which the RSV translates *who first hoped in Christ* could also mean 'who had looked forward with hope to Christ'; i.e. we have to choose between a reference to Jewish hopes before the coming of Christ and a reference to Jewish Christian trust in Christ once he had come. The RSV is here certainly right; for the next two verses deal with the response of Gentile Christians to the gospel once it reached them and require some previous mention of Jewish Christian response. Thus the meaning of the two verses is: 'In Christ also we (Jews) were fore-ordained to be allotted a special role (or 'to be taken as God's special people') within the purpose of him whose power is at work in all history to bring it under the direction of his will, to the end that our action in being the first to put our hope in Christ should redound to the praise of his glory.'

13. It was also *In him* (Christ), and therefore within the eternal purpose of God which had its focus in Christ, that the Gentiles were in due course to be incorporated into the one people of God by responding to *the word of truth*, the truth about God's design and man's place in it. This truth is further defined as *the gospel of your salvation*. The emphasis here is on the pronoun: it is the good news that you (Gentiles) are included in the salvation already accomplished by God and accepted by Jewish Christians.

It is often misleadingly said that salvation in the New Testament always has a future reference. This is obviously untrue, even if we confine ourselves to the noun σωτηρία and its cognate verb, and quite indefensible if we take account of synonyms. Salvation is always three-sided: it is a past fact (Rom. 8^{24}; 11^{11}; 2 Tim. 1^9; Heb. 2^{3-4}; 5^9; Rev. 12^{10}); it is a present experience (Luke 19^{10}; 1 Cor. 1^{18}; 15^2; 2 Cor. 2^{15}; 6^2; Phil. 2^{12}; 1 Pet. 3^{21}); and it is a future hope (Rom. 13^{11}; Heb. 9^{28}; 1 Pet. 1^5). If one of these three aspects is more strongly emphasized than the others, it is, as here, the past fact which can be proclaimed as news.

sealed. Because Paul can speak of circumcision as the seal which confirmed Abraham's justification by faith (Rom. 4^{11}), it has commonly been assumed that here and in 2 Cor. 1^{22} the seal must be baptism. It may indeed have been at their baptism that the Gentile Christians *were sealed with the promised Holy Spirit*, but we must not confuse the occasion with the event; it was God who did the sealing. Their acceptance of the gospel was confirmed by God's gift of the Spirit (cp. Heb. 2^{3-4}). It is taken for granted here, as in Acts, that the coming of the Spirit was accompanied by tokens so obvious as to leave nobody in any doubt about what had happened (cp. Rom. 15^{19}; 1 Cor. 12^7; Gal. 3^2; 1 Thess. 1^5). Paul's attitude to baptism is oddly ambivalent; for sometimes he treats it with deep theological earnestness (Rom. 6^{3-4}; Gal. 3^{27}; Col. 2^{12}), and at others with comparative indifference (1 Cor. 1^{13-17}; 10^2). If he had intended a reference to baptism here he could easily have substituted 'at your baptism' (βαπτισθέντες) for 'at your conversion' (πιστευσάντες), but he is concentrating on their faith and its validation by God. *the promised Holy Spirit* is lit. 'the Holy Spirit of promise', one of the many Hebraisms of this epistle.

14. The Greek word ἀρραβών means more than *guarantee*. It was a Semitic word, presumably borrowed by the Greeks from the Phoenicians. In its Hebrew form it is found in Gen. 38¹⁷⁻¹⁸ meaning 'a pledge or surety'. But in hellenistic Greek it had come to be the ordinary commercial word for an advance on one's pay or for the down-payment which binds both buyer and seller to complete the contract. The evidence for this comes from two papyri, one a contract for the sale of a cow for which the owner is to receive 1,000 drachmae down (*P. Paris* 58), the other a contract for the hire of dancing girls who are to be given an advance on their wages (*P. Grenf.* II. 67). Thus it follows that the Holy Spirit is being described as a foretaste or anticipation of the Christian's final *inheritance* as well as a *guarantee* of the fuller blessing to come (cp. 2 Cor. 1²²; 5⁵).

The phrase which follows (εἰς ἀπολύτρωσιν τῆς περιποιήσεως) is obscure, and the RSV rendering, *until we acquire possession of it*, is a surrender to the difficulty, not a solution of it. Literally the phrase means 'unto redemption of possession', and it is an acute example of typically Pauline compression. The first point to be noted is that ἀπολύτρωσις is always used in the New Testament to denote a redemptive act of God. It is unlikely that the word is being used in a weakened sense to denote man's recovery of what he had forfeited, which seems to be the interpretation underlying the very loose paraphrase of the RSV. The NEB is therefore nearer the mark with 'when God redeems what is his own'. The difficulty with this is that περιπόιησις normally means 'ownership' or 'acquisition', and there is no evidence that it was ever used concretely to mean 'property'. In Mal. 3¹⁷, for example, εἰς περιπόιησιν means 'to take possession of them', and in 1 Pet. 2⁹ the same phrase means 'for God's ownership'. This leaves us with only one other possibility, that the genitive is a genitive of definition or apposition: the redemption consists in the taking of possession. The sense will then be that Christians have been given an advance on their inheritance against the day of full payment, the day 'when God will finally redeem the universe and make it his own'.

The paragraph ends with a reminder that only with the consummation of the great cosmic plan will the Creator's *glory* be fully displayed and call forth the full response of the creation's praise.

1 : 15–23 *Intercession*.

Because Paul has this majestic vision of man's place in God's universal plan, and because he believes that the bringing together of Jew and Gentile in the one Christian community is the first dramatic evidence of God's ability to break down divisive barriers and bring the world to unity in Christ, he is delighted at the news he receives of successful missionary activity in areas where he himself has never worked (vv. 15–16). He prays that these new converts may progress to fuller maturity through a deeper personal experience of God and through an increasing grasp of the opportunity they share with Jewish Christians and of the power now at work in their lives, the very same power which had given Christ victory over death and supremacy over all forms of authority and power (vv. 17–21). In Christ is already seen the full character of God, and that fulness is now being imparted to the church as the first decisive step in the process by which it is to be imparted to the universe at large (vv. 22–3).

15. *For this reason.* What appeared to be the introduction to a general theological treatise, comprehending the full range of God's eternal purpose, turns out to be the ground for a very particular pastoral interest in the spiritual growth of his readers.

Beare has argued that *I have heard* points to a merely mechanical copying from Col. 1⁴, since there the reference is to the report brought by Epaphras, while here no such specific reference is contemplated. This argument would have substance only if we supposed that, before the coming of Epaphras, Paul was ignorant of the existence of churches in Colossae, Hierapolis, and Laodicae. But considering that he had personal friends in at least two of these places, this seems unlikely; and Col. 2¹ is positive evidence that he was kept informed about, and had a pastoral care for, a number of churches which he had neither founded nor visited, just as, at an earlier point in his career, he had received regular news of the church in Rome (Rom. 1⁸⁻¹³).

The word *love* is omitted by many of the oldest manuscripts, and some commentators have thought that it was introduced into the text of later manuscripts to harmonize with Col. 1⁴. On the other hand it is at least equally probable that the word dropped out of the text at an early date through the common error of haplography. This is one of the many places where our estimate of the author's intention matters more than any weighing of manuscript evidence. It is inconceivable that Paul should have congratulated his readers on having a faith directed towards their fellow Christians. Moreover, the *love* which is directed not simply to other Gentiles but *toward all the saints*, the love which is proof of the breaking down of ancestral barriers between Gentile and Jew, is central to the argument of the letter (cp.

2^{11-12}). It is the immediate cause of Paul's thanksgiving, because it is the sign that the divine purpose he has just described is now taking effect.

16. *remembering* is a mistranslation. The noun μνεία by itself can mean 'remembrance', but μνείαν ποιεῖσθαι always means 'to mention'. Paul invariably uses the phrase in connexion with prayer (Rom. 1^4; 1 Thess. 1^2; Philem. 4; in the first two instances the RSV has 'mention'), and in this he seems to have been following a common epistolary convention (see J. A. Robinson, pp. 275–84).

17. *the God of our Lord Jesus Christ*. As in v. 3, the title used for God emphasizes the humanity of Jesus, since God's relation to the human Jesus, as his God and Father, forms the pattern for his relationship with other men. The phrase *Father of glory* is a Hebraism (cp. 2 Cor. 1^3; Jas. 1^{17}), which depicts God as all-glorious in himself, but also as the source of glory, such as he has already conferred on Jesus (1 Cor. 2^8; 2 Cor. 3^{18}; 4^{4-6}), and may be expected to confer on anyone entitled to be called his son (Rom. 5^2; 8^{21}; 15^7; 1 Cor. 2^7; Phil. 3^{21}; Col. 1^{27}; 3^4).

a spirit of wisdom and of revelation. The RSV has taken these words to refer to a human disposition, a capacity to receive and understand (cp. Rom. 11^8; Eph. 4^{23}). It is also possible to see in them a further reference to the activity of the Holy Spirit. The absence of the definite article and the presence of a qualifying genitive are no objection to this (cp. Rom. 8^{15}). As this example from Romans shows, Paul was capable of using the word in both senses in a single sentence. He did not believe that the Spirit of God was so wholly other, so alien to man's spirit, that it was equivocation to use the same word for both. Man's spirit is precisely that aspect of his personality which is open to the influence of God's Spirit, and man is truly human when his spirit is informed by and becomes the vehicle for the Spirit of God (1 Cor. 2^{11}; Rom. 8^{16}). The two interpretations are not incompatible; but that does not absolve us from choosing between them on the grounds that Paul intended both. The decisive point is that *revelation* is always in the New Testament an activity of God, not a faculty of man. It is impossible without straining the words to give any real meaning to *a spirit . . . of revelation*, which could only mean 'a disposition or tendency to make disclosures'. The NEB tries to get round this difficulty by trading on the ambiguity of the word 'vision' ('the spiritual powers of wisdom and vision'). But this is a verbal conjuring trick, for 'vision' may be roughly synonymous with 'revelation' when it means 'something seen', but not when it means 'the faculty of sight'. On the other hand, it is one of the functions of the Spirit, in Paul as in John, to bring home to man's understanding and conscience the significance of the revelation given once for all in Jesus (1 Cor. 2^{10}; Eph. 3^5; cp. John 16^{7-15}), and we must conclude that it is this activity of the Spirit that Paul here invokes.

The help of the Spirit is needed because *the knowledge of* God is something more than knowledge of facts about God. It is a first-hand, personal acquaintance with God, an encounter with him as God. Even the objective revelation of God in Jesus Christ is not of itself enough to produce this knowledge, until the Spirit that was in Jesus becomes a living presence in the believer (cp. Rom. 8^{8-10}; 1 Cor. 2^{11}).

18. In biblical terminology the *heart* is not the seat of the emotions, but stands for the whole inner self, without any tripartite division of will, intellect, and feelings. Since the Jews were unaware of the functions of the brain, they thought of the heart as the organ of knowledge, but of a knowledge which relied for conviction on moral judgment, not on mere empirical verification.

By the illumination of their vision the readers are to attain to a maturer knowledge of God, which is now defined in three parallel clauses. The first needs no elaboration, except that *the hope to which he has called you* does not refer to life after death, as some commentators have thought, but to all the possibilities of spiritual growth that have opened up for those whom God has called. The interpretation of the second clause depends on the meaning given to ἅγιοι (*saints*). Many commentators have taken the word here to mean 'angels', as it frequently does in the Septuagint. But there is not another passage in the Pauline corpus where the word indubitably, or even probably, has this meaning, as against more than thirty instances where it denotes Christians. Here, as in 2^{19}, the reference is more particularly to Jewish Christians, in whose *glorious inheritance* Gentile Christians have now been given a share (cp. Col. 1^{27}). But this clause will be further expanded in 2^{11-22}.

19. It is the third clause which for the present engages Paul's attention. The readers are to discover *the immeasurable greatness of his power* by actually experiencing it at work in their lives. It is hardly surprising in view of his own history that Paul's theology is experiential from start to finish. His convictions about the sufficiency of grace (1 Cor. 15^{10}), continuing efficacy (2 Cor. 12^{7-9}), its universality (2 Cor. 5^{14-15}; Rom. 11^{32}), its creative power (2 Cor. 4^{4-6}), have their basis in the fact, which remained to him a source of abiding astonishment, that mercy had come to him at the height of his rebellion against God. If God could do so much for a persecutor of the church, what limits could be set to the possibilities of his power (Rom. 11^{1})? Similarly, Paul invites the Galatians to judge the truth of his teaching about justification on the basis of their own experience (Gal. 3^{2}). Such a test of truth would be a restricting one if the appeal to past experience were not accompanied by a desire for ever expanding and deepening knowledge (Phil. 3^{8-14}; Eph. 3^{19}). To anyone whose faith is not anchored in a personal acquaintance with God's power, the majestic plan for the unity of the cosmos which Paul has been expounding must seem

grandiose and fantastic. The measure of a man's experience is the measure of his capacity for belief.

20. In a trick of style which is hard to reproduce in English the verb ἐνήργηκεν (*he accomplished*) picks up the sound and sense of the cognate noun ἐνέργεια (*working*) in the previous verse. The activity of God's power experienced by believers is in keeping with its supreme activity in the resurrection and exaltation of Christ. Elsewhere Paul develops in great detail the parallel between the resurrection of Christ and the resurrection of the believer, both to new life in the present (Rom. 6¹¹; 2 Cor. 5¹⁵; Col. 3¹) and to eternal life in the future (Rom. 8¹¹; 1 Cor. 15¹²⁻²²; Phil. 3²¹). Here he gives the comparison a new emphasis by linking it to the theme of Christ's exaltation, because this is the event he associates with Christ's lordship over the cosmos. The two events together are thus represented as a comprehensive victory over the unseen enemies of the spiritual world. It is true that the word 'enemy' is not used, and many scholars have supposed that the list of angelic beings in the next verse includes only hierarchies of beneficent but inferior powers. But this is to reckon without the allusive quality of Paul's Old Testament quotations. The words *made him sit at his right hand* are a fragmentary but obvious citation of Ps. 110¹, a text so frequently quoted in early Christian preaching that Paul could confidently expect his readers to complete it for themselves. God had set Christ at his own *right hand*, i.e. in the place of delegated sovereignty, until all his enemies were reduced to subjection (cp. 1 Cor. 15²⁵, where only the second half of the verse is quoted, but the first half is implied). Paul assumes that the enemies mentioned in the psalm are not human but spiritual ones, and this is why he adds *in the heavenly places*. The scene in which his enemies have hitherto exercised their control must also be the scene in which Christ now asserts his supremacy.

21. What is meant by *rule and authority and power and dominion* can be deduced partly from the words themselves and partly from other contexts in which these and similar terms are used. They denote spiritual beings who preside over all the forms and structures of power operative in the corporate life of men, the guardians of the religious, legal political, and social order (see on v. 10). They are created by God (Col. 1¹⁶), who intended that man should live as a social being, and therefore under various types of authority. But, like everything else in man's world, they have become corrupted by sin so that, though still exercising a divine commission, they constantly act in opposition to God's real purpose. Paul may perhaps have had a mental picture of these beings as angels (cp. 1 Cor. 6³), but their essential character is that they are symbolic representatives of an aspect of human existence. The sin by which they are corrupted, therefore, may be regarded either as their own or as human sin; because they are responsible for all those institutional and corporate wrongs which are human in origin

but cannot be laid at the door of individual sinners. At their best they are responsible for the maintenance of law, though sharing the limitations of the old order they represent (1 Cor. 6³). At their worst they have become 'the world rulers of this present darkness'. Paul is here claiming for Christ that 'all wreaths of empire meet upon his brow', and that his supremacy will enable him in the end to bring under his own control all the forces that permeate the complex existence of man.

Every name that is named can hardly be contemptuous dismissal—'whatever you like to call them' (so Abbott and Beare). Neither in this letter nor elsewhere does Paul treat the powers as trivialities. Robinson is no doubt partly right in his paraphrase: 'every title or dignity that has been or can be given as a designation of majesty' (cp. Phil. 2⁹). But Scott comes closer still in defining the names as 'uttered with reverence'. 'To call on the name' of a deity is a familiar Old Testament expression for worship (e.g. 1 Kings 18²⁴), and the powers which Paul has been speaking included all those beings whom the pagan world regarded as gods. The meaning then will be: 'every other object of man's worship or veneration.'

The distinction between *this age* and *that which is to come* is drawn from Jewish apocalyptic, where the coming age was the future period of deliverance under the reign of God. But in the New Testament the distinction ceases to be a purely temporal one. For in Christ the decisive day of God had arrived. Already he had surrendered himself 'for our sins to deliver us from the present evil age' (Gal. 1⁴), so that Christians could be described as those 'on whom the ends of the ages have come' (1 Cor. 10¹¹). Already the new creation had come into being (2 Cor. 5¹⁷). In so far as the world remained unaffected by Christ, the old age was still in force, controlled by its dark rulers (1 Cor. 2⁶⁻⁸) and its darker god (2 Cor. 4⁴). But in the person of Christ the new age had already broken in upon the present. It is therefore a mistake to translate τῷ μέλλοντι by *that which is to come*, as though from Paul's standpoint it was still wholly future. This age and the age to come already co-exist. Here the point is that Christ's supremacy was achieved in *this age*, i.e. in the very conditions which held other men in bondage, and that under his control even the powers will find their proper place in the new order.

22. As ground for this confidence Paul cites Psalm 8: God *has put all things under his feet.* In his use of this psalm it is likely that Paul was dependent on an earlier Christian tradition.[18] The author of Hebrews, writing independently of Paul, but relying on the same tradition of Old Testament exegesis, assumed that the psalm is to be interpreted in the light of the Jewish distinction between the two ages, and also in combination with Ps. 110. In the present age God had decreed that man should

[18]See C. H. Dodd, *According to the Scriptures*, pp. 32-4.

live in subjection to angels (and specifically that Israel should live under the angels of the Torah); but the age to come was to be under the control of man, who was destined to be crowned with glory and honour and invested with authority over the rest of creation; and in the exaltation of Jesus to God's right hand could be seen the first representative fulfilment of man's destiny (Heb. 1^{13}–2^9). A similar treatment of the two psalms underlies 1 Cor. 15^{24-8}, where the current period in which the regnant Christ is reducing his enemies to impotence is seen as the fulfilment of God's promise to put everything in subjection under man's feet. In the present passage, the combination of quotations from both psalms with an explicit mention of the two ages shows that the same interpretation is presupposed. With the exaltation of Christ the age of man's bondage to angelic powers has ended and the age of his lordship over creation has begun.

has made him the head over all things for the church. The RSV rendering assumes that ἔδωκεν ('gave') is being used in the Hebraic sense of 'appointed', that the headship of Christ is to be explained as part of the 'body' metaphor in the next verse, and that the sense is roughly the same as in Col. 1^{18}. But if Paul had wanted to say that God made Christ head of the church, there were easier ways of saying it than this; and, on the other hand, the translation given is not the most natural way of construing Greek. It can also mean: 'gave him to the church as head over all things'. This translation has two advantages: it allows *all things* in the second half of the verse to have the same value as in the first half, and it maintains unbroken the continuity of the argument. God decreed that *all things* were to be subject to man, he has now established Christ as *head over all things*, and he has given him to the church so that the church may share his supremacy. The idea of Christ as head is not in any way derived from the image of the church as his body, although the two ideas occur together in Eph. 4^{15} and Col. 1^{18}. Paul developed it quite independently (1 Cor. 11^3), drawing no doubt on the metaphorical uses of 'head' in the Old Testament (e.g. Isa. 7^{8-9}; Hos. 1^{11}). That the two ideas of head and body were not inseparable in his mind is proved by 1 Cor. 12, where Christ is the body of which Christians are the several limbs and organs, without any mention of a head, and by Col. 2^{10}, where, shortly after a reference to Christ as head of the body, the church, he speaks of him as 'head of all rule and authority'. This last passage, rather than Col. 1^{18}, is the parallel that illuminates the present usage. It is as head over the whole realm of spiritual power that Christ becomes God's gift to the church.

23. Both in simile and in metaphor Paul compares the church to a *body* many times and with constantly varying emphasis. In 1 Cor. 12^{12-27} he is concerned with the multiplicity of functions required within an organic unity, in Rom. 12^{4-5} with the mutual interdependence of

Christians, in Col. 1¹⁸ and Eph. 4¹⁵ with the common dependence of
Christians on their head, in Col. 1²⁴ with the church as an extension of
Christ's life and character, in Eph. 4⁴ with the need for visible manifestation of the unity which has its roots in the oneness of God, and
here with the unity subsisting between Christ and the church, which
enables the church to share his exaltation.

the fulness of him who fills all in all. Against the weighty authority of
Lightfoot (*Colossians*, pp. 257–73) Robinson has proved that πλήρωμα
(*fulness*) cannot be a passive noun ('that which is filled'), but must
connote either 'that which fills or completes' or 'the resulting fulness
or completeness'. But this still leaves us with three possible ways of
taking the clause:

(a) the church is said to be 'the completion of Christ, who is in the
process of being totally completed';

(b) the church is said to be 'the completion of Christ, who is in the
process of totally filling everything';

(c) Christ is said to be 'the complete embodiment of God who is in
the process of filling all things'.

Both (b) and (c) have the disadvantage that πληροῦσθαι does not
elsewhere occur with an active meaning, but this is a trivial objection
in comparison with the theological difficulty of both (a) and (b),
which imply that Christ is in some way incomplete without his com-
plement, the church. The third interpretation, on the other hand, fits
well with Pauline usage. It is God who is to fill *all in all* (cp. 1 Cor.
15²⁸), and this is to be achieved by his filling Christ with his own fulness (Col. 1¹⁹; 2⁹), in order that he, as the representative of God's
total being, may fill the church (Col. 2¹⁰; Eph. 3¹⁹) and subsequently
the universe (Eph. 4¹⁰). It is Christ then who is here described as *the
fulness* of God the all-filler. God's purpose is being achieved in three
stages: the fulness of his own divine nature has found complete
expression in the man Jesus Christ; he has given Christ, the bearer of
his fulness, as his gift to the church, which is to be the first sharer of
that fulness; and through the church he intends his fulness to pervade
the rest of creation.

2: 1–10 *God's Power in Redemption.*

With the power of God that had manifested itself supremely
in the resurrection of Christ Paul's readers have a direct
personal acquaintance. For by it they have been rescued from
the deadness of their past existence, in which their conduct was
determined partly by their own wickedness, partly by the prevailing atmosphere of worldliness, under the control of that
spiritual power to which they had given allegiance. Nor had

they been in any worse case than the Jews, for the same demonic spirit was still at work in those Jews who had rejected the gospel, and their present condition of disobedience had formerly been shared by Paul and other Jewish Christians, in the days when they had followed the natural inclinations of their unredeemed state and had shared the common exposure of all humanity to the processes of moral retribution (vv. 1–3). It was by God's mercy and love that Jew and Gentile alike had been given a share in the new life of Christ and in his new supremacy over the forces of the spirit world, and they must recognize their responsibility to make public their experience of God's inexhaustible grace (vv. 4–7). Their salvation is the work of grace from start to finish; in them the Creator has begun a new creation, refashioning their lives to make them conform to the character of Jesus, so that they may attain to the life of moral goodness which was God's original design for man (vv. 8–10).

1. *he made alive.* Here as elsewhere (cp. Gal. 2^{3-5}) the impetuosity of Paul's thought runs away with his syntax. The Greek has no main verb, and the accusative phrase *you . . . when you were dead* is left hanging in the air until it is resumed by an almost identical phrase in v. 5. The RSV has followed the AV in supplying a verb from v. 5.

you were dead. Paul uses the metaphor of death in two distinct ways. He can speak, as here, of a spiritual death, which is the inevitable nemesis of sin, because sin cuts a man off from God, the one source of life (Rom. 6^{23}; $7^{10,24}$; 8^{10}; Col. 2^{13}), and in the end gives a sting to physical death by making it a final severance from God (1 Cor. 15^{56}). He can also speak of sacramental death, experienced at baptism, when the old life is allowed to die in order that the Christian, united with Christ in his death, may also be united with him in his resurrection (Rom. 6^{2-13}; 2 Cor. 5^{15}; Col. 2^{20}). These two ideas are not incompatible, but they must not be confused. The argument here is that the Gentile Christians already have some initial experience of the divine power which was operative in Christ's resurrection because they themselves have also passed from death to life. On the face of it the argument appears fallacious, since the two types of death are not comparable: Christ was never dead in his sins, nor have the readers as yet undergone a physical death like his. We cannot escape the dilemma by appealing to Paul's doctrine of sacramental death with Christ, for that is not the type of death here at issue. The solution lies at the very roots of Pauline theology. Believers could, at baptism, accept identification with Christ in his triumph because Christ had already chosen to be identified with them in the full depth of their human predicament, making himself accountable for their sins, even to the point of undergoing in his criminal execution the curse pronounced on all violators of the law of God (Rom. 8³; 2 Cor. 5²¹; Gal. 3¹³; Phil 2⁸). Thus the resurrection of Christ was God's victory over spiritual as well as physical death, and men could experience its power in the new life which it offered to them in exchange for the deadness they were leaving behind.

2. *walked.* This verb, which is used very frequently in the New Testament (31 times by Paul and 15 times in other books) to denote moral behaviour, is a Hebraism. Among the rabbis the exposition of the Scriptures as a rule of life was called *Halakah*, the way to walk.

following the course of this world is a loose translation of a Hebraism (lit. 'according to the age of this world'), which means 'conforming to the standards of the present world order'. Paul uses the expression 'this age' to denote the whole organized system of human life prior to or unaffected by the coming of Christ (Rom. 12²; 1 Cor. 1²⁰; 2⁶,⁸; 3¹⁸; 2 Cor. 4⁴; Gal. 1⁴). He also uses the terms 'the world' or 'this world' in a similar sense (Rom. 3⁶; 1 Cor. 1²⁰⁻⁸; 2¹²; 5¹⁰; 6²; 7³¹; 11³²; Gal. 6¹⁴). To live in the world (Col. 2²⁰) is much the same thing as to be in Adam (Rom. 5¹²⁻¹⁴; 1 Cor. 15²²), or to be in or live according to the flesh (Rom. 7⁵; 8⁴⁻¹³) : it is to be implicated in and dominated by the corporate life of a godless and worldly humanity.

the prince of the power of the air is a title for Satan (cp. 2 Cor. 4⁴; John 12³¹), but one to which no precise parallel can be adduced. The unredeemed world is elsewhere described as 'the domain of darkness' (Col. 1¹³; cf. Eph. 6¹³), where the significance of the metaphor is clearer. The most probable explanation is that *the air* stands for the climate of opinion or, as we should say, the spiritual atmosphere, which inspires men's thoughts and actions. This view is confirmed by the following explanatory clause in which *air* is defined as *the spirit that is now at work.* The connexion between *air* and *spirit* is less obvious in English than in either Hebrew or Greek, where one word does service for breath, wind, or spirit. It is no objection that in biblical theology it is God who breathes into man his animating spirit. Man's spirit may come from God, but man is free to choose whether it shall be an obedient or a rebellious spirit. Paul can even use the same verb (*at work*) for the activity of this spirit as he has used (1²⁰) for the activity of God.

sons of disobedience is a Hebraism (the third in this verse), meaning 'God's rebel subjects' (NEB). The Hebrew *ben* is regularly used as a term of classification, without any trace of its primary meaning ('son'). The reference is not to man's disobedience in general, but to that which has come into effect *now*, i.e. the rejection of the gospel by unbelieving

Jews. Their rebellion against their God has been prompted by exactly the same spirit of worldliness as is found in paganism and must be recognized as the work of the Devil (cp. 2 Cor. 4⁴).

3. Paul can make this drastic assessment of Jewish blindness because he and other Jewish Christians were once in the same condition.

flesh and *body* are translations of the same Greek word, both misleading, since they imply only sensuality. But Paul uses σάρξ (*flesh*) to denote man's unredeemed nature in its totality, and includes among its propensities anger, envy, and ambition as well as sexual vice and drunkenness (Gal. 5²⁰). Paul the Pharisee would have hotly denied that the Jew was in these respects on a level with the Gentile (Rom. 2¹⁷⁻²⁰; Phil. 3⁶); but Paul the Christian had come to see that possession of the law of Moses was no protection against *desires of body and mind*, i.e. the promptings of instincts and false ideas (Col. 2²³; Rom. 2¹). On the contrary, the full sinfulness of sin was apparent in its capacity to adapt even God's law to its own interest (Rom. 7⁷⁻¹³).

children of wrath is yet another Hebraism, reflecting again the *ben* of classification (see v. 2; and cp. Deut. 25²; 1 Sam. 26¹⁶). By *wrath* Paul means the retribution that overtakes wrong-doing, whether it takes the form of judicial sentence in a law court (Rom. 13⁴), of national disaster (1 Thess. 2¹⁶), or of a progressive moral degradation (Rom. 1¹⁸⁻³²). In one sense it is God's will, since it represents his abhorrence of evil. But because it is not God's ultimate will for any man, Paul normally uses the term impersonally, and can even speak of Jesus 'who rescues us from the coming wrath' (1 Thess. 1¹⁰). Thus *children of wrath* means 'liable to divine retribution'.

by nature does not mean that evil is inherent in human nature as God created it, but simply that it is the natural proclivity of fallen men as in fact they are. Neither here nor in Rom. 9²² is there any justification for the idea of Augustine and Calvin that some men are reprobate by God's eternal decree. On the contrary, the point of the argument is that those who by their natural state were exposed to retribution have now by grace been redeemed.

4. The ultimate truth about man is to be found neither in his own natural condition nor in the retribution it deserves, but in God's *mercy* and *love*. In the following paragraph Paul will speak of what Christ has done to reconcile men to God and to one another, but it is characteristic of his theology that the whole process has its origin in God's own love for man.

5. *made us alive together with Christ*. The next verse, together with the parallel in Col. 2¹³⁻¹⁴, makes it clear that the event Paul is speaking of is Christ's own resurrection, not the appropriation of it by the individual believer at baptism. Christ so identified himself with men in his life and death that his death was a representative and inclusive event (2 Cor. 5¹⁴); and therefore his resurrection could be equally

inclusive. When he was made alive, they also were made alive in his representative person. To be associated with Christ is thus to share his new life *by grace*, i.e. by God's free, unearned gift.

you have been saved. The perfect tense has been thought to be un-Pauline. But Paul uses the perfect tense quite correctly when he wants to point, not to the past objective fact of salvation, but to its continuing effects in the present (Rom. 5^2; 6^7; Gal. 3^8). For this reason the NEB translation ('you are saved') is preferable. See also Introduction p. 21f. and the note on Phil. 3^{20}.

6. We have already been told that Christ's enthronement has given him supremacy over all the spiritual powers (1^{20-21}). We are now told that this is no individual prerogative, but one that he has achieved and holds as head of a new humanity. All who take part in his new life can equally claim to *sit with him in the heavenly places*, not yet on the ground of personal experience (1 Cor. 4^8), but because their life lies hidden with Christ in God (Col. 3^3).

7. In the last three verses Paul has spoken of the once-for-all act of God's love in the life, death, resurrection, and ascension of Christ. Now he turns to deal with man's experience of this and the responsibility that flows from it. Christians have been given a new status, a new life, and a new freedom, but only in order that, by accepting the status, living the life, and enjoying the freedom, they may allow God to *show* to the world *the immeasurable riches of his grace*.

This is to happen *in the coming ages*, which means no more than 'in the future'. This use of ἀιών ('age') bears no relation to its technical use to denote either of the two ages of Jewish eschatology (cp. 1^{21}). In his doxologies Paul regularly uses the phrase 'to the ages of ages', just as he can speak of past time as a plurality of ages and generations (Col. 1^{26}). There are indeed some few places in his letters where he speaks as if the world had only a little time to run (1 Cor. 7^{29-31}), but there are others in which he seems to contemplate a long future of indeterminate duration (Rom. 11^{25-32}).

8. Paul repeats what he has already said in parenthesis, that their salvation, past, present, and future, is the work of God's unearned *grace*, because he wishes to emphasize that even the *faith* with which they have responded is not their own achievement, but *the gift of God*. This is not to belittle man, as though he were a mere puppet in the hands of God. It is the man who is apart from God that is the plaything of forces too strong for him to master. Man is truly himself, truly human, only when he lives by grace.

9. By *works* Paul means any conduct by which man tries to earn God's approval or to establish a credit balance in the heavenly ledgers. Anyone who tries to live by such religious book-keeping finds he is never out of debt. But children in God's family do not have to earn their keep. The word *boast*, whether as verb or as noun, occurs over fifty times

in Paul's letters and must be regarded as a characteristically Pauline term. It covers not only open bragging, but the self-congratulation and the sense of moral superiority which are the least attractive by-products of any religion based on merit.

10. *his workmanship* does not refer to man's initial creation at the hand of God, but to the new creation which has made the Christian what he now is (2 Cor. 5^{17}). According to Paul, redemption means something more than the repair of the ravages produced by man's fall or the restoration of a primitive innocence; it is the creation of a new manhood and a new world, such as have hitherto existed only in the purpose of God.

2: 11–22 *The New Humanity*

From a general consideration of God's grace in redemption the letter progresses to a more detailed exposition of its main theme, the unifying power of God. One of the bitterest divisions of the old order was that between Jew and Gentile. If the readers look back on the paganism out of which they came, they will see that it was alienated from what they now know to have been the main stream of history. Racial distinctions had been exaggerated by pagan godlessness and immorality on the one hand and by Jewish superiority and exclusiveness on the other. Formerly estranged from Israel and Israel's God, Gentile Christians now find themselves at peace with Jewish Christians and at peace with God (vv. 11–13). This new unity has been achieved by Christ on the Cross, where he broke down the barrier of hatred, by annulling that legalistic form of religion which had led the Jews to suppose that God's approval must be earned by the observance of moral and ritual rules and, in consequence, to avoid contaminating contact with Gentiles. He has brought into existence a new humanity, in which there is no place for the old divisions, by drawing off on to himself all the hostility that separated Jew and Gentile from each other and from God and letting it die with him (vv. 14–16). In the mission of the church he has come again with his offer of peace to those who are still alienated, bestowing on Jew and Gentile alike the one Spirit and access to the one Father (vv. 17–18). In the church Gentiles share with Jews equal rights of citizenship in God's commonwealth, and equal status in his family;

all, like the apostles with whom the process began, are living stones in the one temple which God is erecting to be the shrine of his own presence in the world (vv. 11–22).

11. It is hard to find any justification for Beare's assertion that 'the exhortation to remember undoubtedly suggests that the readers are in the main Gentile Christians of the second generation'. Is it conceivable that the author of Ephesians, whoever he was, should have described his readers as having formerly been dead in their sins and under Satan's dominion, without Christ, without hope, and without God, if he knew that they had all been born to Christian parents and brought up in the church? This is certainly not the way Paul speaks of children who had even one Christian parent (1 Cor. 7[14]).

In the Greek *Gentiles* has a definite article, which has the effect of assigning them to a class in their own or someone else's eyes (cp. Gal. 6[1]). In this case it is because they are being described throughout from a Jewish point of view. No Greek or Roman thought of himself as a Gentile. It was Jews who called all non-Jews 'the Gentiles'. The barrier was of Jewish making, and therefore had to be broken down from the Jewish side.

Paul uses the phrase *in the flesh* with many different nuances, and it is not easy to determine which is intended here. We may argue, with Abbott, that it must have the same meaning in each clause of this verse, that in the second clause it refers to the outward, physical distinguishing mark of circumcision, and that the verse is to be understood in the light of Rom. 2[28–9], where Paul declares that the outward rite of circumcision makes no real difference unless accompanied by circumcision of the heart. But Paul is not here claiming that the distinction between Jew and Gentile was superficial or unreal. It was so real that nothing less than the death of Christ could break it down. It corresponded to real Jewish advantages and real Gentile deficiencies. The point is rather that Paul regularly uses *flesh* to denote man's unredeemed nature (cp. 2[3]), and regarded *the circumcision which is made in the flesh by hands* as a symbol of the old order in which men, Jews included, had confidence in the flesh (Phil. 3[3–7]), had the mentality of the flesh and lived according to the flesh (Rom. 8[4–7]). He can even say of Christians that they are no longer in the flesh (Rom. 7[5]; 8[8–9]). Robinson is therefore right in taking the first instance of the phrase here to mean 'while these fleshly circumstances lasted.' In the old order the Jews were justified in classifying all other peoples as 'the Gentiles' or *the uncircumcision* and themselves as *the circumcision*.

12. The RSV is probably right in taking *separated from Christ* predicatively rather than adverbially (i.e. 'remember . . . that, when you

were without Christ, you were alienated etc.'). But, if we so take it, we must be prepared to follow through the logic of this punctuation. It implies that, at the time in question, the Jews were not *separated from Christ*. According to Robinson, Paul was thinking of the earliest period of Christian history, when the church consisted entirely of Jews, and when high feelings were generated over the admission of Gentiles. Against this is the reiterated statement of vv. 13–16 that the reconciliation of Jew and Gentile was effected by the death of Christ. We must therefore assume that Paul thought of the Jews of pre-Christian times as already in some sense Christ's people (cp. Rom. 9⁵; 1 Cor. 10⁴; Heb. 11²⁶; 1 Pet. 1¹¹).

The Jews were entitled to regard themselves as God's *commonwealth*, not, as they liked to suppose, because they possessed and lived by the Torah, but solely because they had received *covenants of promise*, i.e. the covenants made with Abraham and his heirs which were based on a promise of future blessing (cp. Rom. 4¹³⁻²¹; Gal. 3¹⁶⁻²²). When the Jews segregated themselves from the Gentiles and called them opprobrious names, they forgot that the promise envisages the inclusion, not the exclusion, of the Gentiles.

having no hope may refer, as in 1 Thess. 4¹³, to the lack of a belief in an afterlife. 'The settled pessimism of the bulk of heathen epitaphs attests the cheerless gloom that brooded like a nightmare over the burial places of a pagan community' (Simpson). But it is more likely that in this context Paul is thinking of the contrast between the Gentile and the Jewish views of history. As Robinson says: 'The golden age of the Gentile was in the past . . . The Jew's golden age was in the future.'

In spite of their pantheon of gods, Gentiles could be called ἄθεοι *(without God)*, because the beings they worshipped were not real gods (Gal. 4⁸). Their *world* was godless because their so-called gods were only parts of it.

13. The use of the Old Testament in the next six verses clearly shows that the author was well versed in rabbinic methods of interpretation. As we can see from v. 17, the words *far* and *near* are taken from Isa. 57¹⁹. In its original context this verse expresses God's offer of peace to all Jews, whether they lived in Palestine near Jerusalem or far away in the Dispersion. But in midrashic exegesis, *near* and *far* were regularly taken to refer to Jews who were near to God and Gentiles who were far from him. 'To bring near' was a technical term for making a man a proselyte; and Isa. 57¹⁹ was actually quoted (*Num. R.* 149ᵈ) to prove that God addresses his offer of peace to the proselyte before the native Israelite.¹⁹ Here the same text is used, but with a difference. The Gentile is *brought near*, not by being turned into a Jew,

---

¹⁹See Strack-Billerbeck, *Kommentar zum Neuen Testament aus Talmud und Midrasch*, iii, pp. 585–7.

but by being included along with the Jew *in Christ Jesus*; and his new status is achieved by *the blood of Christ*, so that it dates, not from his own conversion, but from the death of Christ on the Cross.

14. *he is our peace*. The peace offered to men in the Isaiah prophecy proves to be no abstraction, but a person. It is not a state of mind, but a new state of affairs, brought about by God's new act of creation. Because Christ died for Jew and Gentile and in his death identified himself with both, he has brought both into union with himself, and so has *made us both one*. The fact that *both* is in the neuter here and in the masculine in v. 16 does not warrant any subtle difference in translation; the neuter is often enough used of persons (e.g. 1 Cor. 1²⁷⁻⁸).

14–15. The next nineteen words in the Greek are notoriously difficult. There are four different problems involved: the precise significance of two cumbrous phrases, the punctuation, the source of the metaphor, and the relation of the statement to the actual facts of Jesus's death. For the sake of simplification, let us take these problems in turn.

(a) The Greek for *the dividing wall* is το μεσότοιχον τοῦ φραγμοῦ. Μεσότοιχον is a variant form of the ordinary Greek word for a party-wall between two houses, though it is also used metaphorically. One writer, for example, speaks of breaking through the party-wall between pleasure and virtue. Φραγμός means 'a hedge, fence, or palisade'. Thus the words are roughly synonymous, both meaning 'barrier', but one having an emphasis on separation, the other on protection. We might thus translate the phrase as a whole: 'the dividing wall consisting of a protective fence.' The puzzle is to know why both terms were thought necessary. The second phrase, *the law of commandments and ordinances* (lit. 'in ordinances'), contains three near synonyms. Here the point of the apparent pleonasm seems to be that νόμος (*law*) had both a wider and a narrower sense. In its wider sense it denoted the whole Old Testament revelation of the will and purpose of God, and in this sense Christ fulfilled the law. He annulled it only in the narrower sense, as a system of rules for conduct set out in legal regulations.

(b) Literally translated and without punctuation the sentence runs: ' . . . the party-wall of the fence having broken down the enmity in his flesh the law with its rules and regulations having annulled.' This can be punctuated in three ways:

(i) 'In his flesh he has broken down the dividing fence, the hostility, by annulling the law with its rules and regulations';

(ii) 'He has broken down the dividing fence, the hostility, by annulling in his flesh the law with its rules and regulations';

(iii) 'He has broken down the dividing fence, by annulling in his flesh the hostility, the law with its rules and regulations'.

Many of the older commentators adopted the punctuation of (iii), on the ground that Jew and Gentile were divided by something more than hostility. But, even if the law is regarded as the source of the hostility, it is harsh to identify the two, and harsher still to speak of annulling hostility. The difference between (i) and (ii) is a minor one which hardly affects the theology of the passage. The choice between them depends entirely on considerations of style, and the NEB has adopted the one and the RSV the other.

(c) Most commentators have assumed that the metaphor was derived from the Jerusalem temple where, round the inner side of the Court of the Gentiles, just outside of the great wall surrounding the inner courts, ran a low parapet, four and a half feet high, bearing notices in Greek and Latin, which warned Gentiles not to penetrate further on pain of death (Jos. *Ant.* xv. 11; *B.J.* v. 5). The assumption has obvious attractions, but, whether we believe Paul to have been the author of Ephesians or not, it leads to grave difficulties. Those who have accepted the Pauline authorship have pointed out that Paul had good reason to remember this temple barrier, since he had been accused of taking the Gentile Trophimus inside it (Acts 21[28-9]). But, if this was what Paul had in mind, it would surely have been impossible for him to talk of the destruction of the metaphorical barrier between Jew and Gentile, when his imprisonment was the clearest reminder that the literal barrier still stood. Accordingly, those who deny the Pauline authorship have argued that nobody could have used such a metaphor until the literal barrier has been destroyed in A.D. 70. But this argument proves equally unsatisfactory. For the point of the destruction of the metaphorical barrier in Ephesians is that it enabled Gentiles to enter as equals an area of Jewish privilege; but when Titus destroyed the literal barrier in A.D. 70, he destroyed the whole temple, and left no Jewish privilege for Gentiles to share. There is also a further objection. A copy of the warning notice has been discovered, which runs: *No foreigner to pass the parapet and barrier round the precinct. Anyone caught will have himself to thank for his ensuing death.* The Greek words for 'parapet' and 'barrier' are not those used in Ephesians, and it is hard to see why anyone, wishing to make an allusion to this literal wall, should have gone out of his way to avoid the terms by which it was officially known and to substitute two others much less appropriate.

We come to a different and much more satisfactory result if we assume that the background to the metaphor is to be found in biblical and rabbinic theology. Φραγμός is the word used in the Septuagint (Isa. 5[2]) and in the New Testament (Mark 12[1]) for the protective hedge which God planted around his vineyard, Israel. In Isaiah's parable it is God who breaks down the hedge around Israel and leaves it exposed to punitive devastation. The rabbis occasionally spoke of the law as a hedge which protected Israel from sin (Strack-Billerbeck, iii p. 588). But the closest parallel is provided by the Letter of Aristeas (139), which declares that Moses by his gift of the law 'hedged us about with impregnable ramparts and iron walls, to prevent all contact with any of the other nations, and to keep us pure in body and soul, free from futile speculations, worshipping the one Almighty God above the whole creation.' Paul's point, which has prompted the use of a somewhat cumbersome phraseology, is that the law, intended by God to be a protective hedge, has been turned by Jewish nationalism into a rigid legal system, which has totally isolated Israel from the Gentile world and is thus responsible for the hostility between Jew and Gentile. Only by the annulment of the legal code could the barrier be removed.

(d) The words *in his flesh*, whether taken with what precedes or with what follows, clearly show that the verse has to do with something that happened in A.D. 30, not in A.D. 70. The question that remains is whether Paul's theological estimate of the significance of the Cross has any justification in historical fact. Paul is claiming that Jesus deliberately drew off on to himself the hostility between law-abiding Jews and those whose contaminating company they avoided, that this hostility brought him to the Cross, and that, because he refused to return it, it died there with him. This is a picture substantially borne out by the story of the Gospels. But for Paul the verification of it was plainly to be seen in any Pauline church, where Jew and Gentile mixed freely on equal terms.

15. *create . . . one new man*. A physical barrier may be removed and leave unchanged the people it once separated. But the removal of a barrier of hostility involves a profound personal change, nothing less than a new creation. Paul believed that by his resurrection Christ had become 'the last Adam', the head of a new humanity and the beginning of God's new creation (1 Cor. 15^{45-7}; 2 Cor. 5^{17}). Before that time, all men had belonged to the old humanity of Adam, dominated as it was by sin, death, and the powers of darkness. The point which now concerns him is that divisions of all sorts, of race and religion, of class and sex (Gal. 3^{28}; Col. 3^{11}) belong to that old dying world and have no place in the new humanity of Christ. Those who allow themselves to be identified with Christ must allow themselves also to be identified with one another.

16. Behind every alienation between man and man lies man's deeper alienation from God. Paul normally uses the word *reconcile* of man's relation to God (e.g. Rom. 5^{10-11}; 2 Cor. 5^{18-20}; but see also 1 Cor. 7^{11}), because on this all other forms of reconciliation depend. But the converse is also true, that no man can be reconciled to God who is not ready to be reconciled with his brother (Matt. 5^{23-4}; 1 John 4^{20}).

The *one body* may be interpreted as the church, provided that we think of the church not as an ecclesiastical organization but as the new humanity of v. 15. Nobody may rightly claim to be a member of the *one body* who is not prepared to recognize and express his unity with all other members of it.

17. It was not the earthly but the risen Jesus who *came and preached peace*. Although the early church believed Jesus to be at the right hand of God, they did not therefore regard him as an absentee, who would return to earth only at the end of the world (Matt. 28^{16}; Acts 9^{34}; Rev. 1^{13}). Unlike the more naive among modern scholars, they were well able to recognize the figurative nature of the language they were using to express their faith. *Preached* is a poor translation for a word which denotes a royal proclamation that hostilities are at an end. On *far* and *near*, see v. 13.

18. *access* (προσαγωγή) was a technical term for the right of free approach to a king's presence. A similar idea forms one of the main themes of Hebrews. There the contrast is between the old covenant, in which only the High Priest had the right to enter the Holy of Holies, and the new covenant, in which all believers can draw near to the throne of grace (4^{16}; 7^{25}; 10^{22}; 12^{22}). Here there is no reference to temple, sacrifice, or priesthood. The imagery is political, not liturgical. The point of the implied contrast between the two covenants is that formerly the Jews alone had the rights of citizenship, including the right of audience with the King, while the Gentiles lived in the distant provinces of God's empire; but now Jewish privilege has been abolished, and for both Jew and Gentile *access* to God is available through Christ. The Jewish belief that good conduct is the condition of man's admission to God's presence was divisive. The Christian belief that good conduct is the product of admission to God's presence and of the inner prompting of *the one* Spirit leaves all men equally dependent on the one source of goodness.

19. All ancient peoples distinguished between citizens, foreigners (*strangers*), and resident aliens (*sojourners*). In classical Greek there was a further distinction between resident (μέτοικοι) and transient (πάροικοι) aliens, but in hellenistic Greek this distinction had lapsed, and the second word did service for both categories and is so used in the Septuagint. In theory it was possible for a Gentile to become a naturalized member of the Jewish state by adopting the Jewish religion, but in practice his birth was remembered against him, and he was debarred from becoming a full son of Abraham. The books of Ruth and Jonah are protests against this racialism (cp. Isa. 56$^{1-8}$; 63$^{15-16}$). Jewish opinion on this subject seems to have fluctuated with the international situation, until its final hardening at the time of the Maccabaean revolt (167 B.C.). *Saints* here, as in 1^{18}, means Jewish Christians, whose full rights and privileges have now been opened to Gentiles also.

20. The change of metaphor from commonwealth and family to building and temple is facilitated by the triple meaning of the word οἶκος ('house-

hold', 'house', 'temple'). The habit of moving from one meaning of a word to another is a trick of Paul's style (cp. 1 Cor. 11$^{3-5}$), but it is also common in the Old Testament. Nathan, for example, warns David not to build a house (temple) for the Lord, because the Lord intends instead to build a house (dynasty) for him (2 Sam. 7$^{5-11}$).

the foundation of the apostles and prophets is most naturally taken to mean 'the foundation which consists of apostles and prophets'. But because Paul has said that no other foundation could be laid than Christ (1 Cor. 3^{11}), some defenders of Pauline authorship have felt it necessary to take it as 'the foundation laid by apostles and prophets'. This makes nonsense of the metaphor, since then Christ would be both cornerstone and foundation. If the case for Pauline authorship rested on such devices as this, it would be precarious indeed. But in fact the two passages are not strictly comparable (see Introduction p. 20), and there is not the slightest reason why Paul should not use a building metaphor in two different ways for two different purposes.

That the *prophets* are not the Old Testament prophets but Christian ones is proved by the word order (*apostles* first and *prophets* second), by the evidence of 3^5 and 4^{11}, and by the fact that Paul is here describing the constitution of the new order. *Apostles and prophets* are designated *foundation* members of the church because they were the primary recipients of revelation, the former as eye-witnesses of the earthly, the latter as spokesmen for the heavenly, Jesus. The two nouns share a single definite article, which could mean that Paul had in mind a single category of apostle-prophet. But, in view of 4^{11}, it is more likely that he uses this simple link to couple closely together the two chief types of Christian leader, because, though there were apostles who were not prophets and prophets who were not apostles, others like himself were both. No ecclesiastical system which ignores the place of *prophets* in the foundations of the church gains any support from Ephesians.

the cornerstone, which is here firmly distinguished from the *foundation*, is probably to be identified with 'the headstone of the corner' (Ps. 118^{22}; Mark 12^{10}; Acts 4^{11}; 1 Pet. 2^7), i.e. a large stone placed at the corner of the roof to bind two walls together.

21. As often happens with his more elaborate metaphors, Paul makes no attempt to visualize the picture he is drawing (cp. Rom. 11$^{17-24}$). Although Christ is the culminating stone which gives unity to the whole, the erection of the building is still in process, a new stone being added every time a convert is made. The building is also said to *grow*, just as later the body is said to be built up (4^{16}).

22. The Jews had believed that the temple in Jerusalem was God's earthly *dwelling place*, and this belief was one of the bulwarks of their claim to national privilege. But in the new covenant God's people themselves form the only temple or *dwelling place* God needs; and into

the structure of this temple Gentiles can be built as readily as Jews. The words *you also* provide the proof that the reason why Christ is here depicted as *cornerstone* is that he binds together these two formerly incompatible pieces of building material.

3: 1–13 *The Apostle of the Gentiles.*

Paul now resumes his prayer for his readers, but immediately interrupts it to remind them of the special role that he has been chosen to play in the drama of God's universal purpose. He is in prison, but only because he was appointed apostle to the Gentiles (vv. 1–2). He had received his knowledge of God's secret plan by a special revelation and has written a brief account of it, because he wants his readers to judge the truth of it for themselves, since no such knowledge was granted to previous generations (vv. 3–5). The equal partnership of Gentiles and Jews in the heritage and corporate life of the people of God is at the heart of the gospel he was commissioned to preach, and it was characteristic of God's dealings with men that the peculiar responsibility for the worldwide proclamation of this message should be entrusted to one whose record gave him no claim to any but the lowest rank in the church (vv. 6–9). God's purpose includes in its vast and varied scope the bringing of order and harmony to all the discordant spiritual forces which influence the organized life of men, and it is the task of the church to demonstrate that the process has begun in its own corporate life, with all the freedom and confidence of their newly acquired access to God (vv. 10–12). So Paul's imprisonment is no cause for discouragement, but rather an opportunity to unfold the secret purpose of God to the powers and authorities of the present world order (v. 13).

1. *prisoner for Christ Jesus.* Whereas AV, RV, and NEB use 'of', the RSV uses 'for', thus ensuring that we take the imprisonment literally, to the exclusion of any metaphorical reference (but see Introduction, pp. 1–2). Paul had two good reasons for claiming that his imprisonment was *on behalf of you Gentiles.* It was his insistence that the new covenant had brought an end to the era of Jewish privilege, together with his refusal to have Gentile converts turned into second class Jews by circumcision, that had aroused Jewish antipathy wherever he went,

and led to the final frenetic outburst against him in Jerusalem. But he would not have been in Jerusalem if he had not thought it necessary to accompany the collection which the churches of Greece and Asia Minor had made for the poor church of Jerusalem (1 Cor. 16¹⁻⁴; 2 Cor. 8–9; Rom. 15²⁵⁻³²); and the reason why he set so much store by this collection was that he regarded it as a symbol of the church's unity, an acknowledgment by the Gentile churches of their debt to the mother church and a proof to the Jewish church of Jerusalem that the Gentile churches were genuinely Christian. 'It is no exaggeration to say that Paul died a martyr to the cause of Christian reunion.'[20]

2. *the stewardship of God's grace* is a possible translation of the Greek, but only if we take the phrase by itself, out of its context in the chapter. Here χάρις does not mean *grace*, in the sense of the free, pardoning love shown to all Christians, but denotes rather a special favour granted to Paul. Elsewhere he uses the word five times of the prerogative of his apostolic commission (Rom. 1⁵; 12³; 15¹⁵⁻¹⁶; 1 Cor. 3¹⁰; Gal. 2⁷⁻⁹). Others might share his missionary task, as his colleagues or independently, but no one shared his commission to be the one apostle of the Gentiles. It follows that οἰκονομία cannot mean *stewardship*, but must have roughly the same meaning here as in 1¹⁰; and that the phrase as a whole means: 'the outcome of my special commission from God.'

3. Part of Paul's unique privilege was that he had been admitted to *the mystery*, i.e. God's secret plan for man and his world (see on 1⁹). This happened *by revelation*, and we have to decide whether he is referring to his conversion or to some later experience of prophetic inspiration. The three accounts of Paul's conversion in Acts all associate with it his call to be apostle to the Gentiles, though all in different ways: through Ananias (9¹⁵); in a subsequent vision in the temple (22²¹); or in the words of the heavenly Jesus on the Damascus road (26¹⁷⁻¹⁸). Paul himself can refer to his conversion as 'a revelation of Jesus Christ', in which he received directly from God the gospel he preached and the apostolic commission to preach it to the Gentiles (Gal. 1¹¹⁻¹⁶); and he regularly treats the equality of Jew and Gentile as an integral part of the gospel that came to him in this way (e.g. Rom. 3²⁷⁻³¹). On the other hand, he more often uses the word *revelation* to denote one of the many gifts of the Spirit which he shared with other Christians (1 Cor. 14⁶; 2 Cor. 12¹,⁷), and mentions one case in which his conduct of church affairs was dictated by such an experience (Gal. 2²). There is no reason to doubt that Paul was a prophet (Acts 13¹), and the most probable explanation of his use of the word *mystery*, strongly suggested by this present verse and consistent with other occurrences of the word in his letters, is that a *mystery* was any knowledge of God's will imparted under prophetic inspiration, but particularly through the

[20] J. A. Findlay, *The Acts of the Apostles*, p. 32.

inspired reinterpretation of the Old Testament scriptures (see on 5^{32}). V. 5 seems to be decisive in favour of taking *revelation* in this second sense.

I have written briefly. Since Ephesians is addressed to strangers, it is unlikely that the reference is to previous correspondence. Chapters 1–2 of the present letter are meant. Thucydides (i. 23) uses the same word ($\pi\rho o\acute{\epsilon}\gamma\rho a\psi a$) to refer to the opening chapters of the document he is writing.

4. *you can perceive my insight.* Those who repudiate the Pauline authorship of Ephesians have argued that this verse could have come only from an admiring pupil. According to Beare, 'the words clearly imply that the writer expects this letter at least to be read as theological literature . . . and that he looks upon it as an introduction to Pauline Christianity.' But the words could have been written by Paul without any suggestion of arrogance. He is claiming that the teaching he has just put before his readers is based on divine revelation, and he now invites them to judge for themselves the validity of his claim. He does not expect them to accept his teaching on the grounds of his office alone. He has no authority over them other than the authority of the truth he proclaims. The truth must be allowed to shine with its own light. 'We are interpreting spiritual truths to those who have the Spirit . . . A man endowed with the Spirit can judge the worth of everything.' (1 Cor. $2^{13,15}$).

the mystery of Christ is not Christ's secret but the secret which is Christ (cp. Col. 1^{27}).

5. Up to this point Paul has been arguing that the events of Christian experience have happened in accordance with a purpose of God which had been operative in the world's history since its beginning. Now he is reminded by his own part in these events that man's knowledge of this purpose is something quite new, even though *other generations* had not been totally in the dark. The Jews had received 'the covenants of promise' (2^{12}), even if they had largely misunderstood them. The Christian revelation was 'according to the scriptures' (1 Cor. 15^{3-4}). Paul himself would hardly have been convinced by it, had it not been 'attested by the law and the prophets' (Rom. 3^{21}); and he is able elsewhere to quote Old Testament passages which point to the salvation of the Gentiles (Rom. $9^{25}-10^{21}$). But it was precisely this way of reading the Old Testament that had burst upon Paul with all the amazement of a new revelation. The veil of incomprehension which had lain over the scriptures as long as he read them as a law book had been removed, and the glory of the old covenant had faded into insignificance before the superior splendour of the new (2 Cor. $3^{10,14}$).

sons of men is a Hebraism found in the New Testament only here and at Mark 3^{28}. *holy* (RSV) and 'dedicated' (NEB) are both somewhat misleading translations of ἅγιος. The *apostles and prophets* are not being distinguished from other members of the church, whether by personal sanctity or by ordination to sacred office, but from men of *other generations*. Ἅγιος is a word which applies equally to all Christians, and applies to them solely because they belong to Christ. In the present context, therefore, it comes very near to meaning 'Christian'.

Paul often uses *now* simply to distinguish the present age, inaugurated by Christ's death and resurrection, from the old order that has passed or is passing away. Here, however, it probably indicates a more immediate present. The revelation has been given *by the Spirit*. According to the Fourth Gospel the Paraclete or Spirit of Truth is needed to guide the disciples into all truth, and without his help they cannot expect to understand any of the words or works of Jesus (John 12^{16}; 14^{26}; 16^{12-15}). But in Pauline usage *by the Spirit* almost certainly points to a particular experience of inspiration. If we put the evidence of vv. 3 and 5 together, it would seem that the revelation must have come to other *apostles and prophets* through an inspired utterance of the prophet Paul, which they were able to recognize as the guidance of the Spirit (see also on vv. 7–9). The occasion may well have been similar to that recounted in Acts 13^{1-3}; only then, since the directions given concerned the seconding of Barnabas and Paul for special services, the Spirit must surely have spoken through Symeon Niger, Lucius, or Manaen.

6. *fellow heirs, members of the same body, and partakers*. The Greek says all of this in three words, each a compound of συν. The practice of piling up συν -compounds, many of them apparently coined for the occasion, is a characteristic of the Pauline style (e.g. Rom. 6^{4-8}; $8^{17,22}$; 1 Cor. 12^{26}).[21] Compared with the cosmic range of the plan of God expounded in chapter 1, this revelation of the equality of Jew and Gentile seems limited. But the point of this special revelation that had come to Paul was that in it all else was included in germ. Are the Gentiles *fellow heirs* with Jews and *partakers of the promise*? The promise made to Abraham and his descendants was that they should 'be given the world as their inheritance' (Rom. 4^{13}). Are they *members of the same body*? That *body* is the body of Christ, the new humanity which is replacing the old humanity of Adam (2^{15}) and making it possible for man to be lord of the universe as God always intended (1^{22}), and for the universe to share the glorious liberty of the sons of God (Rom. 8^{21}).

7–8. *Grace* (χάρις) belongs to a group of attitude words which are capable of both subjective and objective meaning. They can be used subjectively of the attitude itself or objectively either of the cause or of the result of the attitude. In English words such as 'wonder' or 'horror' may express either the subjective response or its objective

[21]See also T. R. Glover, *Paul of Tarsus*, pp. 177—80, 212.

cause. Words such as 'kindness' or 'favour' may express either the subjective disposition or the resultant evidence of it in the experience of another person. Thus *grace* can mean either 'the favour that bestows' or 'the favour bestowed'. The two senses are of course very closely allied, and it is not always necessary or possible to draw a hard line between them. Here in v. 8 *grace* clearly has its objective meaning ('privileged position'), whereas in v. 7, as in v. 2, it seems to be a borderline case.

8. *the very least of all the saints* is self-effacement rather than self-depreciation. Paul knew that, by any human standards, his persecution of the church has disqualified him from any but the lowliest status in it. He knew also that, humanly speaking, nobody had done more for the church than he (1 Cor. 15$^{9-10}$; 2 Cor. 11$^{23-9}$). His intention here is not to draw comparisons, but to disclaim all credit for the unique responsibility he had been called to carry and for the way in which God had enabled him to carry it by *the working of his power*.

9. Οἰκονομία (here translated *plan*) means rather 'working out', as in 1^{10} and 3^2; and the NEB correctly translates: 'how this hidden purpose was to be put into effect'. Revelation in the Bible is always performative as well as informative.[22] Whatever is revealed comes thereby into effective operation.

10. It is hardly an exaggeration to say that any interpretation of Ephesians stands or falls with this verse. Most commentators have regarded it as sheer fantasy, too bizarre to be taken seriously by the modern reader. Some have treated it as peripheral embroidery on the theme of the letter. 'God's wisdom in the scheme of redemption is an object of contemplation to heavenly intelligences' (Abbott). Others, like Beare, have detected in it the incipient Gnosticism of the author; for the Gnostics of the second century believed that the heavenly spheres were controlled by powers hostile to man, which would hinder the soul's ascent to God unless it went on its journey armed with the requisite passport of esoteric wisdom. Neither of these views bears any relation to Paul's doctrine of *principalities and powers*, to which he makes some reference in almost every one of his letters. We have seen (1^3) that *the heavenly places* are not some region remote from the life of earth, but the spiritual environment in which unseen forces compete for man's allegiance; and that *the principalities and powers* are beings, neither wholly good nor wholly bad, who preside over the corporate life of man (1^{22}). Paul has already told us that it is part of God's purpose to bring all of these powers under the sovereignty

[22]'Performative' is a term coined by J. L. Austin (*How to do things with words*) to denote any utterance (promise, intention, threat, offer, verdict, etc.) which comes into effect the moment it is spoken and does what it says.

of Christ (1^{10}; cp. Col. 1^{20}). He now tells us that God intends to achieve this end *through the church*. In the context of Ephesians, this can only mean one thing: that the unity of the church, and specifically the reuniting of Jew and Gentile in a single commonwealth and a single family, is to be the demonstration to the world of God's ability to break down all the barriers of suspicion and hatred which divide human society. In his earlier letters Paul spoke only of the defeat of the powers (1 Cor. 2^{6-8}; 15^{24-8}; Rom. 8^{37-9}), but in Colossians, Ephesians, and Philippians he has begun to envisage their redemption. But this is his way of saying that even such structures of power and authority as the secular state are capable of being brought into harmony with the love of God.

11. So far from being peripheral or fantastic, the refashioning of the organized life of man in society through the example and teaching of the church is central to God's *eternal purpose* and, like all other aspects of man's salvation, has already in a representative manner been *realised in Christ Jesus*.

12. The Gentile readers might well be daunted by what they have just been told about the responsibilities of church membership. They are therefore reminded of their qualification for the task. Their faith in Christ has given them *confidence* to approach God without embarrassment. Παρρησία (*boldness*) in classical Greek meant 'freedom of speech' or 'outspokenness'; but in the New Testament it is commonly used to denote the freedom of those who have nothing to conceal. For a man who can stand unashamed in the presence of God the spiritual rulers of this dark world need hold no terrors.

13. Paul's imprisonment might give the impression that he was the victim, not the victor, of the powers of the old world order. He was sensitive to this criticism, because he had previously had to face at Corinth the taunt that he could not be a genuine apostle, because God might have been expected to take better care of his servant (2 Cor. 4^{17-18}; 12^{1-13}), and this verse contains an echo of his reply to the Corinthians (cp. 2 Cor. 4^{16}). There he had contrasted the visible decay of his own poor, battered body with the glory of the inner man, renewed and increased from day to day as he was transfigured stage by stage into the likeness of Christ (2 Cor. 3^{18}; 4^{16-18}). Here he makes the additional point that his sufferings are *your glory*, i.e. the price he has been glad to pay in order to bring the Gentiles into that union with Christ in which they could experience the same process of inner renewal and transfiguration (cp. Col. 1^{24}; 3^{1-4}).

3: 14–21 *Second Intercession.*

Now that the readers have been told the full magnitude of God's redemptive purpose and the part they must play in it, they are in a position to enter into the prayer which Paul makes on their behalf. They know what it means to address God as Father, because in each of their local churches they h ve been brought together, across all the divisions that split human society, to form a single united family; and they have just been assured that God's reconciling love can produce the same family unity among the powers of heaven, the guardians of man's corporate existence (vv. 14–15). Their task is to give to the world an example of the unity which God designs to create in earth and heaven, and for this they need to know God's plan not merely with their minds but in the day to day experience of their lives (vv. 16–17). Such knowledge is not confined to the intellectual elite, nor can it be attained by the individual Christian in isolation. Love can be known only where it is practised. Only the whole community of Christians, with the combined resources and experience of all its members, can do justice to the dimensions of the love which has c me into the world in Christ (vv. 18–19).

The prayer ends with a doxology, which differs from all other doxologies in setting the church alongside Christ as the agent through which the glory of God is to be displayed and acknowledged (vv. 20–21).

14. *For this reason.* The repeated phrase picks up the threads of the prayer interrupted by the long parenthesis of vv. 2–13.

I bow my knees. Though standing was the normal Jewish attitude of prayer (Mark 11[25]; Luke 18[11]), kneeling was not uncommon (1 Kings 8[24]; Ezr. 9[5]; Luke 22[41]; Acts 21[5]). The Greek phrase Paul uses, however, suggests that he may be echoing the words of Isa. 45[23] (cp. Rom. 14[11]; Phil. 2[10]), where the bowing of the knee is the token of homage to the universal King.

14–15. *the Father, from whom every family in heaven and on earth is named.* Paul cannot be using the word *family* literally of human families descended from a common parent, since in this sense there can be no families in heaven, where they neither marry nor are given in marriage (Mark 12[25]). He must be using the word metaphorically, just as in 2[18] he has spoken of Jew and Gentile as together members of the household of God. Each local church was a house of God, a family circle acknowledging God as *Father*. Again, Paul cannot be using the word *named* to make the trite observation that πατριά is etymologically derived from πατήρ. Here as in Hebrew and other Semitic languages 'to name' means 'to constitute', 'to bring into existence'. For instance, the best known of all the Babylonian creation stories begins:

> 'When above the heaven was not named,
> And beneath the earth bore no name.'

Before they were named, they had no existence (cp. Isa. 40²⁶; Eccles. 6¹⁰). So here, those who have learned from Jesus to call God *Father* have thereby been *named* or constituted a family, even if before they had been divided by racial hatred. But what then can be meant by *every family in heaven*? The clue must lie in those earlier references (1³,¹⁰,²⁰; 2⁶; 3¹⁰) where we have found good reason to believe that Paul was thinking of *heaven* as the realm of those spiritual powers which influence human lives. He writes under the effect of an abiding astonishment that Jew and Gentile should have become members of the one household of faith, and in this miracle of grace he has found in microcosm the purpose of the universe. He began by describing that purpose as the uniting of 'all things in Christ, things in heaven and things on earth' (1¹⁰). We now see that he did not have in mind some pantheistic continuum, but the establishment of family unity by the breaking down of barriers. There is to be established among the spiritual rulers of this present darkness the same sort of personal harmony *in heaven* as subsists in an earthly family where God is recognized as *Father*. So interpreted, Paul's address to God forms an admirable summary of the argument that precedes it and an adequate ground for the petitions which follow.

16. Paul uses the expression *the inner man* in two other passages. In Rom. 7²² 'it is synonymous, or almost synonymous, with the "I" that would do good and hates evil . . . and with the "mind".' (Barrett, ad loc.). But there Paul is analysing the experience not of the Christian but of the man who is living under law and is torn in two by the struggle between his mind and his impulses. A better parallel with the present usage is in 2 Cor. 4¹⁶, where he contrasts the outer self, subject to suffering and decay, with the inner self which is renewed daily. To put on Christ (Gal. 3²⁷; Rom. 13¹⁴), to put on the new humanity which is being renewed in the image of its Creator (Col. 3¹⁰), to be transformed by the renewal of the mind (Rom. 12²), are alternative ways of describing the one fundamental Christian experience of new life.

17. Paul more often speaks of Christians as being in Christ than of Christ dwelling in them, perhaps because he does not distinguish between the indwelling Christ and the indwelling Spirit (Rom. 8⁹⁻¹¹; 1 Cor. 15⁴⁵; 2 Cor. 3¹⁷⁻¹⁸). But see also Gal. 2²⁰ and Col. 1²⁷. The translation *rooted and grounded* obscures the double metaphor from horticulture and building (cp. 2²¹; 4¹⁶). The NEB has: 'with deep roots and firm foundations'.

18. Paul is not speaking of any esoteric knowledge such as initiates into the hellenistic cults could boast of. This knowledge is open to *all the saints*, i.e. all members of the church, not as individuals, but as members of the Christian family. Love cannot be known by isolated contemplation, but only by being experienced in a community; and such are the dimensions of *the love of Christ* that it takes the combined experience of *all* Christians to *comprehend* it. In Rom. 8³⁹ *height and depth* are almost certainly astrological terms: stars at their zenith and nadir. But *breadth and length* are never so used, and there is no point in trying to read into these four dimensions here any magical or mystical significance.

19. The attempt *to know* the unknowable is a paradox which is at the heart of all true religion. *Omnia exeunt in mysteria* ('all things run out into mystery'). Man must know God or perish; but, unless he knows him as ultimate mystery, he does not know him at all.

   The fulness of God has already dwelt in Jesus (1²³; cp. Col. 1¹⁹; 2⁹), and we can see now that by this Paul understands the completeness of mutual love and knowledge which marked the relationship between the earthly Jesus and his Father. The second stage in the working out of God's purpose is that this fulness is to be imparted to the church. Finally, through the church, it is to be extended to embrace the whole cosmos.

20. *by the power* does less than justice to the preposition κατά, which means 'to judge by'. Paul's confidence, like his theology, is firmly grounded in religious experience. Christ's love may be beyond his or anyone else's ultimate comprehension, but he has enough acquaintance with *the power* of God *at work* in his own life to be sure that there can be no limits to its achievement (1 Cor. 12⁶; 15¹⁰; Gal. 2⁸; Eph. 1¹⁹; Phil.2¹³; Col. 1²⁹). Neither the majesty of his vision nor his large petitions can overtax God's power, nor is God's activity bounded by the poverty of human imagination or the pettiness of human prayer.

21. This is not the only place where Paul comes near to equating *the church* with Christ (cp. 1 Cor. 1¹³; 12¹²), but it is the only place where *the church* is included in a doxology. A doxology is a fitting climax to the doctrinal section of the letter, which has declared that the glory of God, fully revealed in Jesus, must be appropriated by the whole church and displayed in its life and character for all the cosmos to see and in the end to share.

4: 1–16 *Diversity in Unity.*

Here, as in Romans 12¹–15¹³, the doctrinal section with its closing doxology is followed by a lengthy passage of ethical exhortation. Christian behaviour is not the condition but the consequence of a man's acceptance by God. But Ephesians is unique among the letters of Paul in that the wealth of general ethical instruction which follows in the next three chapters is subordinated to the main theme of the first three. The conduct of the readers must be in keeping with the calling just expounded to them; they must cultivate those qualities of mutual respect, forbearance, and love which make for unity and peace in their life together (vv. 1–3). The unity of the church is not, in the first instance, a task to be achieved or an object of aspiration but a fact, given in the gospel, inherent in the nature of the church and its membership, guaranteed by the one Spirit who inspires it, the one Lord who governs it, and the one God who is the source of its life (vv. 4–6). But this unity must not be misconstrued as uniformity. There must be room for the greatest possible variety if Christians are to be free to exercise the many different gifts of Christ, gifts mentioned in the psalm set for the Jewish Feast of Pentecost which, interpreted as Christian scripture, tells of the ascent of Christ to cosmic supremacy and his return at Pentecost in the person of the Holy Spirit to give gifts to his church (vv. 7–10). Amongst his other gifts were various types of leadership, designed to equip all members of the church for their share in the church's ministry, and so to build up their corporate life (vv. 11–12). Only by the full exercise of these various gifts can the whole company of Christians grow together to form the new humanity and attain to a maturity which is not individual but communal (v. 13). Error is manifold, and the truth is one; but the truth must be lived as well as believed if men are to grow into that perfect organic union with Christ which is possible only when every part of the organism is fulfilling its own distinct function in harmony with the rest (vv. 14–16).

1. The verse begins with the same three Greek words as Rom. 12¹ ('Therefore I urge you'), and the RSV both by changing the word order and by using a different English verb has obscured the parallel. The introduction of ethical teaching by *therefore* is not peculiar to Paul (cp. Col. 3⁵; Jas. 1²¹; 1 Pe. 2¹), but seems rather to have been characteristic of all catechetical instruction in the missionary work of the early church. On *prisoner*, see 3¹.

Although Paul often gives moral precepts in the imperative, he would have resisted any attempt to reduce Christian behaviour to a set of hard and fast rules, since this would have reinstated the very legalism from which Christ had set men free (2^{15}; cp. Gal. 5^1). Conduct must be guided by the Spirit (Gal. 5^{25}), by the mind of Christ (1 Cor. 2^{16}; Phil. 2^5), by love (Rom. 14^{15}). In any situation the Christian must determine what he ought to do, not by looking up the rule-book, but by asking what course of action is *worthy* of Christ (Col. 1^{10}), of God (1 Thess. 2^{12}), or of the gospel (Phil 1^{27}).

2. *Lowliness* ($\tau\alpha\pi\epsilon\iota\nu\sigma\phi\rho\sigma\sigma\acute{\nu}\nu\eta$) is compounded from an adjective which in classical Greek always connoted cringing, abject, servile humility. It was only through the example of Jesus that humility came to be a virtue (cp. Matt. 11^{29}). Here it is that unassuming modesty which never stands on its rights, but always shows consideration for the feelings or views of others (cp. Rom. 12^3; Phil. 2^3). *Meekness* ($\pi\rho\alpha\acute{\nu}\tau\eta s$) is persistent courtesy, even to those who are difficult or unappreciative. *Patience* ($\mu\alpha\kappa\rho\sigma\theta\nu\mu\acute{\iota}\alpha$) is literally 'a long temper', the opposite of a short temper, the ability to make allowances for the weaknesses and faults of others. All three are aspects of the one inclusive social virtue, *love*.

3. *the unity of the Spirit* is that unity which the Spirit creates, just as 'the fellowship of the Spirit' is that fellowship which the Spirit creates (2 Cor. 13^{14}; Phil. 2^1). It is a mischievous distortion of Paul's meaning to use the phrase as though it meant 'spiritual unity' as opposed to 'organic unity', as the next verse makes clear. Though unity is the creation of the Spirit, it requires human diligence to *maintain* it.

4–6. Because of the parallels in 1 Cor. 8^6 and 12^{4-6}, it is frequently stated as though it were a fact that this list is an elaboration of a primitive confession of faith. It may be so, but the modern passion for finding credal and liturgical formulae in the epistles has far outrun the evidence. The fact that not one of these 'formulae' is ever quoted twice in identical words is surely good reason for caution. What is more probable is that Paul in each of these passages is adapting the Jewish confession of faith, the Shema (Deut. 6^{4-9}), in the light of Christian faith and experience.

Like the RSV, most translators supply the words *there is*, though they have no equivalent in the Greek, which has only a string of nouns, each qualified by the adjective *one*. This looseness of syntax is typical of Paul, particularly in ethical passages. In Romans 12, for example, the sentences follow one another in a rapid, staccato style, with little attention to syntax. For a similar phenomenon in a passage of a different kind, see 2 Cor. 8^{23-4}.

4. The corporate unity of the church is not a desirable end, but a datum to which the behaviour of its members must conform. Nobody may claim to be a member of the *one body* unless he is prepared to acknow-

ledge and express his unity with all other members. The idea that the church could be divided was to Paul unthinkable (1 Cor. 1^{13}), and he denounced a refusal to share in the one communion of the Lord's Supper as a denial of the truth of the gospel (Gal. 2$^{11-14}$; cp. 1 Cor. 10$^{16-17}$). Each congregation was to be regarded, not as a part of a larger whole, but as the *one body* in its local manifestation. Thus, although Paul is writing here about the church as a whole, all that he says applies also to the local church in which the unity of the one church becomes visible and real. This outward and visible unity of the church is important not only for its own sake, but because of the *one hope that belongs to your call*, i.e. the hope that through the example of the church God's plan to unite all things under the lordship of Christ may become known and effective throughout the universe (1^{10}; 3^{10}).

5. *one Lord, one faith, one baptism.* These three are probably, as Scott suggests, to be taken together: 'one Lord in whom all have believed and in whose name all have been baptized.' If we try to take them separately, we find ourselves asking why Paul has selected these three as essentials, particularly to the exclusion of the Lord's Supper, which he elsewhere treats as a symbol of unity (1 Cor. 10$^{16-17}$). But the question hardly arises if we take the whole triad to refer the Christian's allegiance given once for all to the *one Lord*. In any case, the absence of any mention of the other sacrament is no argument against Pauline authorship. Since 1 Corinthians is the only New Testament book which explicitly mentions the Eucharist, though we may suspect allusions elsewhere, we have no means of estimating whether its omission here is significant or not. But the omission would present just as much or as little of a problem in a primitive confession of faith or in a pseudo-Pauline epistle as in a genuine letter of Paul.

7–11. This passage is a notorious crux. What is the descent of Christ to which it refers? Is it his Incarnation (cp. John 3^{13}); or his descent into Hades (cp. Rom. 10^{7}; 1 Pet. 3^{19}; 4^{6}); or his return at Pentecost to give his Spirit to the church? Scholarly opinion has on the whole been divided between the first two answers, though we shall find that the evidence points very strongly to the third. Our choice must be guided by the following considerations.[23]

(a) V. 7 introduces and v. 11 continues the theme of Christ's gifts to his church. The intervening verses must be treated as an exposition rather than as an interruption of this theme.

(b) Psalm 68 was one of the psalms appointed for use at the Jewish feast of Pentecost, which had almost certainly by this time come to be

[23]For a fuller statement of the evidence see G. B. Caird, 'The Descent of Christ in Ephesians 4, 7–11', *Studia Evangelica*, ii, pp. 535–45. See also Kirby, op. cit., pp. 97–100.

celebrated as a commemoration of the giving of the law at Sinai. The verse here quoted may originally have referred to Yahweh's victorious ascent of Mount Zion, followed by a procession of defeated enemies, from whom he was to receive tribute; but through its liturgical use at Pentecost, particularly in conjunction with the lection from Exodus 19, it came to be interpreted as a reference to Moses's ascent of Mount Sinai. This interpretation is reflected in the Aramaic paraphrase of the Targum.

'Thou hast ascended to heaven, that is Moses, the prophet;
thou hast taken captivity captive, thou hast learnt the words of the Torah;
thou hast given it as gifts to men,
and also with the rebellious, if they turn in repentance,
the Shekina of the glory of the Lord God dwells.'

(c) In the Old Testament, according to both the Masoretic Text and the Septuagint, the ascending victor was to receive gifts from men, but in Ephesians and the Targum he gives gifts to men: in the one case Moses gives the Torah to Israel, in the other Christ gives spiritual gifts to the church. This agreement cannot be coincidence. Paul must have been familiar with the kind of rabbinic exegesis of the psalm represented by the Targum and be adapting it to Christian ends. We have already come across a similar adaptation of rabbinic exegesis in 2[13-17].

(d) Paul makes two comments on the psalm, and we shall not have interpreted him aright unless we see in what way they contribute to his argument. He remarks:

(i) that the ascent mentioned in the psalm logically implies a corresponding descent; and
(ii) that the ascender and the descender are one and the same person.

It is not easy to see how either the Incarnation of Christ or his descent into Hades could be thought to be logically derived from a belief in his Ascension. In the Jewish tradition Enoch and Elijah had ascended to heaven without first having descended from it or having undergone death and burial. But if the psalm is being interpreted as a Christian Pentecostal psalm, then it makes sense to say that the ascent which is mentioned in the psalm implies a corresponding descent, though this is not mentioned; for the Christ who ascended must have returned to earth to give his gifts to men, just as Moses had to descend to the plain to give the Torah to Israel. Again, it is hard to see why anyone should think it necessary to say that the Christ who descended from heaven at his incarnation or into Hades at his death was identical with the Christ who ascended, since nobody would have questioned this for a moment. But it was worth saying that the visible Christ who ascended was identical with the unseen Lord who descended at Pentecost in the coming of the Holy Spirit; and this identification is thoroughly in keeping with the theology of Paul, who never distinguished between the indwelling Spirit and the indwelling Christ (see on 3¹⁷).

(e) The descent into Hades in later literature was always taken to be the occasion when Christ overthrew the demonic powers of evil. But in Ephesians these powers are said to inhabit the heavenlies (3¹⁰; 6¹²), so that what was required for their defeat was not a descent into the underworld but an ascent to heaven, and this is what Psalm 68 is here taken to affirm. Thus any mention of a descent into Hades would be irrelevant to the theology of this epistle.

(f) There is an illuminating parallel to this passage in 1 Cor. 10⁴. There Paul takes a Jewish midrash, which had found in the rock that followed Israel a reference to the Torah, and adapts it by claiming that the rock was Christ. Here he takes another midrash, which found in Ps. 68 a reference to Moses's gift of the Torah, and adapts it by claiming that it is a psalm of the Christian Pentecost, and that the gifts are the gifts of Christ.

(g) A different midrash on another verse of Ps. 68 underlies the story of Pentecost in Acts 2.

7. *to each of us.* Every Christian has his share in Christ's bounty, but all the shares are different. The church is a living organism, which by its very nature precludes uniformity or regimentation.

8. These words might have provided the occasion for a hymn of praise on Christ's victory over the principalities and powers (cp. Col. 2¹⁵). The fact that Paul has made no use of them in the present context is significant testimony to his concentration throughout the passage on the central theme of Christ's gifts.

9. Some manuscripts add 'first' after *descended*. This reading would exclude a descent at Pentecost after the Ascension, but it is a late gloss, not supported by the best manuscripts. The genitive case in τὰ κατώτερα τῆς γῆς (*the lower parts of the earth*) has been taken by the RSV as a partitive genitive ('the parts of the earth which are below'), because the translators assumed that the reference was to the descent into Hades. But the genitive can equally well be a genitive of apposition ('the region below, namely the earth'). Grammatically there is nothing to choose between the two constructions, except that in the New Testament the partitive genitive, unsupported by preposition or noun of quantity, is rare, whereas the genitive of apposition is used frequently, and particularly so in this letter (e.g. 2¹⁴,¹⁵,²⁰; 6¹⁴⁻¹⁷). But it is the meaning of the passage as a whole that must finally decide which of the two was intended.

10. Christ's descent to bestow his gifts on the church is part of the divine plan *that he might fill all things* (see on 1²³; 3¹⁹).

11. *his gifts were* is a regrettable mistranslation, which implies that the following list of leaders exhausts the gifts. The 'incipient ecclesiasticism' of the epistle, which has been advanced as an argument

against Pauline authorship, is largely the product of this kind of misinterpretation. We have just been told that every Christian has received his due measure of Christ's bounty, in virtue of which he becomes Christ's gift to the church. The fact that the list in 1 Cor. 12$^{28-30}$ consists partly of functions and partly of persons who discharge them, whereas this one consists of five types of persons, is a singularly slender reason for claiming that between the two epistles there has been a greater development of church organization than could have happened in the lifetime of Paul. The correct translation is: 'And it is he who has given some to be apostles etc.' As in 1 Cor. 12, all these functions are charismatic gifts, Pentecostal gifts of the ascended Christ. Men become *apostles*, *prophets*, and the like, not because they are appointed to an office, but because they are endowed with a spiritual gift, each of which carries with it a direct commission from Christ. It is noteworthy that there is as yet no mention of bishops, presbyters, or deacons. Robinson's explanation, that these three 'were primarily local officers, and St. Paul is here concerned with the church as a whole', must be regarded as special pleading, since *pastors* at least must have had a local function. The more obvious inference is that the churches here addressed had not yet reached that stage of ecclesiastical development reflected in Phil. 1^1, let alone that of the Pastoral Epistles.

12. As this verse is punctuated in the RSV, the leaders of the church have three parallel duties. But it is better to omit the first comma and read: 'to equip the saints for the work of the ministry'. The *ministry* is Christ's own programme of service to the world, which he entrusts to the whole membership of the people of God, not to a group of clergy within the church. The *building up* of *the body of Christ* is not achieved by pastoral concentration on the interior life of the church, but by training every member for his part in the church's mission to the world. On *the body of Christ*, see 1^{23} and 4^{15}.

13. The destination of the church is described in three parallel clauses. First, the unity which has been proclaimed as a given fact is now presented also as the goal of Christian endeavour, a goal which by its very nature can be reached only by *all* together. Most commentators have taken the genitives in this first clause to be possessive ('the unity that properly belongs with faith in the Son of God and knowledge of him'). But they could also be genitives of reference ('unity in faith and knowledge'). This interpretation is strongly supported by the contrast with doctrinal vacillations in the next verse, and also by the teaching of 3^{18}, that it is only in company with all God's people that the Christian can comprehend the profundities of his faith.

Mature manhood is not to be an individual attainment but a corporate one. All men are by nature born into the old humanity of Adam, but may by grace be incorporated into the new humanity of Christ. This 'new man' (2^{15}) has been created in Christ, 'but he has a long growth before him' (Robinson). The maturity of this growth is to be measured by nothing less than *the stature of the fullness of Christ*. This phrase could be a Hebraism, i.e. 'the complete stature of Christ'; but it is more probably intended to pick up the idea, already adumbrated in 1^{23}, 3^{19}, and 4^{10}, that Christ, filled himself with the full being of God, is to communicate that *fullness* first to the church and through it to the world.

14. The opposite of maturity is infantile gullibility, which Paul describes in one of his most splendidly mixed metaphors (see Introduction, p. 28). *Cunning* ($\kappa \upsilon \beta \iota a$) is literally 'dice-playing'. So Christians are warned not to be babies, in an open boat at the mercy of wind and wave, driven off course by the roll of the dice. The last phrase in the verse is hard to translate. *Craftiness in deceitful wiles* implies that the warning is against deliberate dishonesty, but the three preceding metaphors suggest rather that the danger envisaged is a haphazard and misguided cleverness. Young children tend to believe anything they are told. A rudderless boat goes where wind and wave happen to drive it. A game of dice depends on sheer luck. $\Pi a\nu o\upsilon\rho\gamma\iota a$ can mean *craftiness*, but often, particularly in the Septuagint, it simply means 'cleverness', without necessarily any pejorative overtones. $\Pi\lambda a\nu\eta$, here translated *deceitful*, normally means 'error', i.e. a going astray rather than a leading astray of others. $M\epsilon\theta o\delta\iota a$, apart from its use here and in 6^{11}, is used only to denote a system of tax collection, but the cognate $\mu\epsilon\theta\delta\delta\iota o\nu$ can mean 'an ingenious surprise' (Petron. 36). The preposition $\pi\rho\delta s$ seems to be used in a sense not unlike that of John 11^4: 'this illness is not unto (i.e. enough to cause) death'. An even closer parallel is provided by James 4^5, which should be translated: 'the spirit which God has planted in us has longings to the point of envy' ($\pi\rho\delta s$ $\phi\theta\delta\nu o\nu$). It is therefore possible to translate here: ' . . . by the passing fads of men, by a cleverness verging on misguided ingenuity.

15. *speaking the truth in love*. Paul is not recommending frankness of speech tempered by consideration, nor is he suggesting that the claims of *truth* and *love* must be held in some sort of tension. There is no Christian *truth* which is not 'rooted and grounded in love', and *love* is the only legitimate test of men's adherence to the truth of the gospel and of their freedom from the dangers of misplaced ingenuity. Those who perpetuate the divisions of Christendom on the grounds of their loyalty to truth can draw no support from this epistle.

When children literally *grow up*, they become more and more distinct in personality from their fellows. But the metaphorical growing up from spiritual infancy to maturity is a process of closer and closer mutual identification in love within the inclusive manhood of Christ.

15–16. We commit a grave anachronism if we suppose that Paul called Christ *the head* because that is the seat of the brain which controls the rest of the body. The functions of the brain and central nervous system were unknown to the ancient world, and Jews and Greeks alike regarded the heart as the seat of intelligence. Nor is there any suggestion here or in Col. 2^{19} that the head is being thought of as the source of nourishment. In classical Greek κεφαλή ('head') was not used metaphorically,[24] and Paul is here, probably quite unconsciously, interweaving three of the senses which this Greek word acquired in the Septuagint as a translation of the Hebrew *rōsh*. *Rōsh* can mean: (a) the anatomical head; (b) the top of anything; (c) a chief or ruling person; (d) the first of a series; (e) a source. In the last two senses it is often translated in the Septuagint by the Greek ἀρχή. In 1 Cor. 11^{2-10} there is an elaborate argument involving a play on three of these meanings. Because Eve was taken out of Adam, man is the head (e) of woman. The husband is therefore the head (c) of his wife. If a woman leads public worship with her head (a) uncovered, she dishonours her head (c and e). Whatever we may think of the logic of this argument, it helps us to see why Paul can speak of Christ as *head* out of whom (ἐξ οὗ) *the whole body . . . makes bodily growth*. That this is the explanation of his imagery is put beyond doubt by 5^{23-33}. The metaphor of Christ as *head* is thus quite independent in origin of the metaphor of the church as body, though the two have been brought together in Ephesians and Colossians. We can also see that the mixture of metaphors from anatomy and building here and in 2^{21} was easier for Paul, inasmuch as he thought of bodily structure in architectural rather than biological terms (cp. Ps. 139^{13-15}; Job. 10^{9-12}; Ezek 37^{7-8}).

4: 17–24 *The Old Life and the New.*

Although the church must have room for a great variety of talents, temperaments, interests, and backgrounds, and although its faith is no sterile orthodoxy but a fruitful alliance of many minds in the service of Christ, it stands out in sharp distinction from the pagan world around it, and the difference should be plainly discernible in the conduct of its members. The futility of paganism has its origin in idolatry (v. 17), which has blinded men to the true purpose of life. It has alienated them from God, and therefore from the one true source of life. Their whole society has come to be controlled by a prevailing ignorance, and their moral judgement is so stultified that they

[24]But see C. K. Barrett, *The First Epistle to the Corinthians*, on 1 Cor. $11^{3\text{ff.}}$, for the evidence that in hellenistic Greek it had come to mean 'source'.

are progressively less and less able to discriminate between good and evil (v. 18). This is the root of all the moral corruption of the pagan world. Because of their lack of all moral sensitivity men have abandoned themselves to habits which outrage public decency and show complete disregard for the rights and feelings of others (v. 19). Christian conduct, on the contrary, is based on the example of the historical Jesus (vv. 20-1). Guided by his death and resurrection, with which they have been identified in their baptism, the readers will leave their old behaviour behind them, by the drastic method of peeling off their old nature, exposed as it was to decay and mortality because of its own delusive passions; and they will put on the new nature, which the Creator has now provided as a means of restoring them to their right minds and to the just and holy life for which he has designed them (vv. 22-4).

17. In the New Testament the verb *testify* has lost its association with the law court and simply means 'solemnly declare'. *in the Lord* means 'as a Christian to Christians', taking their common allegiance for granted. *futility* (ματαιότης) and its cognate adjective and verb were parts of the vocabulary of Jewish polemics against Gentile idolatry. The gods of the heathen were vanities, and their worship could give rise only to a view of life equally void of reality, meaning, and purpose; and this in turn manifested itself in conduct lacking in any moral principle or restraint. That Paul uses the word with these Jewish overtones is clear from Rom. 1²¹, where he tells us that it was because men refused to acknowledge the one true God and their own dependence on him that all their thinking was reduced to *futility*.

18. Here, as in Romans 1, paganism is depicted as a hopeless and, humanly speaking, irreversible deterioration. By every denial of the truth the mind is *darkened*, made less capable in future of apprehending truth. Every surrender to temptation encrusts the *heart* (i.e. the will) and narrows the range of its future choice. To reject God is to be *alienated from the life of God*, the only source of moral and mental health. *Ignorance* has ceased to be a private condition of mind and has become a disease endemic in pagan culture (for *that is in them* read 'prevailing among them').

19. It is because this spiritual decline has made them *callous*, dead to all proper feeling, that pagans abandon themselves to vice. The diagnosis remains the same as in Romans 1, but here it is subordinated to the

theme of this letter by a concentration on antisocial behaviour. *Licentiousness* (ἀσέλγεια) is conduct so scandalous as to shock public opinion. *Greed* (πλεονεξία) is a settled determination to have one's own way, regardless of the cost to others.

20–24. The syntax of this sentence is chaotic, and any translation is bound to be a makeshift. The RSV has cut the knot by inserting a full stop at the end of v. 21 and taking the accusative and infinitive at the beginning of the next verse as an imperative (*Put off*). Some commentators treat v. 21 as a parenthesis, but this leaves the infinitive of v. 22 dependent on a positive verb (you have learnt) to be deduced from the negative verb of v. 20. It is probably best to allow the infinitive to be dependent on *were taught*, even though that renders the accusative pronoun ὑμᾶς redundant. *as the truth is in Jesus* can hardly be the correct sense, since the noun has no article and therefore should be the predicate rather than the subject of the clause; yet it is hard to find a plausible alternative rendering. *learn Christ* is an odd phrase, unparalleled elsewhere, and particularly odd when it is immediately followed by an apparently contrasted use of the name *Jesus*. There are other passages like this in the epistles where Paul's mind seems to have run away with his tongue or pen, so as to leave large holes in his argument. When this happens, our only recourse is to try to reconstruct the underlying train of thought from such clues as he has afforded us.

(a) Paul uses the name *Jesus* by itself only rarely, and without any uniform principle. Sometimes it is just shorthand for a longer title appearing beside it in the same context (Rom. 8¹¹; 2 Cor. 4⁵). But in other places he seems to use it as an indication that he is looking back beyond the living Lord, present and known in the church, to the earthly, historical Jesus (2 Cor. 4¹⁰⁻¹⁴; Gal. 6¹⁷; Phil. 2¹⁰). Such a distinction seems inescapable in the present context.

(b) In the parallel passage in Colossians (2²⁰–3¹⁴), the command to put off the old life and put on the new is accompanied by a reminder that the readers have already put off the one and on the other at their baptism (cp. Gal. 3²⁷). They have in that sacramental act died and risen with Christ, so that their old nature has been nailed with him to the Cross and transformed into the new manhood of his risen life. A similar sequence of ideas, expressed in terms of a new birth, is found in 1 Pet. 1²³–2³ and in James 1¹⁸⁻²¹. It is nowadays generally agreed that this is not a case of two later writers borrowing from an earlier one, but of three independent writers all drawing on the common stock of catechetical formulae used throughout the early church. In writing to the church of Rome, which he had not founded, Paul assumes that their understanding of baptism will be the same as his own (Rom. 6³); and the same assumption, though unexpressed, underlies the present passage. To *learn Christ* then is, to judge from these parallels, a portmanteau expression into which a great deal of content has been packed. What the readers are expected to have learnt is that union with Christ which is symbolized by baptism is union with him in his death and resurrection, and that those who accept Christ accept with him the crucifixion of their old nature and its passions (cp. Gal. 5²⁴).

(c) The sacramental death and resurrection of the Christian is possible only because of the real, historical death and resurrection of *Jesus*. He had borne the old nature (Rom. 8³) and carried it with him to a real, literal death on the Cross. In him man's aspiration after death-and-resurrection, death-and-rebirth, had come true, and in such a way as to make it come true for others also. It must be to this that the last obscure clause of v. 21 refers: 'I assume that you have received the usual catechetical instruction and have learnt that your union with Christ (*in him*) entails a death to the old ways, just as was literally true in the case of Jesus.' The whole truth about the unseen Christ in whom they are to have their new being is embodied in the historical life, death, and resurrection of the man Jesus.

22. *Corrupt through deceitful lusts* suggests to the English reader only moral depravity. But the Greek connotes also a literal corruption. The old nature has been started, by the misguided gratification of its passions, on the road of decay that leads to death.

23. Because the decay was initiated by the futility of *minds* alienated from God, the reversal of the process must begin with the renewal of the mind.

24. Although Christians are told to *put on the new nature*, their transformation is in no sense their own responsibility or achievement. It is God the Creator who has inaugurated the new creation (2¹⁵; cp. 2 Cor. 5¹⁷), and who is recreating them continuously until they conform to the pattern of Christ, which is God's own *likeness* or image (cp. Col. 3¹⁰).

4: 25–52 *General Rules of Christian Conduct*.

The responsibilities of life in the body of Christ are now spelt out in detail, with particular attention to those disruptive tendencies which would imperil the unity of the church. Falsehood undermines the mutual trust on which any society depends for its very existence. To cherish resentment even overnight is to play into the hands of the devil, who can easily work it up into a lasting animosity. Theft of course is excluded, but so is any other less obvious parasitism on one's neighbours (vv. 25–8). All talk that gives offence is to be avoided in favour of such as builds up the community and conveys a blessing on its members. Any breach of these rules is a menace to the common life created by the Holy Spirit. Bitter or harsh feelings are incompatible with the forgiving disposition which is required of those who have been forgiven by God (vv. 21–32). In short, those who wish to be members of God's family must take after their Father, and that means a self-forgetful love like that which turned Christ's death into a sacrifice offered to God (5^{1-2}).

25. For *members one of another*, cp. Rom. 12^5. Most of the injunctions of this passage are ethical commonplaces, which can be paralleled in other epistles, and the first two are actually drawn from the Old Testament (Zech. 8^{16}; Ps. 4^4). They are probably part of a general stock of catechetical material in use throughout the early church, drawn from Jewish and Gentile, as well as from specifically Christian, sources. Passages such as this draw our attention to the constant problems of the missionary in Gentile society. Jewish converts had been brought up on the strict moral code of the Old Testament, and the teaching of Jesus shows us how he was able to take this for granted and then go beyond it (Matt. 5^{21-48}). But it could not be assumed that Gentile converts had any such solid grounding. The so-called 'Judaizers' who wanted Gentiles to be circumcised before they could be admitted to church membership could argue that circumcision was a means of bringing converts under the elementary discipline of the Torah, after which it would be time enough to introduce them to the more advanced teaching of the Christian gospel. Paul resisted this argument on the grounds that legal religion is incompatible with a religion of grace. But he and other missionaries who accepted his main principle knew that they must put something in the place of the Torah. Paul was inflexibly opposed to any attempt to reduce Christian behaviour to a set of rigid regulations, but he was ready to supply simple guide-lines to help beginners. These guide-lines appear in Ephesians with a difference, for to each of them is attached a reason which links it with the theme of Christian unity.

28. This verse is a forceful reminder that many of the members of the Gentile churches came from the dregs of society (cp. 1 Cor. 1^{26-9}; 1 Pet. 4^{15}). Particularly among slaves thieving was regarded as normal (cp. Philem. 18). The warning to *the thief* to change his ways must therefore be taken quite literally. But at the same time Paul enlarges the scope of the eighth commandment. The opposite of theft is *honest work*, and any attempt to live at the expense of others is a kind of stealing. It is theft not to pay a worker a fair wage, but it is also theft on the worker's part to take his money without doing a fair day's work in return. Even so, there will always be cases of genuine and deserving

need, and Christian love demands that a man should work hard enough to have something to spare over and above the provision he makes for himself and his family.

29. *Grace* here is used with a double meaning which cannot be reproduced in English. Good and seasonable talk gratifies the hearer, but also conveys a deeper benefit.

30. On *the Holy Spirit* as a seal see 1¹³⁻¹⁴. The common life which the Spirit creates is intended to be a preparation for the perfect society of *the day of redemption*. As with all the other vocabulary used to express the idea of atonement, Paul can use *redemption* (ἀπολύτρωσις) of the past objective act of God achieved once for all in Christ (Rom. 3²⁴; Eph. 1⁷; Col. 1¹⁴), of the present, continuous experience (1 Cor. 1³⁰), and of the ultimate hope (Rom. 8²³; Eph. 1¹⁴).

31. *Malice* can take many forms, of which five examples are given: silently harboured grudge, indignant outburst, seething rage, public quarrel, and slanderous taunt.

1. The imitation of God is a general ethical principle taken over from the Old Testament by Jesus (Lev. 19²; Matt. 5⁴⁸; Luke 6³⁶; Mark 8³³; cp. 1 Pet. 1¹⁶). But here Christians are particularly to be *imitators of God* in his forgiveness. It is this forgiveness that has made them a family, and as *beloved children* they must preserve the family unity by mutual forgiveness.

2. Paul makes sparing use of the imagery of sacrifice, and more often uses it in ethical and personal sections of his letters than in the doctrinal. He has no sacrificial doctrine of the atonement. In any literal sense Christ's death was not a sacrifice. It was a miscarriage of justice in which Jew and Roman honestly believed that they were acting for the best. But it was Jesus' willingness to accept what others forced upon him and to see it as a *sacrifice* which he could offer *to God* that transformed an act of human sin into an act of divine redemption. Here Christ's sacrifice is held up as an example of self-giving love. There can be no forgiveness which is not costly to the giver and acceptable to God.

5: 3–20 *From Darkness into Light.*

If Christians are to avoid sins which contradict their calling, how much more must they renounce those which disqualify them for it. There can be no compromise with the gross sensuality and ruthless self-indulgence of paganism or the intellectual atmosphere these vices breed in. Anyone who argues that the natural appetites are subject to their own laws and therefore irrelevant to the spiritual life has failed to reckon with the grim evidence of moral retribution already overtaking those who flout the laws of God (vv. 3–6). Converts must therefore make a clean break with their disreputable past. Their former lives derived their quality from the prevailing moral darkness, but their present lives take their quality from the light of Christ, and they must behave accordingly, doing only what would have his approval. As in the natural world, so in the moral, light makes for healthy growth, whereas darkness is sterile (vv. 7–11). Though Christians may well be ashamed even to talk about the worst excesses of paganism, they must not hesitate to expose them for what they are by comparison with their own behaviour. Once let in the light, and it has the miraculous power not only to reveal but to transform, as is recorded in the familiar baptismal hymn (vv. 12–14).

Christians must never act without thinking, but must always be considering how to make best use of their limited opportunities. Instead of drifting with the tide, they must be able to decide for themselves what God wants them to be (vv. 15–17). They can leave drunkenness to the dissolute, for they will have all the stimulus they need in the heightening of faculties and feelings which comes from the inspiration of the Spirit, and this they may experience to the full in the corporate worship of God (vv. 18–20).

3. For the second time (cp. 4^{19}) Paul links sexual immorality with πλεονεξία, which must mean more than *covetousness*. It is the arrogant assumption that everything and everyone exist for one's own gratification. He can hardly intend *not even be named* to be taken literally, or it would be a rule very frequently broken in the New Testament. These vices are not to be subjects of conversation or even of curious interest.

4. Contemporary pagan literature shows how readily ribald, scurrilous, or flippant talk could pass for wit. Where vice is universally regarded as amusing the practice of it is likely to come easy. The mention of *levity* (εὐτραπελία) leads to a word-play with thanksgiving (εὐχαριστία).

5. *Be sure of this* (lit. 'knowing know') is one of the many Hebraisms of this epistle; cp. below 'sons of disobedience' (v. 6) and 'children of light' (v. 8). The *covetous* man is an idolater because he makes a god of anything he sets his heart on.

   Elsewhere (1 Cor. 6^{9-10}) Paul has said that immoral people will have no place in the future reign of God. Here he uses a more complex phrase, *the kingdom of Christ and of God*, because he wishes to add that they have no place in the church. Christ's *kingdom* is a present reality, into which Christians have already been transferred (Col. 1¹³), but it is ultimately due to be surrendered to God (1 Cor. 15²⁴⁻⁸). Thus *the kingdom* is Christ's here and God's hereafter.

6. Some of the second century Gnostics argued that, because matter is inherently evil and hostile to spirit, and because the body is hopelessly corrupt, the spiritual man must indulge in sensuality to show his total contempt for the body, safe in the assurance that its activities could not hamper the progress of the soul. The letters of Jude and 2 Peter are a vituperative attack on an argument of this kind, and some such defence of immorality may be covered here by *empty words*. But this is no reason for assigning a late date to Ephesians. Paul had already faced at Corinth the specious argument that free indulgence in bodily appetites is justified since God would not have given them to us unless he had meant them to be satisfied (1 Cor. 6¹²⁻¹³).

By *the wrath of God* Paul means the principle of retribution built into the structure of God's ordered universe. It may operate through the punitive functions of the state (Rom. 13⁴), through political disaster (1 Thess. 2¹⁶), or through the moral deterioration that ensues upon a rejection of God (Rom. 1¹⁸⁻³²; Eph. 4¹⁷⁻¹⁹). But the essence of it is that God allows men to reap the harvest of their own disobedience (Gal. 6⁷⁻⁸).

8. *Darkness* and *light* are universal symbols for moral condition and influence. Darkness makes everything in it dark, and light makes everything light. As pagans the readers had been part of the darkness they lived in, contributing to the low moral standards of society and helping to influence the lives of others. Now as Christians they are part of the light, and must see that their moral influence conforms to their new character.

9–10. In Gal. 5²² Paul describes all the Christian virtues as fruit of the Spirit. Where the Spirit is present, they grow naturally and spontaneously on the Christian character. So here goodness is *the fruit of light*. It cannot be produced by obedience to a book of rules. Evil tends to run true to type and can be regulated by law. But concerning the harvest of the Spirit Paul says that 'there is no law dealing with such things as these'. What is required rather is a renewed mind (4²³), an informed moral judgment capable of discerning the will of God (Rom. 12²), the mind of Christ (1 Cor. 2¹⁶), or, as he says here, *what is pleasing to the Lord*.

11–13. There is no contradiction between the two commands to *expose* the excesses of paganism and not *even to speak* of them. *The works of darkness* are to be exposed by the light, i.e. by what Christians are, not by what they say. They are not being licenced to scold, or even to score off, their fellows. Exposure to the light may be painful to those who have always lived in darkness, but it is the first necessary step towards transformation into light.

14. This couplet is introduced with a formula of quotation such as is usually reserved for Scripture, but it cannot come from anything other than a Christian writing. It is generally agreed that it is taken from one of the hymns mentioned in 5^{19}. Since baptism was held to be a symbolic dying and rising with Christ, the hymn was probably one used in that connexion. The command to *awake* has then a double reference to the sleep of death and to the dark night of the old life that is being left behind.

15. Christians are *wise* because they have been given a share in the many-splendoured wisdom of God ($1^{8,17}$; 3^{10}), but, so far from being a mystic or recondite experience, it turns out to have immediate practical effects.

16. Up to this point Paul has been painting on a large canvas. In the majestic cadences of his liturgical style he has unfolded the whole counsel of God. Now suddenly for the first time comes a note of urgency; *the time* for the realization of God's mighty plan is desperately short, and Christians must use their God-given wisdom to make *the most of* it. It had been one of the tenets of Jewish apocalyptic literature that the new age would be ushered in by a period of unparalleled suffering—the birth pangs of the Messiah. The Christian church took over this belief (John 16^{21}; Gal. 1^4; 2 Tim. 3^1; Rev. 12^2), but with a difference. For them the new age had already begun; *the days* were *evil* because the old order was already tottering to its doom under the weight of its own corruption (1 Cor. 2^6; 7^{26}; Eph. 4^{22}; 1 John 2^{17}). They were evil because the devil was still in power (Barn. 2^1; cp. Luke 4^6; John 12^{31}; 2 Cor. 4^4; Eph. 2^2; 6^{13}), and critically evil because he now knew that his time was short (Rev. 12^{12}). He had been given notice to quit and would not surrender his tenancy without a struggle.

18. The contrast between being *drunk with wine* and being *filled with the Spirit* is yet another point of contact between this letter and the account of Pentecost in Acts 2 (cp. notes on 4^{7-11}).

19. Public worship at Corinth had neither presiding minister nor set order of service. Any member might read Scripture, preach, pray, speak with tongues, or strike up a hymn at the prompting of the Spirit (1 Cor. 14^{26}). The same procedure seems to be presupposed here. At least it is clear that the public worship of the church is still to be Spirit-controlled.

5: 21–6: 9 *The Christian Family*.

If the church is to present itself to the world as the united family of God, the quality of its life must be reproduced in microcosm in every Christian home. The general rule in the church is mutual subordination, each member showing more concern for the needs and rights of others than for his own (v. 21). In the home there must, to be sure, be one head of the household, whose authority is accepted by the rest. But this natural structure of the family must be infused with a distinctively Christian character. There is a close, though not perfect, analogy between the relation of husband to wife and the relation of Christ to the church. The subjection of the church is to Christ's self-sacrificing love, and the same must be true of a wife's subjection to her husband (vv. 22–4). Where such love exists, subordination becomes nothing less than identification, and it is the same sort of identification we have in mind when we describe the church as the body of Christ (vv. 27–30). The possibility that two persons might be thus fused into one is already envisaged in Scripture, which declares that a man must leave the natural solidarity into which he was born and with his wife establish the new solidarity of marriage. This Old Testament text enshrines a far-reaching principle, which finds its highest expression in the mutual love of Christ and the church. But that is not to say that husbands and wives ought not also to take the text at its face value (vv. 31–3).

Children are to obey their parents as a natural duty, laid down in the Ten Commandments, and in their own best interests. But fathers are to deserve their children's respect and bring them up to be responsible members of the Christian community (vv. 1–4). Slaves are to obey their masters, not regarding obedience as wrung from them by compulsion, by threat of punishment or expectation of favour, but transforming their duties into a voluntary act by doing them enthusiastically as a service to Christ, remembering that social status counts for nothing in the sight of God. Masters are to share this attitude and treat their servants as fellow slaves in the service of the one impartial Master (vv. 5–9).

21. The verb in this verse is a participle, which appears to be syntactically dependent on the previous sentence, but the RSV has rightly taken it to be the beginning of a new section and has translated it as an impera-

tive. One reason for doing this is that v. 22 has no verb of its own and needs an imperative to be supplied by implication from v. 22. But in any case the use of the participle as an imperative is common enough in ethical passages of the New Testament (Rom. 12^{3-19}; 1 Pet. 2^{18}; $3^{1,7-9}$), and seems to have developed out of a similar use of the participle in late Hebrew.[25] It is no objection to this punctuation that the mutual subordination required in this verse cannot be exactly equated with the one-way subordination of wives, children, and slaves to the head of the household. Paul is basing his instructions on a code of household rules in common use throughout the early Gentile mission of the church, adapted from Jewish and Stoic patterns.[26] All over the ancient world the paterfamilias wielded an unquestioned authority; and Paul, though the first to insist that the discrimination against slaves and women had been made obsolete by Christ (Gal. 3^{28}; Col. 3^{11}), and that mutual subordination is the general rule of Christian ethics, shows no disposition to tamper with the basic structure of ancient society. What he does is to require that the code of subordination shall be properly baptized with the spirit of Christ. The whole passage is an excellent illustration of the general ethical principle (cp. vv. 16–18) that the Spirit-filled man must and can discern the will of God within the limitations imposed by a defective social order.

22. *Wives* are to accept the subordinate role society has allotted them, but not, as pagan moralists would have urged, because it is part of the natural order. This is to be their way of practising that submission which all Christians have just been told to show to one another. In this way the demands of social custom can be transformed by being treated as a service *to the Lord*.

23. On the metaphorical use of *head*, cp. 4^{15}. The argument is a midrash on Gen. 2^{18-24}. Woman was created to be man's companion, and man was the source (*head*) from which she was derived. She must therefore accept her subordinate status. The comparison of man and wife with Christ and church is a good example of reciprocal metaphor. When metaphors drawn from human relationships are used of God, the immediate purpose is to illuminate the unknown by comparison with the known, but the secondary effect is that the character of the divine father, judge, king, etc. becomes the norm by which the behaviour of the human father, judge, or king must be regulated. So here Paul is using marriage to throw light on the relation between Christ and the church, but at the same time establishing a norm for the behaviour of

[25]See Appended Note by D. Daube in *The First Epistle of St. Peter* by E. G. Selwyn, pp. 467–88.

[26]See P. Carrington, op. cit., H. Schlier, ad loc., and J. E. Crouch, *The Origin and Intention of the Colossian Haustafel.*

husbands and wives. For the use of the same metaphor in the Old
Testament see Hos. 1–3; Jer. 2²; Isa. 54⁵⁻⁸.

The last clause, *and is himself its Saviour*, is introduced to show that
the analogy is not a perfect one, since the husband is not saviour of
his wife. The proof of this is that the next verse begins with a strong
adversative (ἀλλά), which the RSV has omitted. The NEB makes the
point very neatly: 'Christ is, indeed, the Saviour of the body; but . . . '

24. The church's submission to Christ, as Paul never tired of pointing
out, is not obedience to his dictation, but faith; and faith is the acceptance of his free and unconditioned grace and of the constraints of love
which that grace entails (e.g. 2 Cor. 5¹⁴).

25. *Christ loved the church* 'not because it was perfectly lovable but to make
it such' (Westcott).

26. The phrase *the washing of water with the word* sounds like an allusion to
baptism, but it can hardly be intended as a simple reference to the
sacrament and the accompanying word spoken over or by the convert.
For here it is not individual Christians but the whole church that is
cleansed and consecrated. Language reminiscent of baptism is being
used to describe something more comprehensive and universal. *The
word* means the gospel, Christ's declarative act which has effectively
made the church his own and set it on the road to perfection.

28. Under the influence of the example of Christ the notion of subordination gives place to that of identification.

29–31. The change from body to *flesh* involves no subtle variation of
meaning, but simply prepares for the quotation from Gen. 2²⁴, where
'one flesh' has been correctly taken by the RSV to mean *one* person.
The idea of corporate solidarity is so strong in the Old Testament that
a family, clan, tribe, or nation may be regarded as a single entity.
But all these are examples of a natural solidarity into which men are
born. Marriage is the most obvious instance of voluntary solidarity,
and it is therefore regularly used in the Old Testament to denote the
solidarity between God and Israel, established by God's free act of
grace and Israel's free response of faith.

32. The word *mystery* has been used four times in this letter to denote
God's secret plan for the world, revealed to Paul by prophetic inspiration (1⁹; 3³,⁴,⁹). Here it is a secret meaning which he has detected in a
passage of Scripture. But it is possible that the use of the word con-
stitutes a claim to inspiration and that all Paul's mysteries involved an
inspired reinterpretation of the Old Testament (cp. Rom. 11²⁵).

33. *however.* The analogical application of the text does not cancel the
literal.

1. There is good manuscript evidence for omitting the words *in the Lord*.
If we do so, there are then two significant differences between the
instructions given to children and those given to wives. *Children* are to
obey, not just to accept a subordinate position in the family; and they

are to do this because *this is right*, i.e. a natural duty. This is a most important distinction. The subordination of wife, children, and slaves to the head of the household was part of the accepted social order. But, whereas the subjection of child to parent was part of the natural order established by God, that of slave to master was not. It was part of an order corrupted by sin. But is the subjection of the wife like that of the child or like that of the slave? Paul could have settled this question by reference to Gen. 3[16], which declares plainly that the subjection of woman to man is one of the consequences of the Fall, but he does not do so. His use of Gen. 2[18-24] might seem to suggest that he regarded women's subordinate role as part of the created order. Elsewhere however he declares that the difference of status is abolished in Christ (Gal. 3[28]; cp. Col. 3[11]), and he can hardly have believed that there was any discrepancy between what God intended in creation and what he achieved in Christ. Inherited presuppositions may have made it hard for him to be wholly consistent, but his change of tone in addressing the children shows how very close he had come to believing in the equality of the sexes.[27]

2-3 The fifth commandment is the only one in the Decalogue *with a promise* attached to it, but Paul is thinking of the whole body of law to which the Decalogue forms an introduction.

4. Goodspeed (*Key*, p. vii) has argued that this verse is incompatible with Pauline authorship. 'For Paul, expectations of the return of Jesus as the Messiah and of the establishment of God's kingdom are still too vivid and imminent to warrant the projection of long-term programs of religious education.' But a Jew, accustomed to the daily repetition of the Shema (Deut. 6[4-9]) could hardly have conceived of any crisis so acute as to render the religious instruction of children inappropriate. In any case this verse scarcely amounts to an elaborate syllabus.

5. Paul does not advocate cringing and obsequious humility; *fear and trembling* are proper responses to God to whom their service is to be offered, not to their human master (cp. Phil. 2[12]; Col. 3[22]). *in single-ness of heart* means without hypocrisy or ulterior motive.

6. Work done only when the master is looking is *eye-service*; *men-pleasers* do what they are told not from any genuine desire to please, but to curry favour.

7. Jesus taught his followers to go the second mile, so that what began as compulsory service might end by being voluntary (Matt. 5[41]). The slave is to achieve a similar result by performing his duties *with a good will* as a service to Christ. For a more general treatment of Paul's attitude to slavery and the problems it raises, see the Introduction to Philemon.

[27]See G. B. Caird, 'Paul and Women's Liberty', *Bulletin of the John Rylands Library*, liv, pp. 268–81.

9. *do the same*, i.e. show your slaves the same consideration, share the same attitude that has been recommended to the slaves.

6: 10–20 *The Christian Soldier.*

In the first half of his letter Paul has prayed that his readers may come to know the power of God which was operative in the resurrection of Christ and in his victory over the forces of evil (1^{17-21}); has reminded them that they have already had some acquaintance with this power in their conversion, which was a resurrection from the deadness of the past and a deliverance from the prevailing forces of paganism (2^{1-2}); and he prayed again for the deepening of their experience of it (3^{16}). Now he reminds them that in the future they will have to learn to rely on this same power. There is a battle to be fought, part of the long campaign of God against that arch-strategist the devil, and there can be no hope of victory unless it is fought with God's own weapons. The Christian soldier may be tempted to think that his enemies are human and to fight them with worldly weapons, but the real enemies are the spiritual forces that stand behind all institutions of government and control the lives of men and nations (vv. 10–12). When the battle reaches its climax, all that the soldier can do is to stand his ground and trust his armour. Every item of his equipment is a variation on the central theme of the gospel: the truth of man's destiny as it is revealed in Jesus (cp. 4^{21}), the righteousness of the new humanity created in the likeness of God (cp. 4^{24}), the good news that peace has been established where before there was hostility (cp. 2^{15}), the faith which appropriates the gift of grace and brings men into unity with God and with one another (cp. 2^8; 4^{13}), the salvation which is both present possession and future hope (cp. 2^8), and the word of God, the only offensive weapon he is allowed to use (vv. 13–17). The good soldier keeps watch against the approach of danger, and for the Christian this must be done in prayer, not for himself alone but for all his fellow Christians. Accordingly Paul asks a special prayer for himself in his imprisonment that he may be able to wield to good effect the verbal weapons of his warfare (vv. 18–20).

92

10. *Finally* (τὸ λοιπὸν). This reading is not as well attested as τοῦ λοιποῦ ('from now on'). This paragraph does not deal with the normal situation of the present evil days mentioned in 5¹⁶, but with a coming crisis (see below on v. 13), for which the Christian must be on the alert. It will call for all the spiritual resources he can muster.

11. A comparison with Isa. 59¹⁷ shows that *the whole armour* is not merely supplied by God; it is God's own armour, the armour God himself uses against his enemies. The slightly disparaging translation *wiles* for μεθοδίας (cp. 4¹⁴) suggests that Paul did not take the devil seriously and is hardly in keeping with the sustained military metaphor. 'Stratagems' would give the required combination of tactical shrewdness and ingenious deception.

We gravely mistake Paul's meaning unless we recognize that *not against flesh and blood* is an instance of Hebraic hyperbole (cp. Hos. 6⁶). Paul is not contrasting the Christian's outward struggle against the threats of his pagan neighbours with his inner struggle against temptation and saying that the second is the only one that matters. He is warning his readers that, when they are under attack from human enemies, they must identify the real enemies, the spiritual forces in the background. *The heavenly places* are the territory in which invisible powers compete for man's allegiance and the control of his life (cp. 1³). *Principalities* and *powers*, as their names indicate, are the forces which operate in all systems of human government, authority, or organization. *World rulers* (κοσμοκράτορες) is in origin an astrological term for the planets, which the ancient world regarded as spiritual beings exercising an inflexible rule of law over human affairs. Paul himself had no belief in astrology, but he recognized the grip it held on the mind of pagan man, who felt himself to be at the mercy of a malignant cosmic order, against which he himself was powerless to struggle; and he was convinced that pagan man was right in thinking himself the helpless victim of forces which were sweeping him to an unavoidable doom. The old order was corrupt and tottering (1 Cor. 2⁶; 7³¹), and the dawn of a new day was soon to break upon *this present darkness*. The argument that Paul could not have written this verse because he believed the *powers* to have been already vanquished by Christ on the Cross (Col. 2¹⁵) is inept. Christ's victory was a representative victory, which had to be repeated in the lives of his followers; and it was precisely because he had shown the possibility of successful resistance that they were now able, in his strength, to carry on the contest.

13. *the evil day* is not identical with *this present darkness*. It denotes a future intensification of the onslaughts of the powers of evil. The Christian church had already good reason to be prepared for a crescendo of hostility. The powers of the old order were in the process of being dethroned by Christ (cp. 1 Cor. 15²⁵) and would not surrender their authority without desperate counter-attacks.

14–17. This list of weapons is a sustained metaphor, not an allegory. We need not look for subtle reasons why *truth* should be identified with the soldier's belt or *righteousness* with his coat of mail. The passage is a patchwork of Old Testament allusion: to the divine warrior who fights his own battle when there is no man to act as his champion (Isa. 59^{15-17}; cp. 1 Thess. 5^8); to the anointed king who is to bring in the reign of justice (Isa. 11^{4-5}); and to the herald sent to proclaim the advent of peace (Isa. 52^7). Thus the armour of God is not merely that which God supplies, but that which God himself uses in his age-long war against evil. The list is as remarkable for what it omits as for what it contains: for the divine warrior of Isa. 59 put on vengeance as a tunic and wrapped himself in the cloak of fury; and, in a passage based on the same Old Testament text, the Lord is said to carry 'stern wrath for a sword' (Wisd. 5^{20}).

15. It is a striking paradox that the soldier should be equipped for battle with a declaration of *peace*.

16. For the uses of *flaming darts* in ancient warfare see Herod. viii. 52; Thuc. ii 75; Liv. xxi. 8. A wooden shield could be set on fire by them, unless covered by a layer of hide.

17. For the idea that God needs no other weapon than the spoken word, cp. Hos. 6^5; Isa. 11^4; Rev. 1^{16}; 19^{15}. Here *the word of God* is called *the sword of the Spirit*, partly because in Isa. 11^4, in both Hebrew and Greek, the word used for 'breath' could also be translated 'Spirit', and partly because Jesus promised his disciples that the Spirit would put words into their mouths in moments of crisis to confound their adversaries (Mark 13^{11}; Luke 12^{11-12}).

18. The instruction to *keep alert* (lit. 'awake') was a part of the early catechetical teaching (1 Cor. 16^{13}; Col. 4^2; 1 Thess. 5^6; 1 Pet. 5^8; Rev. 3^2; 16^{15}) which had its roots in the teaching of Jesus (Mark 13^{33}; Luke 21^{36}). The Christian soldier is reminded that he is not engaged in single combat.

6: 21–4 *Closing Greetings.*

The letter closes with a commendation of the bearer, Tychicus, almost identical with that sent to Colossae, and with a brief benediction.

21. On *Tychicus*, see Col. 4^7.

22. *Encourage* implies that some of his readers may have been worried or alarmed at the news of Paul's imprisonment.

23–24. The benediction is in the third person because the letter is intended as an encyclical. The last phrase, ἐν ἀφθαρσίᾳ, has no parallel in any other New Testament benediction and is difficult to construe. Literally it means 'in immortality'. The RSV takes it as an adverbial phrase qualifying the verb *love* and renders it *with love undying*. The NEB takes it with χάρις: 'grace and immortality'. Neither of these constructions is very probable, nor is Beare's suggestion that the phrase simply means 'for ever'. The difficulty probably arises from the compression of a complex idea into the brevity of a benediction: 'those who love our Lord Jesus Christ and share in his undying life'. If so, Robinson's comment would be fully justified: 'So the epistle which opened with a bold glance into the eternal past closes with the outlook of an immortal hope.'

INTRODUCTION

I. PHILIPPI AND THE PHILIPPIAN CHURCH

Philippi was named after its founder, Philip II of Macedonia, the father of Alexander the Great. It lay at the eastern edge of a small, fertile plain in the country then known as Thrace, surrounded by mountains, but less than ten miles from the sea. It owed its importance at first to the gold mines of Mt. Pangaeus, but also, and increasingly, to its strategic position commanding the great overland route from Europe to Asia, which the Romans later called the Via Egnatia. There was a Thracian village on the site, known as Krenides (The Springs), and it had been occupied in 361 B.C. by settlers from the nearby island of Thasos, led by an Athenian exile, Callistratus (Diod. XVI. iii. 7). But two years later Philip succeeded to the throne of Macedonia and began the spectacular series of conquests which was to carry his son as far as the Punjab. To secure control of the mines, from which he drew an annual revenue of 1,000 talents, and to protect his eastern frontier, he converted Krenides into a walled garrison town and changed its name to Philippi. After the battle of Pydna in 168 B.C., when Macedonia came under Roman rule, Philippi was assigned to the first of its four administrative districts; and twenty years later Macedonia became a Roman province. In 42 B.C. Antony and

Octavian defeated Brutus and Cassius at the battle of Philippi, and Antony celebrated the victory by settling some of his veterans there and making the city a Roman colony with the title Colonia Victrix Philippensium (Strabo, vii. 331; Plin. *N.H.* iv. 42). The Roman population was considerably augmented after the defeat of Antony at Actium in 31 B.C. Octavian decided, for his own security, to settle his veterans in Italy, and many of the families who were dispossessed to make room for them were resettled in Philippi or Dyrrachium. The name of the city was now changed to Colonia Julia Philippensis, and in 27 B.C., when Octavian was given the title Augustus by the Senate, it became Colonia Augusta Julia Philippensis.

A Roman colony differed from all other forms of municipality in the provinces in having a large nucleus of Roman citizens, who retained all the rights of their citizenship, and a civic administration modelled on that of Rome. The two chief magistrates were called *duumviri iure dicundo*,[1] were attended by lictors, and generally held an authority comparable to that of the praetors in Rome. Under them were quaestors, aediles, and Augustales (priests of the imperial cult). The city was a miniature Rome, its official language was Latin, and its inhabitants thought of themselves as Romans (Acts 16[21]), even if they were in fact descended from Greek, Macedonian, or even Asiatic stock. The most impressive proof of this is to be found in the archaeological records of religious observance. Thracian and Greek deities were still worshipped, but for the most part under the names of their Latin counterparts. The Thracian goddess Bendis, for example, whom the Greeks had identified with Artemis, was now known by her Latin name Diana. Some few deities had indeed resisted the process of Romanization, particularly the Asian Cybele, the Egyptian Isis with her retinue of lesser gods, and the native Thracian Sabazius (the Most High God of Acts 16[17]). But there were also cults of purely Italian origin.

[1]Luke, however, is quite correct in calling them by their popular title of στρατηγόι in Acts 16[20].

The Jewish community in Philippi must have been very small. There was no synagogue within the walls, and the congregation which met at the place of prayer by the riverside consisted mostly, if not entirely, of women. One of them at least was not a Jewess but a God-fearer, i.e. a Gentile who had been attracted to Judaism without taking the final step of becoming a proselyte (Acts 16$^{13-14}$). This is of some importance for our understanding of Paul's letter, since it suggests that the warnings of 3$^{2ff\cdot}$ were occasioned by his own experiences in Rome rather than by information he had received about Jewish activities in Philippi.

From the story of Paul's missionary career we may infer that his strategy was to concentrate on the large urban centres and leave any further expansion to the churches he founded in them (cp. Rom. 15$^{18-24}$). He had no intention of reaching Macedonia when he left Antioch with Silas in A.D. 49, for there were more important cities nearer at hand. Two years previously, when he landed from Cyprus at Perga with Barnabas, he probably had it in mind to make his way to Ephesus; for he tells us that it was only the need to recuperate from an illness that drove him into the highlands of Galatia (Gal. 4^{13}). Ephesus must again have been his goal on his second journey, when he was 'forbidden by the Holy Spirit to speak the word in Asia' (Acts 16^6). His second choice was either Nicomedia or Nicaea in Bithynia, but again the Spirit intervened. In what form the veto of the Spirit came we are not told. Luke's story has an air of breathless haste which leaves many details unclear. The one clear point is that Paul was driven to Philippi by divine Providence alone.

Sir William Ramsay conjectured that the Macedonian whom Paul saw beckoning in a vision at Alexandria Troas was Luke himself.[2] Certainly, if we take the 'we' passages in Acts to be an indication of the presence of the author, Luke joined the party at Troas, remained behind in Philippi, and joined Paul again at Philippi seven years later (Acts 16^{10,40}; 20^6). On the

[2]*St. Paul the Traveller*, pp. 200–8.

other hand, Luke cannot have had a home or even close friends in Philippi, or the missionaries would not have had to rely for hospitality on their new acquaintance, Lydia. Luke also garbles one piece of information he was given, calling Philippi 'the first city of the district of Macedonia' instead of 'a city of the first district of Macedonia (Acts 16^{12}).'

From his own correspondence we know that the church Paul founded in Philippi was the one which gave him the most satisfaction and least trouble. His letter to it brims over with affection and gratitude, with hardly a hint of criticism. He calls the church 'my joy and crown' (4^1). His friends there had from the start regarded themselves as his partners (1^7), and had demonstrated this by regular gifts of money, which began as soon as he reached Thessalonica (4^{15-16}). When he was organizing the collection for the Jerusalem church, their generosity was an example to others, especially as they were poor and hard pressed at the time (2 Cor. 8^{1-5}). His last letter to Corinth may well have been written from Philippi during the visit mentioned in Acts 20^1 (cp. 2 Cor. 4^{13}; 7^{5-7}). He had not expected then to see his Philippian friends again, for his intention was to spend some time in Corinth, to sail from there to Palestine, and then to set out for Rome and Spain (Acts 20^3; Rom. 15^{24-8}). But a plot against his life caused a change of plan and gave him the chance of spending the Passover season in Philippi (Acts 20^6). Then for a while the Philippians lost touch with him. But as soon as they heard that he was in prison in Rome (or that he was on his way to Rome under arrest), they sent Epaphroditus with a further gift of money (Phil. 4^{10-18}). Epaphroditus had a serious illness from which he almost died (2^{30}), and Paul, having decided that he must send him home, wrote a letter to send with him.

2. AUTHORSHIP AND INTEGRITY

Philippians was declared spurious by F. C. Baur in 1845 on grounds which even his disciples of the Tubingen school found unconvincing.[3] Of his arguments J. B. Lightfoot (*Philippians*, p. 73) wrote: 'I cannot think that the mere fact of their having been brought forward by men of ability and learning is suffici-ent to entitle objections of this stamp to a serious refutation.' Since then no men of ability and learning have come forward to take up such a forlorn cause. For Philippians is the most personal of Paul's letters and bears the marks of authenticity in every sentence. It is not surprising that C. L. Mitton, in his attempt to prove that Ephesians was not by Paul, should have chosen Philippians as his control and norm. The letter may have been known to Clement (c. A.D. 97) and Ignatius (c. A.D. 115), and was certainly known to Polycarp (c. A.D. 117), since he explicitly refers to it in his own letter to the Philippians (iii. 2).

We cannot be so sure, however, that our Philippians was originally written as a single letter. 2 Corinthians is almost certainly composite, pieced together out of fragments of two or three letters. It is quite likely that Romans 16 was originally addressed not to Rome but to Ephesus. Similarly, it is widely held that Philippians, in the form in which we have it, is the work of an editor, presumably the man who collected the letters into a corpus. There are two main lines of argument.

(a) Paul would hardly write a letter of thanks for a gift of money and leave all mention of it until the last paragraph. Nor would he wait several months before acknowledging the gift. Yet enough time has elapsed for Epaphroditus to fall ill, for word of his illness to reach his friends in Philippi, and for word of their anxiety on his account to be brought back to Rome. This difficulty would disappear if 4^{10-20} were part of an earlier letter.

(b) There is an abrupt change of tone at 3^2. Two chapters of affectionate intimacy are followed suddenly by a passage of scathing denunciation. Nobody doubts that Paul was capable of writing in both veins. The question is whether he could do so in a single letter. Some scholars hold that the editor has roughly

[3]*Paulus der Apostel Jesu Christi*, pp. 485ff.

fitted together parts of two letters, 1^1–3^1, 4^{21-3} and 3^2–4^{20}. Others prefer to treat $3^{2ff.}$ as an interpolation from a much earlier letter, introduced by the editor into the letter from Rome.

If we accept both these arguments, then Paul wrote three letters to Philippi which have been combined in our epistle. But neither argument is wholly convincing. The view taken in this commentary is that Epaphroditus fell ill on the way to Rome and nearly died because he insisted on completing his journey. In that case word of his illness could have reached the Philippians before he himself reached Rome, and a report of their anxieties could have reached Rome before he had time to recover. Thus belief in the integrity of the letter involves no great delay between the receipt and the acknowledgment of the gift. It would be natural for Paul to be disinclined to write until he had good news to report and Epaphroditus was well enough to travel. In any case it is not true that the only reference to the gift is in the last paragraph; there are preparatory allusions to it in 1^5 and 2^{30}. The break at 3^2 appears obvious enough, though the notes will show that even this depends on the way the verse is translated. But the trouble with all theories of partition or interpolation is that no two critics can agree where the break ends: some say 3^{19}, others 4^1, 4^3, 4^9, or 4^{20}. There are moreover breaks just as abrupt in other Pauline letters, e.g. after 1 Cor. 15^{58} and Gal. 6^{10}. The change of tone is not sustained through the third chapter and is not indicative of a change of attitude to the Philippians themselves.

There is one other critical point on which there is a far greater measure of scholarly agreement. In 1928 E. Lohmeyer wrote a monograph (*Kyrios Jesus*), to prove that Phil. 2^{6-11} was not written by Paul but was a pre-Pauline hymn, which the apostle adapted to the purpose of his letter. His arguments may be summarized as follows.

(a) The passage can be arranged in six three-line stanzas, each having one main verb, and each line having three stresses. Paul's hymn to love in 1 Cor. 13 is neither so regular nor so compact.

(b) The vocabulary is un-Pauline: it contains words which Paul never uses at all (μορφή, ἁρπαγμός, ἴσος, ὑπερυψοῦν, καταχθόνια), and others which he does not use in the same sense (κενοῦν, σχῆμα, ταπεινοῦν).

(c) The theology is un-Pauline. There is no mention of the resurrection, Christ is depicted as Lord not of the church but of the cosmos, and the identification of Christ with the Servant of the Lord of Isa. 53 belongs to the theology of the pre-Pauline church.

(d) The passage interrupts the flow of ethical exhortation, since the last three stanzas have no particular relevance to the theme of safeguarding one another's rights.

(e) The stilted Greek suggests that the author was more at home in Aramaic and that Greek was only his second language.

Lohmeyer's arguments have received so much acceptance that some scholars treat his conclusion as though it were a demonstrable fact. It is therefore well to recognize that there is something to be said on the other side.

(a) Those who follow Lohmeyer's thesis of strophic arrangement do not agree whether it consists of two groups of three stanzas or three groups of two. The division into stanzas is achieved only by excising the words 'even death on a cross' as a Pauline gloss, and it must be admitted that these words, if included, would stamp the whole as undoubtedly Pauline, since no other New Testament writer uses σταυρός (cross) as a theological term. Moreover, in his commentary, published two years after his monograph, Lohmeyer arranged no fewer than 48 of the 104 verses in the epistle in poetic form, and thus robbed his case for putting 2^{6-11} in a special category of much of its weight.

(b) Even if we were to agree that the passage is a hymn with recognizable strophes, this would not mean that it was therefore not written by Paul; or, if not by him, that it was therefore pre-Pauline. It might have been written either by Paul himself or by one of his younger disciples.

(c) The list of non-Pauline words is misleading. Paul does not, to be sure, use ὑπερυψοῦν in his other letters, but he is exceedingly fond of compounds of ὑπέρ, using 19 all told, of which 13 occur in only one letter. Several of the other words occur in cognate forms in the other letters. But even if we take the list as it stands, the proportion of unusual words is almost exactly the same for this passage as for the letter as a whole.

(d) Lohmeyer found the theology of the passage un-Pauline only because he chose to interpret it in an un-Pauline sense. Apart from the excised phrase, the theology is in three respects quite distinctively Pauline. The basic idea is a contrast between Adam, who aimed at eqüality with God and was humbled, and Christ, who set aside his heavenly claims in order to be equal with man and was exalted; and an Adam-Christ typology is found nowhere else in the New Testament except in Paul's letters. The idea that acceptance of the human form involved servitude is not derived, as has constantly been asserted, from the prophetic figure of the Servant of the Lord, who admittedly plays no part in Paul's theology, but from the peculiarly Pauline doctrine of man's bondage to the principalities and powers. And only Paul attributes to the pre-existent Christ an act of choice and makes that choice an example to be imitated by Christians (cp. 2 Cor. 8^{8-9}).

(e) When Paul quotes from the Old Testament, he uses exactly as much as he requires and no more. In the one place where he indubitably quotes an early Christian hymn three lines are enough for him (Eph. 5^{14}). We have no reason to suppose that Paul would ever have allowed an unnecessarily extended quotation to interrupt the flow of his argument. On the other hand, he frequently interrupts his own flow by following up thoughts as they well up spontaneously in his mind.

(f) Lohmeyer's conjecture of an Aramaic-speaking author was based on faulty exegesis. He took the expression ὡς ἄνθρωπος, for example (RSV, 'in human form'), to be a literal rendering of the Aramaic $k^e bar$ $^e nash$ ('like a son of man'). But in Dan. 7^{13} and Rev. 1^{13}; 14^{14} the preposition 'like to' is an indication that what is being described is visionary experience and not ordinary sight, whereas here we have to do with a straightforward statement of historical fact, the publicly attested manhood of Jesus.

(g) In some quarters Lohmeyer's theory has gained considerable support from association with Reitzenstein's myth of a Heavenly Redeemer, though this was no part of Lohmeyer's own argument, nor did Reitzenstein apply his theory to Phil. 2 $^{6-11}$. Reitzenstein claimed to have discovered in the Hermetic tract *Poimandres* evidence for the existence of a widespread Graeco-oriental myth of a primal man, who came down from heaven to redeem mankind from its fallen condition. He admitted that in *Poimandres* the myth was 'incompletely reproduced', but thought that he could supply the deficiencies from certain Gnostic documents and from Philo. In his later works he adduced further evidence from Manichaean and Mandaean sources and tried to demonstrate the Iranian origin of the myth.[4] The vitality of this theory has been remarkable, considering the damaging criticism to which it has been exposed.

(i) Much of the evidence is post-Christian, and that drawn from Gnostic and Manichaean sources is clearly the product of Christian deviations.

(ii) In none of these systems was there any descent of a *redeemer*. Redemption was to be accomplished by Gnosis, i.e. knowledge of the revealed truth about man's origin and destiny. The descent of the heavenly man was part of a myth about man's *creation*, which embodied the saving truth about his origin. It is therefore probable that the heavenly primal man was conceived as a symbol of a general truth, not as an individual person.

(iii) Philo, who believed that God created a whole ideal, heavenly cosmos, not just a heavenly man, before the creation of the material universe, makes it plain that this cosmos, which he identifies with the Logos, existed only in the mind or predestining purpose of God; for he compares the pre-existent Logos to the plan of a city in the mind of the architect (*De*

---

[4] R. Reitzenstein, *Poimandres*, pp. 81ff.; *Das Iranische Erlosungsmysterium*, pp. 115ff.; *Die hellenistischen Mysterienreligionen*, 3rd ed., pp. 168ff.

Opif. Mundi, iv. 17–18). The primal man of *Poimandres* certainly originated in Jewish speculations of a similar sort, appropriated by a syncretistic sect in Egypt.[5]

(iv) If Paul knew anything about such speculations, which is not very likely, he dissociated himself from them by his assertion that Christ, as heavenly man, was not first but second. He became heavenly man by his resurrection (1 Cor. 15[47]).

(v) In Phil. 2[6–11] Christ did not pre-exist *as man*. He pre-existed in the form of God and became man by his own choice. This passage therefore stands with Pauline theology as it is represented in the other letters and against all the extraneous evidence amassed by Reitzenstein and his followers.

(h) Provided we do not suppose that the hymn was inserted in Paul's letter by a later hand (and for that there is no manuscript evidence whatever), the hypothesis we are considering ought not to make any appreciable difference either to the integrity of the letter or to its interpretation. Whether Paul wrote the passage in the course of writing his letter or quoted his own or someone else's hymn, it was he who put it in its present context; and he did so because he believed that it said what he himself wanted to say. Here as always we must pay proper respect to the law of contextual determination, that words, singly or in combination, mean what the writer or speaker on any given occasion intends them to mean. The meaning of this passage *in Philippians* is the meaning Paul intends it to have, the meaning he has imposed on the ambiguities of its language. If we say with Beare that 'the hymn belongs to the realm of soteriology, not of Christology or of ethics', we must be aware that we are talking about the hymn in its conjectural previous existence, not about the hymn as it stands in its present context in Philippians, which is both Christological and ethical. To isolate these verses from their context is to remove them from the epistle and so from the New Testament. There may be some justification for doing this when we are speculating about early Christian origins, but not when we are expounding a letter of Paul.

[5] See C. H. Dodd, *The Bible and the Greeks*, pp. 145–69.

ANALYSIS

1	1: 1–2	Address.
2	1: 3–11	Prayer.
3	1: 12–26	Paul's Imprisonment.
4	1: 27–2: 4	An Appeal for Unity.
5	2: 5–11	The Example of Christ.
6	2: 12–18	The Response to Grace.
7	2: 19–30	The Apostle's Plans.
8	3: 1–11	Reminiscences of a Converted Pharisee.
9	3: 12–16	The Race of Faith.
10	3: 17–4: 1	Citizens of Heaven.
11	4: 2–9	Final Instructions.
12	4: 10–23	The Present from Philippi.

COMMENTARY

1: 1–2 *Address*

For the form of greeting and the meaning of *saints* see Eph. 1[1–2]. In the address of his letters Paul includes the name of any colleague known to the recipients who happens to be with him at the time of writing (see esp. 1 Cor. 1[1]). But this is an act of courtesy and does not necessarily mean that Timothy is co-author of this letter.

1. All Christians are *servants* (or slaves) *of Christ Jesus* (cp. 1 Cor. 7[21–2]; Eph. 6[6]), because they belong to him and owe him an unconditional allegiance (1 Cor. 3[23]), which sets them free from all other forms of control (Rom. 6[18–22]). But Paul also uses the expression in a narrower sense, to denote those who are called to particular service within the church (Rom. 1[1]; Gal. 1[10]; Col. 4[12]). This double usage is derived from the Old Testament. In the Hebrew monarchy all the king's subjects were his slaves, including the highest ministers of state (e.g. 1 Sam. 28[7]; 1 Kings 1[47]). Similarly all the worshippers of God were his slaves (2 Kings 10[23]), but particularly those entrusted with special responsibility (Exod. 14[31]; Amos 3[7]). Thus, as slave of Christ, Paul is writing with a combination of humility and authority.

The use of *bishops and deacons* to translate ἐπισκόποις καὶ διακόνοις is misleading, since the plural form is enough to show that the words are not being used in their modern sense; but it is not easy to find an alternative rendering. 'Επίσκοπος was used in classical and hellenistic Greek as a title for a variety of officials with administrative, judicial, or financial duties. In the Septuagint it is used of inspectors appointed by Antiochus (1 Macc. 1⁵¹), of Abimelech's deputy (Judg. 9²⁸), of army officers (Num. 31¹⁴; 4 Kingd. 11¹⁵), and of various officials associated with the temple, vergers (Num. 4¹⁶), watchmen (4 Kingd. 11¹⁸), treasurers (4 Kingd. 12¹¹), and superintendents (Neh. 11⁹). The earliest New Testament use of the word, and the only Pauline one, is here. In the Pastoral Epistles ἐπίσκοπος appears to be a synonym for πρεσβύτερος ('elder') in Tit. 1⁵⁻⁷, and the suggestion that the latter was the title of the office and the former descriptive of its function ('the man who exercises oversight') would gain some support from Acts 20¹⁷·²⁸ and from 1 Clement 42–4. When Ignatius wrote his letters (c. A.D. 115), the one ἐπίσκοπος had come to be distinguished from the πρεσβύτεροι and διάκονοι who shared with him the ministry of the local congregation. Attempts have been made to derive this Ignatian 'bishop' from the *meᵇbaqqer* or overseer of the Qumran community, but this derivation is unlikely, since all the New Testament evidence, including the address to the Philippians, shows that at first there was a plurality of ἐπίσκοποι in the local church. Διάκονος is used in the New Testament in the general sense of minister, applied to Christ and the apostles, as well as to their assistants; but it is also used in the Pastoral Epistles to denote a particular office. Besides these lexicographical uncertainties, there is the further difficulty that Paul nowhere else mentions any officers in the churches he writes to, but refers to the leaders in very general terms, as though they had assumed leadership in virtue of their gifts or initiative rather than by appointment (1 Thess. 5¹²⁻¹³; 1 Cor. 16¹⁵⁻¹⁶; Gal. 6⁶). It is improbable that Paul mentions the officers of the church solely because of the gift of money he had received, since a small church would not have needed two ranks of treasurers. Perhaps, as Beare suggests, we have here 'an indication that the Roman penchant for organization had already given the Philippian church a regular system of office-bearers.' The evidence hardly justifies any dogmatic conclusions, and it is safest to assume that the terms are here being used in their broadest, functional sense of 'overseers and assistants'.

1: 3–11 *Prayer*

Paul begins most of his letters with a prayer of thanksgiving,[6]

[6]According to A. Deissmann (*Light from the Ancient East*, pp. 179ff.), this was a common practice of ancient letter-writers.

but none of the others can compare with this in personal intensity. Other churches caused him trouble and anxiety (2 Cor. 11²⁸), but not the church at Philippi. Every time he thinks of his friends there, he is filled with joy (v. 4), gratitude (v. 5), affection (vv. 7–8), and confidence (vv. 6, 9–11).

3. *in all my remembrance of you* is too stilted. The phrase is good colloquial Greek for 'every time I think of you'.
4. The note of joy is sounded repeatedly throughout this letter (1¹⁸,²⁵; 2²,¹⁷,¹⁸,²⁸,²⁹; 3¹; 4¹,⁴,¹⁰).
5. Paul is writing to acknowledge a gift of money, and *partnership in the gospel* is a first delicate reference to it (cp. 2³⁰; 4¹⁴⁻¹⁸). It had been his practice never to accept money from any church in which he was working (1 Thess. 2⁹; 1 Cor. 4¹²; 9¹⁵⁻¹⁸; 2 Cor. 11⁷⁻⁹). No one was to be allowed to say that he had charged for the gospel. But the Philippians had overcome his scruples by sending money to help his missionary work elsewhere. There had been more than one gift while he was in Thessalonica (4¹⁶), one at least while he was in Corinth (2 Cor. 11⁹). Now they have sent a further present to help him in prison.
6. The *good work* is their salvation, which is God's doing from start to finish. It involves a continuous transformation of character and conduct (2 Cor. 3¹⁸), which leaves ample room for human effort and aspiration (Rom. 12²; Eph. 4²²⁻³; Phil. 2¹²⁻¹³; Col. 3¹⁻¹⁴), but none for human merit. It is not because of their splendid record that Paul is assured of the ultimate *completion* of the process, but because God does not leave his work half done.

Christians can face *the day of Jesus Christ* (i.e. the day of judgment) without anxiety, because they know that the verdict does not depend on their deserts but on God's grace and mercy. Paul frequently mentions this day without any suggestion that he expected it to happen soon (1 Cor. 1⁸; 3¹³; 5⁵; 2 Cor. 1¹⁴; 5¹⁰; Phil. 2¹⁶; 2 Thess. 1¹⁰). The widely accepted view that the whole early church believed in an imminent advent of Christ is based on a superficial reading of the evidence. The advent was imminent only in the sense that it might happen at any time, not because it must happen within a given period.⁷ The decisive act of God had already happened in the death and resurrection of Christ, and from then on men must live their lives under the shadow of the end. But the end would come when God's purposes were complete, and this was something only he could decide (Mark 13³²; Acts 1⁷).

⁷For this important distinction see A. L. Moore, *The Parousia in the New Testament* (Supplement XIII to *Novum Testamentum*), pp. 108–74.

7. *It is right.* Moffatt's rendering brings out more sensitively the exact nuance of the Greek idiom: 'it is only natural'. It is possible to take the words *I hold you in my heart* the other way round: 'you hold me in such affection' (NEB). But the Greek word order and the context are both marginally in favour of the RSV interpretation. For *partakers* it is better to read 'partners', since there is an intended echo of the 'partnership' of v. 5. Here *grace* is not the general favour of God to all Christians, but, as so often in Paul's letters, the special privilege of his apostolic mission (see on Eph. 3²). By their help and sympathy they have taken partnership shares in his commission. Both *defense* and *confirmation* are legal terms and refer, no doubt, to Paul's appearances in court. But he writes as though not he but the gospel were on trial. The evidence he gives on his own behalf not merely defends but vindicates the gospel. The verse thus contains a double surprise and shows how free from egotism Paul was. Another man might have thanked his friends for sympathizing with his troubles and being with him in spirit as he stood trial. Paul congratulates them on being partners in his privilege of acting as advocate for the gospel.

8. *God is my witness* should not be regarded as a solemn oath, as though some members of the church were disposed to doubt his affection or at least the impartiality of it. Paul uses a similarly unemphatic turn of phrase in Rom. 1⁹; 2 Cor. 11³¹; 1 Thess. 2⁵; and in each case it is best translated 'God knows'. Where he wants to make an emphatic asseveration of truth, he uses a longer formula (Rom. 9¹; 2 Cor. 1²³; Gal. 1²⁰; 1 Thess. 2¹⁰).

I yearn means that he wants to be with them. But his longing also has its source in *the affection of Christ Jesus.* He loves them as Christ loves, and therefore, as Barth says, 'without that self-seeking that seems to cling like a curse to even the most real human love.'

9. From human affection Paul's mind moves to *love*, which is the distinctively Christian quality because it is God's own love bestowed on men by the Holy Spirit (Rom. 5⁵). This *love* is to manifest itself in the way the Philippians form their moral judgments. Moral decisions are only rarely a matter of distinguishing right from wrong. They require *knowledge* of the character and purpose of God and *discernment.* What is right in itself may be wrong in the circumstances. What is good may not be best. Often it is necessary to weigh the claims of conflicting loyalties. Only *love* can impart the necessary grasp of general principles and the sensitivity to particular needs.

10. The verb δοκιμάζειν can mean *approve*, but the sense required here is rather 'to learn by experience'. Ethical judgment becomes mature only by constant exercise. Τὰ διαφέροντα (*what is excellent*) was a technical term of Stoic moral philosophy, which had passed into popular usage, denoting 'the things that really matter'.

'Απρόσκοποι can mean either *blameless* or harmless, either 'not

stumbling' or 'not causing others to stumble'. In Acts 24¹⁶ it has the
first meaning and in 1 Cor. 10³² the second. Either would fit the context here. Paul could be warning his friends against heedlessness or
against the moral rigour which does what is right regardless of the
damage to others. The RSV has chosen the first, but the second interpretation would be more characteristically Pauline and more in
keeping with the emphasis on love.

11. The RSV takes the verb as passive (*filled with the fruits*), which gives
tolerable sense. But it could also be middle ('bearing a full harvest'),
and this perhaps fits the metaphor slightly better and the list of
Christian attitudes which it concludes. For *righteousness* does not mean
moral uprightness, but the state of being justified or declared right
with God; and it is from this seed that the harvest of Christian character grows. It is God's free, unearned gift *through Jesus Christ*, but it
enables man to bear the harvest he ought and so to give God the *glory
and praise* that are his due.

1: 12–26 *Paul's imprisonment*

Paul knows that his friends are worried about the outcome
of his trial and writes this letter partly to reassure them. So far
from hindering his missionary work, imprisonment has actually
furthered it, and that in two ways. Through the soldiers who
guard him word has spread to the whole praetorian guard, and
indeed to the general public, that he has committed no crime,
but is in prison because he is a Christian. The members of the
church in Rome might have taken his imprisonment as a
warning to do nothing that would attract the attention of the
authorities; but most of them have instead gained from it a new
access of confidence and are preaching the gospel with renewed
vigour (vv. 12–14). It is true that his presence in the city has
affected them in various ways. Some are prompted by good-
will towards him and are concerned only to emulate his success.
Others are interested in success for its own sake. Jealous of the
apostle's reputation, they are determined to show that the
church's mission can prosper without him, under the impression that he will feel deflated at discovering himself to be dis-
pensable. But the result is the same, whatever mixture of
motives may have produced it (vv. 15–18).

As for his own prospects, Paul is sure that the outcome of his
trial will be vindication by God. He has the prayers of his

friends and the generous support of the Holy Spirit to ensure his continuing loyalty to Christ. Whether the verdict of the court is life or death, the one thing that matters to him, now as always, is that he should demonstrate the greatness of Christ (vv. 19–20). Life for him now means union with Christ, and this transforms the prospect of death from loss to gain. He recognizes however that God may still have work for him to do on earth and is hard put to it to decide which verdict he would prefer. If he thinks only of his own benefit, he chooses death and the closer presence of Christ. If he thinks of his friends, he would rather be granted a further span of useful service (vv. 21–24). This debate leads him to the conclusion that he will be acquitted, because it is so important both to himself and to the Philippians that they should see one another again (vv. 25–6).

13. The *praetorian* guard was the Emperor's bodyguard of nine cohorts, the only troops stationed in Italy after the settlement of Augustus. They had their headquarters in Rome, near the Viminal Gate. The RSV is probably right in assuming that this is what Paul means by πραιτώριον. But the Latin *praetorium*, of which this is a Greek transliteration, has a number of meanings, and several of them would fit the context almost as well. It can mean: (a) the headquarters of a general in the field; (b) the headquarters of the praetorian guard in Rome; (c) the guard itself; (d) a detachment of the guard overseas; (e) the residency of a Roman governor in a provincial capital (Mark 15[16]; John 18[28,33]; 19[9]); (f) a palace (Acts 23[35]). Although no Roman would have used this word of the Emperor's palace on the Palatine hill in Rome, a visitor from the eastern provinces might well have done so. Senses (b), (c), and (f) are all consonant with a Roman origin of the letter, (d) and (e) with an Ephesian one.

Paul does not claim to have made converts among the *guard*, but only to have made plain to them the true cause of his arrest. According to Acts, Paul had been accused first of sacrilege (21[28]), then of being a political agitator (24[5]), and he had been informed that in Rome no one had a good word to say for the Christian religion (28[22]). He had therefore been at pains to prove to all he met that loyalty to *Christ* was his sole offence. In this he had shown more concern for the gospel than for his own safety. The time had not indeed yet come when it was a criminal offence to be a Christian. But it was always dangerous to belong to an outlandish cult, particularly if that cult forbad participation in the official Roman religion. The Romans regarded religion as a department of state. Refusal to worship the gods was both atheism and treason, and the only people exempt from this requirement were the Jews. As long as Christianity was officially thought to be a brand of Judaism, it enjoyed the security of this exemption. But once it was known to be a new, and therefore illegal, religion, the security of its

14. adherents was removed. It follows that the new boldness of the Roman Christian must have been inspired by Paul's fortitude in the face of danger, not by any certainty of his release.

15–17. Paul seems to have as little contact with his supporters as with his rivals. This is one reason for believing him to be in Rome, where he was a stranger, rather than in Ephesus, where most of the Christians were his close friends. Lightfoot was sure that the opponents who were prompted by *envy and rivalry* were Judaizers, like those who set the Galatian churches by the ears. But it is hardly credible that Paul should have said three times of such false teachers that they *preach Christ*. In writing to the Galatians he had refused to allow that the gospel preached by Judaizers was a genuine gospel (1^{6-9}), and had warned those who were tempted to follow it that they would be severed from Christ (5^4). The two types of Christian in Rome are not distinguished by doctrine or conduct, but only by their personal attitude to Paul. All that he is saying of them is that, while most of the members of the Roman church have been stimulated by his imprisonment to greater efforts of evangelism, in some the stimulus has taken the form of *love* and in others of *rivalry* or *partisanship*; and in both cases he is content to have been the means of advancing the work of the gospel. The only fault he imputes to his rivals is that they have acted *not sincerely*, i.e. with mixed motives, fancying that their success would make him jealous and bring home to him the frustrations of his enforced inactivity.

From the tantalizing glimpses of the church in Rome that this letter affords we may judge that it was far from being a united family, and this corresponds with what we know of other religious groups in the capital during the first century A.D.[8] Foreign immigrants contrived to maintain their language, religion, and racial or national solidarity by living together in tenement houses (*insulae*). But because of the *lex Julia de collegiis*, which banned all society meetings except those licensed by the Senate, these groups tended to be isolated from one another. There were at least thirteen Jewish synagogues in the city, and the likelihood is that each one catered for Jews from a different part of the empire. It is a reasonable conjecture that the church in Rome never had a founder, but came into existence through the immigration of Christians from many provinces; and that they, like

[8] See G. la Piana, 'Foreign Groups in Rome during the First Centuries of the Empire', *Harvard Theological Review*, xx (1927), pp. 183ff.

other immigrants, had their closest contacts with other Christians from the country of their origin. Political and social influences would have combined to keep such groups apart, and it would have taken effort and determination to establish any community of spirit.

18. *in pretence.* Paul is not accusing his rivals of preaching a gospel they do not believe, but of using their laudable devotion to the gospel as a cover for their less reputable motive of putting him in the shade and causing him chagrin. The efficacy of the gospel happily does not depend on the character or motives of the preacher.

19. *this will turn out for my deliverance* should be printed as a quotation. Paul is quoting Job 13[16] in the Septuagint version, and his words are liable to misinterpretation unless we recognize their source. As the next verse shows, Paul has no confidence in his acquittal by an earthly court. Like Job, he is sure of vindication when his case is presented in the heavenly court of appeal, because his own faith will there be reinforced by the *prayers* of the church and *the help of the Spirit of Jesus Christ,* who appears here in the Johannine role of advocate (John 14[16,26]; 15[26]; 16[7]).

20. Paul turns his thoughts from the heavenly to the earthly law court. The second half of the verse makes it plain that he is now speaking of his demeanour before the Roman judge and not of his hopes for the Day of Christ. It follows that *ashamed* is an over literal rendering of the Greek verb, which here means 'to be daunted, intimidated, or put out of countenance'. It stands in contrast to the *full courage,* which cannot be silenced by the threat of wordly reprisals. Paul has never lacked that *courage* in the past, but he is too well aware of his own weakness to be sure that he can command it *now as always* without drawing on resources greater than his own. *Christ will be honoured* is a possible translation of the Greek, but the verb ($\mu\epsilon\gamma\alpha\lambda\acute{\nu}\nu\epsilon\sigma\theta\alpha\iota$) belongs to a class of verbs in which the passive is regularly used also in an intransitive sense, and this is what is required here: 'Christ will display his greatness'.[9] It is Christ, not Paul, who is to be the agent of the expected triumph. *my body* is to be understood as 'my person' (cp. Eph. 5[28]).

21. Paul is facing a judicial verdict of life or death, but these earthly distinctions have come to mean little to him. 'I have been crucified with Christ; it is no longer I who live, but Christ who lives in me' (Gal. 2[20]). The only death that matters is the one he died when he was baptized into the death of Christ (Rom. 6[3]). What men call death is now *gain.* In saying that *to die is gain* Paul is not at this stage in his reflections contrasting death with continuing bodily life, as though that were something from which he would be glad to escape; *to live is*

[9] See G. B. Caird, 'The Glory of God in the Fourth Gospel; an Exercise in Biblical Semantics', New Testament Studies, xv, pp. 265–77.

Christ, and death can neither add to that union nor subtract from it. The contrast is rather between the Christian and the pagan views of death. Christ has transformed both life and death, so that, *if to live is Christ*, then *to die is gain*.

22. Paul is prepared to consider one reason for not regarding death as preferable, but it is not clear what the reason is. Καρπὸς ἔργου can mean either *fruitful labour* in the future or 'the fruit of past labours'. Either rendering would provide a good reason for wanting to stay alive. In the one case it would be because God had new work for him to do, in the other because his presence was needed to reap the harvest of his life-work. The syntax of the sentence as a whole is obscure, and there are three ways of taking it:

(a) 'If my living on in the body means that I could reap the fruit of my past toil, then I do not know which to prefer.'

(b) 'If I am to live on in the body, that will mean that I can reap the fruit of my toil. Yet I do not know which to prefer.'

(c) 'What if my living on in the body means that I could reap the fruit of my toil! I do not know which to prefer.'

The third is Lightfoot's suggestion and has been adopted by the NEB.

Yet which I shall choose. Paul is not claiming that he actually has a choice. The decision lies with his Roman judge. His dilemma is that he does not know which verdict to hope for.

23. The words *depart and be with Christ* are a notorious crux and have called forth a bewildering variety of explanations. In his earlier letters Paul has taught a single consistent doctrine of life after death. Christians who die remain in a state of sleep until the Advent of Christ, who will then raise them to eternal life, transforming their mortal nature and clothing it with immortality (1 Thess. 4^{13}–5^{10}; 1 Cor. 15^{35-55}; 2 Cor. 5^{1-10};[10] Rom. 8^{18-25}). This verse seems to present the contrary view that those who die 'in the Lord' go directly into his presence (cp. Mark $12^{18\mathrm{ff}\cdot}$, which appears to require that Abraham, Isaac, and Jacob already enjoy life eternal in the presence of God). But this impression is called in question by 3^{21}, which shows that Paul's belief in the resurrection or redemption of the body at the Day of Christ has remained unchanged. The following solutions have been proposed:

(a) that Paul expected some unique provision to be made for himself, as had been made for Enoch and Elijah;

(b) that he expected special provision to be made for martyrs;

(c) that he is not referring to life after death but to the closer identification with Christ achieved in a martyr's death;

[10]There is no good case for holding that the doctrine of this passage is different from that of the other epistles cited here. The parallels with 1 Cor. 15 are very striking.

(d) that he is referring to the intermediate state in which the dead wait for the resurrection at the Parousia;

(e) that, because he had a Semitic mind, he was capable of holding mutually contradictory views together in tension, allowing each to qualify the other. None of these proposals has much to be said for it. There are no grounds for supposing that Paul, with his strong emphasis on salvation by grace alone, would have put himself or anyone else in a special category. He would hardly have described the sleep of death as *far better*, and in any case those who sleep in the grave cannot be said to be *with Christ* who has left it. And ought we to resort to paradox before the possibilities of reason are exhausted? There is however one further possibility, that Paul believed in a real analogy between sleep and death. Sleep is the experience which negates the passage of time. When a man falls asleep, the next thing he is conscious of is waking. Similarly, when a Christian falls asleep in death, the next thing he is conscious of is the great awaking of the Day of Christ. In this way it could be true both that a man passes into the presence of Christ immediately at death and that this happens for all simultaneously. In other words, this image of sleep could be a Pauline solution to the problematic relation of time and eternity. Such a notion should not be dismissed as too sophisticated for the ancient world, for there is an impressive parallel in 2 Esdras 5⁴², where the angel guide explains that the Day of Judgment is like a circle, in which all points on the circumference are equidistant from the centre. Every man's death is equidistant from the Day of the Lord.

25–26. Throughout this paragraph Paul has been discussing the outcome of his trial lightheartedly, almost playfully, as though it were a decision that lay in his own hands. Now he brings the discussion to a close by saying, in effect: 'I have convinced myself by my own arguments that I had better stay alive, because I know how proud of me you are.'

1: 27–2: 4 *An appeal for Unity*

Thus far Paul has concentrated on his own condition and prospects, because he knows that these are uppermost in the minds of his friends and that their greatest need is to be assured that he is in good heart. But now the pastor in him comes to the fore. Whether he is able to visit them or not, they are to discharge their duties as citizens of the heavenly commonwealth, and the first of these is to present a united front to the world. If they can do this without being intimidated, this will be God's way of demonstrating that their opponents are on the road to perdition, while their Christian victims are on the road to salvation. To face hardships for the sake of Christ is a privilege inherent in the Christian calling, part of the one great struggle against the powers of evil in which Paul was engaged when he first came to Philippi and is still engaged in Rome (vv. 27–30).

Unity is important not only because of threats from outside, but also because the Christian life is a shared life. In Christ they have experienced the spiritual power that stirs the heart, the love that reassures, the fellowship created by the Spirit, the affection and compassion which Christians learn from their Lord, and they know that all these contribute to the same result—a community bound together by a common way of thinking and feeling. In such a community there can be no place for rivalry or self-esteem. Each member must put the needs, interests, and rights of others before his own (vv. 1–4).

27. *let your manner of life be*. This is a translation of a single word, πολιτεύεσθε. By derivation this verb means 'to exercise the rights and duties of citizens', 'to take part in government', 'to have a particular kind of government'. In hellenistic Greek it could be used with the weakened meaning 'to behave' (Acts 23[1]), and the RSV has assumed that this is so here. But there are two reasons for thinking that Paul may have had an ear for the word's etymology: he uses the cognate noun in 3[20] with its full sense of 'commonwealth', and he is addressing the residents of a city which has a deep civic pride in its status as a colony. He is reminding the Philippians that the gospel is the charter of the Christian commonwealth and asking them to live up to its claims. Michael has drawn attention to an irregularity of expression in this verse, which suggests that, for all the bravado of the previous paragraph, Paul has no very strong hopes of acquittal. We should have expected him to say: 'Whether I come and see for myself or have reports brought to me while I am absent from you, I want to be satisfied that you are standing firm.' What he has in fact said is: 'Whether I come and see for myself or not, I want to hear reports about you that you are standing firm.' He does not really expect to see, only to hear.

Paul rarely uses sustained metaphor. He prefers to string together a variety of metaphors with a single point (cp. Eph. 4[14]). Here the Philippians are told to conduct themselves like good citizens, to *stand firm* like good soldiers, *striving side by side* like good athletes in the stadium (συναθλοῦντες). These three images together drive home the need for concerted action.

28. *a clear omen* is hardly strong enough for ἔνδειξις, which Paul uses elsewhere in the sense of 'demonstration' or 'proof'. The unflinching unity of the church in the face of persecution is to be God's way of proving something to the persecutors, and the proof has to do with man's final destiny of *destruction* or *salvation*. The persecutors are to be furnished with evidence, as once happened to Paul himself (Acts 9⁵), that God is against them and on the side of their victims, and that there are eternal consequences in store for both. But the NEB ('a sure sign to them that their doom is sealed') goes too far. The point of believing in a Last Judgment is that, until then, no man's doom is sealed. Paul and at least one member of the Philippian church (Acts 16³³) had been involved in the persecution of Christians without thereby forfeiting their chance of eternal bliss. Paul would scarcely have called the solidarity of Christians a proof, *and that from God*, if he had not thought it possible that some would be convinced by it. The unity of the church is to be 'a clear proof to them—and that from God—of the perdition in store for them and the salvation for you.'

30. The athletic metaphor of v. 27 is picked up in the word *conflict* (ἀγών). To be a Christian is to be entered for a contest against powerful adversaries, not only the human ones but the superhuman forces of evil which dominate the darkness of the present world order (cp. Eph. 6¹²). There is, however, no evidence that the Philippian church was undergoing official persecution by the Roman authorities, let alone martyrdom. Their contest was of the same kind as *you saw . . . to be mine* on the occasion of his first visit to their city, when the opposition had come from frustrated commercial interests.

1. Most translators and commentators take the words *encouragement in Christ* closely together, as the RSV has done, and so find themselves in difficulties with the syntax of the clause, which has no verb. It is easier, with the NEB, to take the words *in Christ* with the list as a whole: 'if you have found in Christ (i.e. in the common life of the church) any encouragement etc.' Παράκλησις (*encouragement*) is a technical term of New Testament catechetical instruction with a wide range of use. Frequently, as here, it denotes 'the moral strengthening which comes from the presence or guidance of those who are strong in the faith'.[11] *Incentive of love* is an improbable rendering, first proposed by Lightfoot, and taken over by the RSV from Moffatt. Paul undoubtedly believed that the experience of *love* in the church was a persuasive argument in favour of unity, but the list as a whole shows that he has in mind here the experience itself and not its persuasiveness. What is required is the normal meaning of the word: 'consolation' or 'reassurance'. *participation in the Spirit* is part of what is covered by κοινωνία Πνεύματος, for the Spirit is Christ's gift to his church in which all

[11]E. G. Selwyn, *The First Epistle of St. Peter*, p. 262.

members share alike. But elsewhere κοινωνία means 'fellowship' or 'communion'. In the threefold benediction of 2 Cor. 13¹⁴, the balance of the three phrases requires that all three genitives be taken as subjective: 'the grace which Christ supplies, the love which God bestows, and the fellowship which the Holy Spirit creates.' In the present context the absence of the definite article does not seem an adequate reason for adopting a different translation. It is impossible to experience *participation in the Spirit* except through the fellowship which is the Spirit's distinctive creation.

2. *being of the same mind*. This is a regular Greek idiom for living in agreement. Paul is not asking for doctrinal orthodoxy or uniformity of opinion, nor is he here referring to the process, well attested in the early church, by which the Spirit brought members of an assembly to a common mind (Acts 15²⁸). He is asking for a harmonious disposition, which he further defines in the next two verses. He is so emphatic in his demand for unity that he repeats himself over and over again in different words. This has led some commentators to imagine that he had heard news of serious quarrels in Philippi, which were the one blot on their record. But the only evidence for this in his letter is that two of the women have not been seeing eye to eye (4²). If the whole church were really beset by squabbles, it is strange that he should have singled out that one for special mention. Moreover, the natural interpretation of 2¹² is that the church has always in the past obediently followed the pattern of unity through humility which Paul has just illustrated by the example of Christ. It is surely far more likely that the emphasis on unity is the reflexion of his unhappy dealings with the divided church in Rome, just as, at an earlier date, his letter to Rome reflected the debates with the churches of Galatia and Corinth.

3. By using two different words to translate ἐριθεία, here (*selfishness*) and in 1¹⁷ ('partisanship'), the RSV has obscured the connexion between Paul's warnings to Philippi and this Roman experience (cp. 2²¹). *humility* was not generally regarded in the ancient world as a virtue, but as the token of a slavish disposition. As Lightfoot has said: 'it was one great result of the life of Christ to raise "humility" to its proper level.' Christian *humility* is not self-disparagement, which is either dishonesty or inverted pride, but self-effacement.

4. *his own interests . . . the interests of others*. The Greek has two much vaguer phrases, literally translated in the AV as 'his own things' and 'the things of others'. The RSV has chosen one way of filling out the empty word 'things', but there are other ways: it could refer to possessions, gifts, rights, or points of view. Perhaps Paul deliberately used a vague expression in order to include them all. But the following description of the example of Christ leaves no serious doubt that the emphasis is on rights. The real threat to the harmony of a community does not come when each member is wrapped up in his own interests, protects

his own property, parades his talents, or defends his opinions, but when each stands on his dignity and demands his rights. The Christian is to be more concerned about the rights and dignity of others than about his own.

2: 5–11 *The Example of Christ.*

This disposition, in which concern for others leaves no room for self-concern, must be characteristic of the common life of the church, because that life is lived in Christ, and this was Christ's own disposition (v. 5). He might have insisted on the honours and dignities proper to his divine nature, but for man's sake he chose to forgo them. Unlike Adam, who aimed at equality with God and was humbled, he surrendered the status which was his by right and brought himself down to the level of man. He accepted all that manhood entailed, including man's bondage to the powers which dominated man's dark world. He carried his identification with sinful man consistently through to the end, accepting not merely the death which is the wages of sin, but death by criminal execution (vv. 6–8). All the divine honours which the heavenly Christ had renounced, and to which the self-assertive Adam had aspired in vain, were now lavished by God on the man Jesus, and through him on mankind, and the greatest honour of all is that henceforth the whole creation is to pay its homage to God in the name of Jesus and to offer its worship to God by confessing his lordship (vv. 9–11).

5. *this* is retrospective, i.e. 'this frame of mind I have just described'. The words *you have* are not in the Greek, and it is not clear how the RSV intends them to be taken. The translation could mean 'which you have (exemplified) in Christ Jesus', and in that case it would agree with the AV ('which was also in Christ Jesus'). The objection to this interpretation is that it gives an unparalleled sense to the phrase *in Christ Jesus*, which Paul regularly uses to designate the corporate life of the church. The other possible meaning of the RSV version is 'which you possess in Christ Jesus'. But this is to make the whole sentence pleonastic: 'have in your relations with one another what you already have in your corporate life in Christ.' These difficulties do not arise if we take the Greek exactly as it stands, without supplying a verb ('which also in Christ Jesus'), and treat the words 'which also' (ὃ καί) as the Greek equivalent of the Latin *id est*: 'this is the disposition which

must govern your common life, i.e. your life in Christ Jesus, because he . . . '

6–11. For the theory that these verses are a pre-Pauline hymn, see Introduction, pp. 100–104. Whether it was written by Paul or by another, there is general agreement that it refers to the pre-existence of Christ, attributes to him a divine nature, and represents him as capable of exercising choice. In this last respect it may be said to contain a higher Christology than even the prologues of Hebrews and the Fourth Gospel, both of which speak of the pre-existent Christ without ascribing to him any personal action. We are given no hint, however, of the process of thought which led the author to formulate such a remarkable belief about one whom many of his contemporaries had known in the flesh. Indeed, the term pre-existence is somewhat glibly used in theological discussion without any clear definition of its significance. When Jewish theology spoke of persons or things as existing before the Creation, this was always to be understood in one of two ways. The pre-existent Wisdom, for example, was the personification of an attribute of God, and her apparently independent personal existence could readily be recognized as a figure of speech (Prov. $8^{22\text{ff.}}$; Ecclus. 24; Wisd. $7^{22\text{ff.}}$). To say that Wisdom was God's agent in creation is nothing more than a picturesque way of saying that God in his wisdom created the world. Other persons or things said to pre-exist did so in the mind or predestining purpose of God. Thus in 2 Esdras, the pre-existent Messiah is 'kept until the end' (12^{32}); but the identical phrase is used of the wings of the eagle, which represent Roman emperors (12^{21}). Thus the Jewish background, important as it is for the development of Christian doctrine (cp. notes on Col. $1^{15\text{ff.}}$), provides no complete explanation of the origin of this belief in a personal pre-existence of Christ. For reasons given in the Introduction we can dismiss the alternative hypothesis that Christians came to believe in the pre-existence of Christ through identifying him with the heavenly man of pagan myth. In the present passage Christ does not pre-exist as man; he becomes man. The probability is that it was Paul who first taught his fellow Christians to think of Christ as pre-existent, that he himself began with the Jewish ideas about the pre-existence of Wisdom and the Torah on which he had been brought up, and that it was the person of the historical Jesus that compelled him to take the further step of thinking of that pre-existence as personal. At least we know that Paul believed in Christ's personal act in choosing to be incarnate, and that he reached that belief long before Philippians was written (cp. 2 Cor. 8^9).

6. This verse is compounded of three phrases (*the form of God*, *equality with God*, and *a thing to be grasped*), each in its own way so ambiguous that it is not surprising to find almost as many interpretations as interpreters. The RSV uses the same word *form* for μορφή here and for σχῆμα in v. 7.

Lightfoot, though recognizing that the two words are partial synonyms, pointed out that they were distinguished by the philosophers, and claimed that a similar distinction should be observed there. The one denoted 'what He is in himself', the other 'what He appeared in the eyes of men'. He had to admit, however, that in 3²¹ 'the difference is not obvious at first sight'. The RSV is probably right to reject such subtleties, though it does not necessarily follow that the two Greek words are best translated by the same English one. But even if we were to accept Lightfoot's contention, it would not greatly help us to determine what being *in the form of God* involved. Was it the same as *equality with God*, or was *equality with God* a higher status to which the pre-existent Christ might have aspired? We should be in a better position to answer this question if we knew the intended meaning of the third term, ἁρπαγμός, which can mean either 'a grasping', 'a snatch', 'a robbery' or 'a thing grasped', 'booty', 'a prize or catch'. There are four main ways of reading the verse:

(a) Christ, being in the form of God, was equal with God and counted this status his by right, not by usurpation (snatching);

(b) Christ, being in the form of God, was equal with God, but did not count this a prize to be clutched;

(c) Christ, being in the form of God, was equal with God, but did not think that this equality was to be construed in terms of grasping;[12]

(d) Christ, being in the form of God, did not count the higher status of equality with God a prize to be grasped.

It is possible to object to each of these interpretations on the ground that the idea could have been more simply expressed. For this reason it is likely that the choice of terms (and particularly the choice of ἁρπαγμός) has been dictated by an implied contrast between Christ and some other person who attained or aspired to *equality with God*. One suggestion is that the contrast is with the divine heroes of the hellenistic world, such as Heracles or Alexander the Great;[13] but this theory fails on two counts, that it does not explain the use of ἁρπαγμός, since the Greek heroes were granted divine status without snatching at it, and that it provides no adequate basis for the ethical instruction in humility, which is the point of the whole passage. There has been considerable support for the more plausible idea that the contrast is with Satan, but here again there are two insuperable objections. The myth of Satan rebelling against God is not found in the Bible. Lucifer, who says, 'I will ascend to heaven . . . I will make

[12]See C. F. D. Moule, 'Further Reflexions on Philippians 2:5–11' in *Apostolic History and the Gospel*, ed. W. Ward Gasque and Ralph P. Martin, pp. 264–76.

[13]See W. L. Knox, 'The "Divine Hero" Christology in the New Testament', Harvard Theological Review, xli (1948), pp. 229–49.

myself like the Most High' (Isa. 14$^{12-14}$), is not Satan but the Day-star, Venus, which the prophet is using as a symbol to depict the fruitless aspirations of the king of Babylon. But the decisive point is the rhetorical balance of the passage as a whole: he who renounced *equality with God* to become man can be adequately contrasted only with a man who aimed at *equality with God*. The contrast therefore is with Adam, and it is because he grasped at *equality with God* that Christ is said not to have done so. The logic of this balance further requires that Adam, who grasped at a dignity to which he had no right, should be contrasted with Christ, who renounced a status to which he already had every right; only so could he provide the ethical example required by the context. There is nothing praiseworthy in not usurping a status to which one has no title. To this it may be added that an Adam-Christ typology is distinctively Pauline (1 Cor. 15$^{21-2,45-9}$; Rom. 5$^{12-14}$; Eph. 4$^{22-3}$; Col. 3$^{9-11}$), and that there is at least one passage where it seems to have determined the form of an argument without being explicitly expressed (Rom. 7$^{7-11}$).[14] For these reasons the verdict must lie between interpretations (b) and (c), with a slight bias in favour of (b).

7. *emptied himself.* There is no justification here for what in modern times has come to be known as Kenotic Christology, the idea that Christ could not have become man without divesting himself of the attributes of deity, particularly those of omnipotence, omniscience, and omnipresence. Paul is not talking about these matters, but about Christ's renunciation of rank, privilege, and rights. 'The supposed *locus classicus* for Kenoticism, literally interpreted, has in fact no direct bearing on the question.'[15]

The order of the clauses clearly shows that *the form of a servant* is a mistranslation, and that no reference to Isaiah 53 can be intended. Other New Testament passages no doubt assert that Christ, as one man among many, chose to fulfil the vocation of the Servant of the Lord. Here Christ's voluntary actions as man are described in v. 8. This verse deals with his Incarnation, and the 'form of a slave' which he accepted in becoming man must be an inevitable concomitant of manhood. There is nothing in man's nature which makes it inescapable for him to be servant of God. But in Paul's theology every son of Adam is inevitably born into a world dominated by powers of evil. In Romans 5–8 these powers are identified as sin, death, and law. The man who sins puts himself in the power of sin, and therefore under the law which condemns him and the death which is sin's wages and the law's sentence; and all men are implicated by their common humanity

[14]See also M. D. Hooker, 'Adam in Romans 1', *New Testament Studies*, vi (1960), pp. 297–306.

[15]E. R. Fairweather, 'The "Kenotic" Christology', an appended note in Beare's commentary, pp. 159–74.

in one another's slavery. Christ accepts involvement in this triple bondage; he came 'in the likeness of sinful flesh' (Rom. 8³), was born under the law (Gal. 4⁴), and submitted to the control of death (Rom. 6⁹). Elsewhere Paul includes this human bondage in the more general enslavement to principalities and powers, the elemental spirits of the universe (see on Eph. 1¹⁰). To this also Christ submitted, allowing them to crucify him, so that his death might free himself and the rest of mankind from their domination (1 Cor. 2⁶⁻⁸; Col. 2²⁰).

Neither here nor in Rom. 8³ does the word likeness (ὁμοίωμα) carry any hint of mere semblance or unreality. Christ was *born* like other men, and his involvement in the common life of sinful humanity was genuine. Unless he had shared all the conditions of human servitude, he could not have broken it.

8. The story moves from the decision of the heavenly Christ to the decision of the man Jesus. *Humbled* echoes 'humility' in v. 3 and makes the parallel explicit: Christians are to exhibit the humility of which Jesus was the supreme example. Those who believe that this is a pre-Pauline hymn have objected that there is no real comparison between the mutual renunciation of rights between members of the church and the humility of Jesus, which took the form of obedience to God. But this is a shallow criticism. How could obedience to God require of Jesus that he should submit not only to death but to criminal death, unless that death was in some sense vicarious, the renunciation for the benefit of others of his own right to live? Admittedly this is not stated in so many words. But there are other passages in Paul's letters where his nimble mind jumps a step in the argument on the assumption that his readers will have the wits to follow him (cp. Rom. 5¹⁵ff.).

obedient unto death means 'obedient to God to the full length of accepting death'. Paul thinks of death not biologically but spiritually, not as the terminus of physical existence but as 'the wages of sin' (Rom. 6²³). Sin cuts a man off from God, and death is the judicial sentence which makes that severence complete and final. 'The decree from of old is, "You must surely die!" ' (Ecclus. 14¹⁷). Christ's identification with sinful man is so total that he accepts not only death but execution. Because the *cross* has been transformed into a symbol of Christian piety, we are apt to forget that in Paul's day it was the symbol of degradation, reserved by the Romans for the most serious crimes. Lohmeyer's attempt to bracket the words *even death on a cross* as an intrusive gloss, on the grounds that they do not fit the strophic scheme of his hymn, is the reductio ad absurdum of his theory, since the words in fact constitute the climax to which the last three verses have been pointing. The self-abnegation begun in heaven is complete on Golgotha, and so also is Christ's enslavement to the legal powers of the present world order, operating through Jewish and Roman jurisdiction.

9. *Therefore* indicates that what follows is not simply a reversal of fortune,

nor even a reward for obedience, but a direct consequence of Christ's earthly career. What he obeyed was no arbitrary dictate, but God's plan of salvation, that the innocent should die for the guilty. His earthly life and death made it possible for God to do what otherwise he could not have done. It is the man Jesus of whom it is said that *God has highly exalted him*. The heavenly Christ returns to the high dignity he possessed before, but with this difference that he returns as man, and as a man who by his self-humbling has made common cause with his fellow men and become their representative. The glorious destiny which Adam lost by grabbing for it Christ has gained for himself and others by receiving it as the free gift *bestowed* by God's grace. The name is not just a title, but carries with it rank and authority. In particular, Christ now takes precedence over all those cosmic powers to which in his earthly life he was subservient (cp. Eph. 1[21]). The immediate repetition of the word *name* in the next verse strongly suggests that *the name which is above every name* is Jesus ('Saviour'). There is an obvious difficulty, however, in identifying a name given at Christ's exaltation with that by which he was known to his contemporaries during his earthly life. For this reason the majority opinion is that the new name is 'Lord' (cp. Acts 2[36]).

10. *at the name of Jesus* could give the false impression that the homage is to be offered to Jesus instead of to God, and it is better to keep to the literal rendering, 'in the name of Jesus'. Here, as in Rom. 14[11], Paul is quoting from Isa. 45[23]: 'By myself I have sworn, from my mouth has gone forth in righteousness a word that shall not return: "To me every knee shall bow, every tongue shall swear." ' The bowing of the *knee* is the token of surrender to the victorious God, and it is noteworthy that here in Philippians the inhabitants of *heaven* as well as *earth* need to be brought to submission. The thought of this passage is thus closely in line with that of Col. 1[20], where the heavenly beings reconciled to God by the cross are the principalities and powers listed earlier in the same paragraph. So to the prophet's vision of world wide homage to God Paul has now added two fresh elements: that it will include the acceptance of God's sovereignty by the angelic rulers in the heavens, as well as by the living inhabitants of *earth* and the dead in Hades *under the earth*; and that it is to be offered to a divine sovereignty totally redefined through the revelation of God in Jesus. For the point of the exaltation of Jesus is not that he has been promoted from humility to greatness, not that he has become something quite different from what he was on earth, but rather that his self-forgetful love has been declared by God to be the only true greatness, to be indeed the very character of God himself. And this is why his example provides the rule for the common life of the church.

11. *Jesus Christ is Lord* appears to have been the earliest confessional formula of the primitive church (Rom. 10[9]; 1 Cor. 12[3]). Κύριος ('lord'),

or rather its Hebrew equivalent, was the normal style of the kings of
Israel (cp. 1 Sam. 24^{10}; 2 Sam. 13^{33}), and therefore of the messianic
King whose coming the Jews had long awaited. But it had also been
used in the Septuagint as the Greek equivalent of the divine name
Yahweh, and it had a long and varied history as a divine title in many
pagan cults. It is not surprising therefore that at an early date it
became the most popular designation for Jesus, or that its ambiguity
provided a setting in which Christian devotion to Jesus could expand.
But Paul at least never took the step of calling Jesus God. He retained
his Jewish monotheism to the end. Even if Jesus could be described as
equal with God, even if 'the highest place that heaven affords' belonged to him by right, yet at the last he must surrender his sovereignty
to God, so that God may be all in all (1 Cor. 15^{28}). Similarly here he
remains subordinate to *God the Father*. The universal acknowledgment
of Jesus is not an end in itself, but fulfils the role for which the world
was created, to reflect *the glory of God*.

2:12–18 *The Response to Grace.*

Paul's hymn to Christ has provided not only an example of
that obedience to God which takes the form of self-forgetful-
ness, but also a reminder that the Christian life is the work of
God's grace from start to finish; and it is this point which he
now develops. As Christ obediently accepted the plan which
God had laid down for him, so in the past the Philippian church
has been obedient. Now, if they are to remain true to their
splendid record, they must remember that it is not on Paul's
presence that they must rely. Whether he is free to come to
them or not, the realization of God's purpose of unity in their
common life depends on God's own activity in their midst,
inspiring both will and effort; and their active response must
be accompanied by a thrill of awe as they recognize the presence of God in their fellow Christians (vv. 12–13). Like Israel
in the wilderness they are on pilgrimage, but there the resemblance to Israel must end. There must be no rebellious
grumblings or arguments, such as once earned Israel the name
of being a crooked and perverse generation. This description
now fits the pagan world in which Christians must live, but
they must dissociate themselves from it by conduct that is above
reproach. It is their task by faithfulness to the gospel to offer to
the dark world the light it needs. If they do this, then when

Paul stands before his Master at the Day of Judgment, he will be able to point with pride to them as proof that his life-work was not wasted (vv. 14–16). If now he is to die, they must not think of his death as tragic loss. Provided that their faith is fit to be offered as a sacrifice to God, he is content that his life should be poured out as a libation to crown the sacrifice. In that way there should be room only for mutual rejoicing and congratulations (vv. 17–18).

12. *Therefore* resumes the appeal for unity in vv. 1–4, but in the light of the intervening passage. *obeyed* picks up the 'obedient' of v. 8: they have shown in the past that they have learnt Christ's lesson. The contrast between *presence* and *absence* must be interpreted at two levels. Superficially it means *presence* and *absence* from Philippi, but, if that had been all he had in mind, Paul would hardly have written *now . . . much more*. It was over four years since he had been in Philippi, and even before that his *presence* with them had been only intermittent. He appears to be thinking of the past as the period of his *presence* and of the future as the period of his *absence*, because he cannot avoid the suspicion that his absence is about to become permanent. As long as he is present in this life, the Philippians can turn to him for help and advice, but, once he is absent, they will be thrown on to their *own* resources, and therefore on to the grace of God.

your own salvation must refer to the spiritual well-being of the church as a whole. After his passionate plea that they should put self-concern behind them, it is inconceivable that Paul should instruct the Philippians to concentrate on their own individual salvation—the most selfish of all supposedly religious pursuits, expressly condemned by Jesus (Mark 8[35]; Matt. 10[39]; Luke 17[33]). Salvation in the New Testament is always an intensely personal, but never an individual, matter. It is God's gift in Jesus Christ; and only in Christ, i.e. in the community of which he is head, can it be experienced. It follows that *fear and trembling* are not to be understood as the nervous apprehension with which men might be supposed to face the Last Judgment; this, so far from being a Christian virtue, is tantamount to unbelief (cp. Rom. 8[1]). The word translated *fear* ($\phi\delta\beta\sigma\varsigma$) does not here denote alarm or dismay in the face of threat, danger, or loss, but, as often in the New Testament, the awe which men experience in the presence of the divine. With *trembling* awe they must recognize the presence of God in the corporate life of the church and in one another. The unity of the church is secure, as Paul knew from experience, only when its members see each other in this light. When the dispute over the admission of the Gentiles to the church was at its height, the Jerusalem apostles recognized that the God who was at work in Peter's mission to the Jews was also at work in Paul's mission to the Gentiles, and all other differences shrank into insignificance before that one salient fact (Gal. 2^{8-9}).

13. The RSV has seriously misconstrued the Greek by assuming that the verb *is at work* (ἐνεργῶν) is intransitive, and that God is the subject of the two infinitives *to will* and *to work*. The verb is transitive, and the two infinitives are its objects: 'it is God whose activity inspires in you both the will and the effort necessary for the accomplishment of his purpose.' *Good pleasure* (εὐδοκία) denotes not just any conduct which happens to be pleasing to God, but his whole gracious plan for mankind, revealed and made possible by Jesus (cp. Eph. $1^{5,9}$). In Philippians, as in Ephesians, the unity of the church is very close to the centre of that purpose as Paul has come to understand it.

14. Paul does not elsewhere use the word *grumbling*, but he uses the cognate verb in a passage which recalls the complaints made, with disastrous effects, by Israel to Moses in the wilderness (1 Cor. 10^{10}). Since he goes on to quote in v. 15 from Moses's farewell address to Israel, it is probable that he already had the Old Testament parallel in mind here also. *Grumbling* and *questioning* are symptoms of a defective faith in the power or the wisdom of God.

15. Moses's farewell to Israel opens with a bitter indictment: 'They have sinned, they are not God's children, they are to blame, a crooked and perverse generation' (Deut. 32^5 LXX). Paul, in what he knew might well be his farewell letter, echoes these words, but with exactly the opposite effect. He is confident that his friends can be *blameless* and that they are *children of God; a crooked and perverse generation* is a description which still applies to the surrounding world of paganism, but not to the Christians of Philippi. The word used for *lights* is most commonly used of the heavenly bodies (cp. Gen. 1^{14}), and this meaning fits the context admirably: they stand out against their pagan environment like stars against the night sky.

16. *holding fast* is the correct translation if in the previous verse Paul intends only a contrast. But the Greek word can also mean 'proffering', and, if this is the sense Paul intended, he would be reminding his readers of their missionary calling to be the light of the world (cp. Matt. 5^{16}), and defining the light with which they were to shine as the *word of life*, i.e. the gospel. This rendering has the double advantage that it is more in keeping with the star metaphor than the other, and also that it better sustains the general theme of living for others rather than for oneself.

I may be proud. This is a distinctively Pauline idea. The Greek word and its cognates (καύχημα, καύχησις, καυχᾶσθαι) are found fifty times in the Pauline letters and only four times in the rest of the New Testament. Paul's frequent use of them is without doubt a legacy from his

Pharisaic days, when he was convinced that a man's destiny at the Judgment depended on his record (Rom. 2¹⁷,²³; Gal. 6¹³⁻¹⁴; Eph. 2⁹). At that time it was not enough for him to pass the divine scrutiny, he must pass with distinction (Gal. 1¹⁴). When he became a Christian, he resigned all claim to that sort of boasting. Salvation depended on God's free grace alone, not on achievement or merit, and all pride was excluded (Rom. 3²⁷). But he did not therefore relax his determination to excel or to have something to show for himself *in the day of Christ*. The Christian must appear before the tribunal of Christ (2 Cor. 5¹⁰), not indeed to determine his eternal destiny, but to render account of his stewardship to his Lord (1 Cor. 4¹). There is no condemnation in store for those who are in Christ (Rom. 8¹), and, if a man's life work is proved worthless, he does not thereby lose his chance of eternal life; but he does lose something (1 Cor. 3¹²⁻¹⁵; cp. 5⁵). Thus the doctrine of justification by faith goes hand in hand with a profound sense of responsibility from which self-concern has been expelled. The one thing that matters is the approval of Christ.

17. Jewish as well as pagan sacrifices were normally accompanied by *a libation* of wine (2 Kings 16¹³; Jer. 7¹⁸; Hos. 9⁴). The high priest Simon, for example, is said to have 'poured a libation of the blood of the grape' at the foot of the altar to complete the sacrificial liturgy (Ecclus. 50¹⁵). All literal priesthood and sacrifice have been made obsolete by the once-for-all offering of Christ. But Paul can still use the language of sacrifice metaphorically. As Apostle of the Gentiles he has the priestly task of presenting them to God as an acceptable offering (Rom. 15¹⁶). All Christians are required to offer their very selves to God as a living sacrifice (Rom. 12¹). Here *of your faith* is not a genitive of apposition ('the offering which consists of your faith') but a subjective genitive ('the sacrifice offered by your faith') and *the sacrificial offering* refers to the blameless life they are called to lead, without disruptive grumbles. The regular use of the expression 'blood of the grape' for wine makes it easier for Paul to think of his death as *a libation* crowning the sacrifice.

2: 19–30 *The Apostle's Plans*

Paul intends shortly to send Timothy to reassure the Philippians about him and to bring back news of them. But they must be patient for a little. Timothy cannot for the moment leave Rome, and there is no one else available who shares his pastoral care for the Philippian church. All others are too much engrossed in their own affairs to take time for the business of Christ. But Timothy is worth waiting for; they know his record. With Paul he has been like a son apprenticed to his father in the service of the gospel (vv. 19–22). The reason why he cannot come immediately is that he must wait for the outcome of Paul's trial. Then he will come at once, and, if the verdict is acquittal, Paul himself will follow, as soon as he regains his liberty (vv. 23–4). In the meantime he is sending this letter by Epaphroditus, their own messenger, who has been acutely homesick, because word has come that his family and friends are worried about his illness. He was so ill that he nearly died, and that would have been a crushing sorrow to Paul. His task is not yet complete, but Paul has judged that he should be sent home at once, to relieve the anxiety at home and take a load off Paul's own mind. They are not to think any worse of him for coming home prematurely. He fell ill on the road from Philippi to Rome, and it was his determination to complete the journey and to discharge his commission that nearly cost him his life. And so Paul bids his friends goodbye (vv. 25–30).

19. *soon*, but not immediately, for he must await the verdict of Paul's trial (v. 23). In the difficult verses that follow Paul explains why they must be prepared to wait for Timothy. He assumes that, when Timothy returns with *news*, he will *be cheered* by it. This is a clear answer to those who have thought they could read between the lines of this letter a gnawing anxiety about divisions in the Philippian church.

20. *like him.* All that Paul says is, 'I have no one of like mind', and he uses a rare poetic word ($ἰσόψυχος$), which may be taken either as a noun or as an adjective. If it is an adjective, he has left the reader to supply the comparison. There are four possibilities:
(a) 'I have no confidant who . . . '
(b) 'I have no one who shares my regard for you who . . . '
(c) 'I have no one who shares Timothy's devotion to duty who . . . '
(d) 'I have no one in sympathy with your outlook who . . . '
The reason usually given for adopting (c), as the RSV has done, is that for any of the others Paul ought to have said, 'I have no one else . . . ' But Paul is here writing in his usual compressed style in which many things are taken for granted. There is much to be said for (d). Paul has just commended the Philippians for having always in the past obeyed the rule not to put their own rights first, and it would be natural for him to feel that they would not take kindly to the sort of person described in v. 21.

21. The close similarity of wording is a further indication that the

warnings of vv. 1–4 were occasioned by the behaviour of the Christians in Rome and not by what Paul had heard of those in Philippi. The sting of the remark is somewhat diminished when we remember how exacting were Paul's demands, both on himself and on his colleagues. In this instance he was expecting some member of the church in Rome to drop all his other commitments in order to undertake a return journey of 1,600 miles on foot. Thus what at first sight appears to be a bitter complaint is in fact an apology to the church in Philippi. If he had had a really dedicated colleague available, he would have sent him at once. As it is, they will be better served by waiting until Timothy is free.

22. *you know*. Timothy was well known in Philippi. He was with Paul when the church was founded (Acts 16¹) and had visited it at least twice since (Acts 19²²; 20³⁻⁶). The common pattern of family life in the ancient world was that *a son* should learn his trade from his *father*, and Timothy has learnt all that Paul can teach him.

23. *I hope therefore to send him*. The Greek uses a more emphatic word order: 'so he is the one I mean to send.'

24. *I trust*. But he cannot have had much confidence in his release, or he would not have needed to send Timothy.

25. To judge by his name, Epaphroditus must have been a Gentile convert, the child of parents devoted to the worship of Aphrodite. He is unknown to us apart from this epistle (Glover's attempt to identify him with the Epaphras of Colossians is without foundation), but the description of him as *fellow worker* and *fellow soldier* shows that he was not previously unknown to Paul. The NEB correctly takes *messenger and minister* as a hendiadys: 'whom you commissioned to minister'. The Greek words are ἀπόστολος and λειτουργός, which in other contexts can be used of forms of ministry in the church. But there is no need to import these associations into the text here, as though Epaphroditus had been ordained to a priestly office.

26. Enough time had elapsed since Epaphroditus's departure for him to reach Rome, for the Philippians to hear *that he was ill*, and for a report to come to Rome that they were anxiously awaiting news of his health. This is one of the reasons why some commentators have thought that the letter must have been written from Ephesus, since this would greatly reduce the travel involved. But the argument is ill-conceived. It assumes that Epaphroditus fell ill after his arrival in Rome. But the obvious interpretation of v. 30 is that he fell ill on the road and nearly killed himself by completing his journey while he was unfit to travel. If the onset of the illness came before he reached Dyrrachium, the family could have heard about it before ever he reached Rome. Moreover, as Beare observes, 'if Epaphroditus could have slipped back for a weekend, there would not be all this circumstantial discussion about his return.'

27. Paul already had enough on his mind without the additional *sorrow* of knowing that he had unwittingly been the contributory cause of a friend's death.

28. It is not clear why these arrangements should make Paul *less anxious*, unless Epaphroditus's homesickness and the agitated reports from Philippi have been preying on his mind.

29. There is a note of apology in the words *receive him*, as though Paul was doubtful about Epaphroditus's reception. The church had commissioned him not only to carry a gift of money but also to remain in Rome and look after Paul. They are to understand that his early return is not dereliction of duty but Paul's own choice.

30. See on v. 26 above. The RSV has made no attempt at translating the word ὑστέρημα ('deficiency'). Literally translated, the last clause runs: 'gambling with his life to fulfil the deficiency of your service to me'. There is however no suggestion that the Philippians have done less than they ought, only that they have done less than they wanted or planned. The meaning presumably is: 'to render me the service you could not give in person.' They could send a present, but they could not give him personal attention, and it was chiefly to do this, not just to deliver the money, that Epaphroditus had travelled on at the risk of *his life*. See also Col. 1[24].

3: 1–11 *Reminiscences of a Converted Pharisee.*

Now that these tiresome details are disposed of, Paul can return to the theme of joy which is uppermost in his mind. He does not care how often he repeats himself, for joy is the best possible safeguard against counterfeit religion. The dangers against which it offers protection are illustrated by those strict Jews who pride themselves on their superiority to others and call themselves the Circumcision, a title which properly belongs to those who do not rely on their own resources but on the Spirit, whose pride and confidence are in Christ and not in outward privilege and achievement (vv. 1–3). This is a subject on which Paul can speak with the authority of personal experience. Whatever claims any Jew can make, Paul can cap them. If it is a question of pride of race, he was born to strict Jewish parents with a carefully preserved pedigree, and was brought up to speak the ancestral language. If it is a question of pride of achievement, he had interpreted the law with Pharisaic exactitude, proved his devotion to it by persecuting those who were undermining its authority, and held an irreproachable record for legal observance (vv. 4–6). But his conversion made him regard all his previous assets as liabilities. He is still prepared to write everything else off as sheer loss in comparison with the profit of knowing Christ, for whose sake he has in fact forfeited everything. He has learnt to count everything a waste that does not help him to win the prize of finding himself in union with Christ, gaining God's approval not by his own achievements in keeping the law, but simply by faith in Christ. All that matters to him is to know Christ, to experience both the power of his resurrection and the fellowship that comes from sharing his sufferings, to undergo a constant inner transformation into the likeness of the crucified Lord, and so in the end to be raised to life eternal (vv. 7–11).

1. The interpretation of this verse is difficult, partly because of two ambiguities of language, partly because it depends on the theory we adopt about the writing of the letter as a whole. The phrase translated *Finally* (τὸ λοιπόν) is also used in a much vaguer sense, 'and so';[16] and the word translated *rejoice* can also mean 'farewell'. The view adopted in this commentary is that the whole chapter can and should be read as an uninterrupted composition. But there has been much support for the view that there is a break at this point, either because an interruption set Paul off on a new train of thought, or because 3²ff· belongs to a different letter altogether. Those who believe in such a break disagree about v. 1ᵇ, some taking it with what precedes, some with what follows. There are thus three ways of translating v. 1ᵃ, each of which corresponds to a different solution of the literary problem.

(a) 'Finally, friends, I bid you farewell in the Lord.' This must have been intended as the end of the letter, and v. 1ᵇ then becomes the introduction to what follows, whether that was a disconnected postscript or part of a different letter.

(b) 'Finally, friends, rejoice in the Lord.' V. 1ᵇ is then an apology for the repetition of this injunction, and the break comes after it.

(c) 'Well, my friends, rejoice in the Lord.' No break follows, and there should be no paragraph division between v. 1 and v. 2.

The integrity of the letter has been discussed in the Introduction, but there are supplementary reasons for believing that (c) is correct.

(i) It is misleading to say that χαίρετε can mean either 'rejoice' or 'farewell'. Its meaning is 'rejoice', though in some contexts this mean-

[16]See C. F. D. Moule, *An Idiom-Book of New Testament Greek*, pp. 161f.

ing is attenuated into a formal salutation. This is the justification for the attempt in the NEB to take it both ways at once: 'And now, friends, farewell; I wish you joy in the Lord.' As a salutation it is appropriate to any occasion, but it is far more frequently used on meeting than on parting, and there is no example in any extant letter of its use as a closing formula.[17] In the infinitive this verb was used in the almost invariable epistolary formula of opening greeting (see notes on Eph. 1^{1-2}). But even at the beginning of his letters Paul never uses it, preferring to fill out the conventional style of address with theological meaning. For these reasons it is highly improbable that the imperative has its attenuated meaning here or in the other contexts in which it is used in this letter (2^{18}; 4^4).

(ii) There is no reason to suppose that $3^{2ff.}$ was occasioned by any new threat to the church or by any situation different from that reflected in the first two chapters. In v. 19 Paul explicitly says that the warning is one he has frequently given before, and the natural inference is that this holds also for v. 2.

(iii) If v. 2 is interpreted as a vituperative attack on dangerous enemies, why is the attack not sustained? There is no subsequent reference to anything they have done or may do in the future. On the contrary, they are mentioned only in passing, and the rest of the chapter is quietly reminiscent and personal. It is in striking contrast to the persistently polemical tone of Galatians or 2 Cor. 10–13.

(iv) Read as a whole, the chapter exactly fits its context. It is a deeply theological justification for rejoicing in the Lord, even in the face of probable death; and those who do not share the convictions out of which this joy spontaneously arises are introduced only by way of admonitory contrast.

Paul apologises for repeating *the same things*. By translating χαίρετε in 2^{18} as 'you should be glad' the RSV has obscured the need for this. The repetition is *safe* for the Philippians because joy of any kind is a safeguard against the utilitarian attitude which judges people and things wholly by the use that can be made of them; and Christian joy, the exaltation of spirit that flows from acceptance of the free gifts of God's grace, is the best protection against that book-keeping mentality which assumes that every good thing must be a reward for virtue and offers no halfway house between smugness and a bad conscience.

2. *Look out for*. The RSV has softened the rendering of the AV and RV ('Beware of'), but has hardly gone far enough. When the Greek

---

[17]In the papyri nearly all letters end with 'Good luck!' (εὐτύχει) or 'Good health!' (ἔρρωσο) or, more formally, 'I pray for your good health' (ἐρρῶσθάι σε εὔχομαι); cp. Xen. *Cyr.* IV. v. 33 and Plat. *Ep.* I. ii. 410.

βλέπειν means 'beware', it is always followed by an object clause ('beware lest') or by the preposition ἀπό. There is no instance of its use in this sense with a direct object (Mark 13⁹ and 2 John 8, where it governs a reflexive pronoun, are not cases in point). Paul uses the verb four times elsewhere in the imperative with a direct object, and in each case the meaning is 'consider', 'take due note of', or 'pay attention to' (1 Cor. 1²⁶; 10¹⁸; 2 Cor. 10⁷; Col. 4¹⁷). The only reason which could be urged in favour of the traditional translation is the strong emphasis of the threefold repetition, but this is not strong enough by itself to weigh against the evidence of usage. In other words, Paul is not warning his friends to be on constant guard against Jewish menace, but holding the Jews up for their consideration as a cautionary example. The correct translation is: 'consider' or 'learn your lesson from'.¹⁸

The persons cited as a warning are described in three phrases. Either of the first two, by itself, would be ambiguous: *dogs* could mean watchdogs, self-constituted guardians of a moral and religious code, for ever barking at real or supposed danger, or pariahs, excluded because of their unpleasant habits from decent society; and the word translated *evil* could mean morally bad (RSV), malicious (NEB), or simply harmful. The ambiguities are removed, however, by the third phrase, *those who mutilate the flesh*. The Greek for this is ἡ κατατομή ('the mutilation'), and the following sentence shows that Paul intends a punning reference to persons who prided themselves on being ἡ περιτομή ('the circumcision'). We can thus dismiss the theory that the persons concerned were Judaizers, Christians who favoured the adoption of circumcision. The only people who called themselves 'the Circumcision' were Jews (cp. Gal. 2⁷⁻⁹; Col. 4¹¹). The three phrases are therefore best taken as abusive adaptations of language regularly used by the Jews about themselves or others. The strict Jew regarded all Gentiles as unclean and called them *dogs*, because they associated the pariah both with carrion (e.g. 1 Kings 14¹¹; 21¹⁹) and with immorality (Deut. 23¹⁸; 2 Pet. 2²²; Rev. 22¹⁴). Paul is allowing the term of contempt to recoil on the heads of its authors, just as Jesus warned his disciples to avoid the contaminating contact of the Pharisees who were proud of their freedom from taint (Mark 8¹⁵; Luke 11⁴⁴). The Jewish sense of superiority came from that obedience to the law which Paul elsewhere calls 'works'. They are therefore the *workers*, and Paul calls them bad *workers*, not because they do what is morally wrong, nor because they act out of malice, but, as the sequel shows, because their reliance on 'works' is in the end harmful both to themselves and to others. The offensive word 'mutilation' carries a

---

¹⁸See also '*Βλέπετε* Philippians 3²' by G. D. Kilpatrick in *In Memoriam Paul Kahle* (ed. M. Black and G. Fohrer), pp. 146ff.).

reference to the levitical law which excluded mutilated persons from the priesthood (Lev. 21^{5,20}; cp. Deut. 23^1). It is precisely their emphasis on purity that makes them pariahs, their emphasis on good works that makes them bad, their claim to special privilege that disqualifies them.

3. *For* ($\gamma\acute{\alpha}\rho$), as often with Paul, conceals a jump in the argument. It introduces the reason, not for the warning contained in the previous sentence, but for the language in which it is couched: 'Consider the Mutilation. I refuse to call them the Circumcision, which is their self-designation, for we are the Circumcision.' The word *true* has no counterpart in the Greek and should be omitted. The claim that metaphorical and not literal circumcision is the real thing is more fully expounded in Rom. 2$^{28-9}$ and is well founded in Old Testament teaching (Deut. 10^{16}; 30^6; Jer. 4^4; cp. Lev. 26^{41}; Jer. 6^{10}; 9^{25}; Ezek. 44^7). Of these Old Testament passages the one in the forefront of Paul's mind is Jer. 9$^{23-5}$, which combines the idea of true circumcision with that of glorying in the Lord (cp. 1 Cor. 1^{31}; 2 Cor. 10^{17}).

who worship God in spirit. There are three variant readings, and the RSV text has adopted neither the earliest nor the best attested. The earliest manuscript, the Chester Beatty papyrus, omits the word 'God', and must be translated: 'whose worship is spiritual' (NEB). But the main weight of textual evidence favours the reading: 'who worship by the Spirit of God' (RSVmg). The contrast is not merely between a Jewish worship which is external and a Christian worship which is spiritual, but between a physical circumcision, which is the symbol of obedience to a code of law, and a circumcision of heart, i.e. an inner transformation brought about by the gift of the Holy Spirit. The majority reading must be accepted, because the point of the ensuing argument is that Christian salvation, Christian conduct, Christian progress are all the product of God's free, undeserved grace and not of human achievement, not even of human spirituality. The Christian is one whose actions, including his worship, are not dictated by a law which stands over against him, but by the Spirit of God within him. The verb here translated *glory* is from the same root as the word translated 'be proud' in 2^{16} (q.v.). *flesh* carries an incidental allusion to circumcision, but here, as in Eph. 2^{11}, this rite is regarded as the symbol of the old way of life from which the Christian has been rescued by Christ. What Paul means by *confidence in the flesh* becomes clear in the following verses: it is any claim to superiority, whether it is based on inherited privilege or on personal success.

4. Paul's disparagement of proud self-reliance is not the envy of the have-not. He does not choose to boast of anything except what Christ has done for him (cp. Gal. 6^{14}); but, if anyone challenges him to a boasting match on other grounds, he has no doubt of his ability to win it *in the flesh also*. Here is proof, if further proof be needed, that the

'dogs' of v. 2 are an admonitory example and not a group of menacing enemies against whom the Philippians must be on their guard. For they are allowed to drop into the background, and the contrast from now on is between Paul the Jew and Paul the Christian.

5. Paul lists first the four privileges which came to him by birth.

(a) He was born to orthodox parents who had him *circumcised*, as the law required, *on the eighth day*.

(b) He was 'an Israelite by race'. Here the RSV translation, *of the people of Israel*, is imprecise. Proselytes belonged to the people (λαός), and Paul uses another word (γένος) to show that he is speaking of racial descent.

(c) Priests were required to prove their lineage, and the father of any girl who was to marry a priest had to prove his Israelite descent for three generations. Apart from this Jews do not appear to have been any more scrupulous than others in tracing their genealogy.[19] Many of the tribes had long since ceased to be anything more than ideal entities. The claim to be *of the tribe of Benjamin*, therefore, indicates a special pride, particularly as that tribe was one of the two southern tribes which remained true to the house of David and to Jerusalem as the one legitimate centre of Israelite faith. It is possible that the parents named their child Saul after the first king of Israel, also a Benjamite.

(d) The claim to be *a Hebrew born of Hebrews* probably relates to the use of the sacred language of Scripture. Paul was clearly brought up speaking Greek as his first language, and he also spoke Aramaic (Acts 21[40]). But the way in which he uses the Old Testament strongly suggests that he knew it in the original Hebrew as well as in the Septuagint version. It was more than three centuries since Hebrew had given place to Aramaic as the vernacular language, but it was still studied in the rabbinic schools and had never quite ceased to be a spoken language. If, as Acts tells us, Paul was a student of Gamaliel (22[3]), he must have used Hebrew in his studies at Jerusalem. But what he here asserts is that he learnt it from his parents in his home in Tarsus.

The verse division, which includes Paul's claim to the title Pharisee among his inherited advantages, has been influenced by the statements in Acts that his parents were Pharisees (22[3]) and that he himself followed the Pharisaic regimen in Tarsus as well as in Jerusalem (26[4-5]). All this may be true, but it is not the point Paul is here making. He has turned from what he was by birth to what he became by choice, conviction, and achievement, as the punctuation of the RSV correctly signifies.

The Pharisees were a small sect—about 6,000 in the reign of Herod

[19]See Marshall D. Johnson, *The Purpose of the Biblical Genealogies*.

(Jos. *Ant.* XVII. ii. 4)—who took very seriously Israel's call to be the holy people of God, and tried to apply the levitical standards of purity to the laity as well as to priests. It was not enough for them to obey the Law of Moses. The application of every commandment to daily life must be spelled out in detail in accordance with a cumulative tradition of legal interpretation. The strictest of them scrupulously avoided even accidental violations of the Law by leaving a margin of safety (*Pirke Aboth* i. 1) and doing more than was commanded. In order to avoid defilement by even a chance contact with those who were less meticulous than themselves, they formed fraternities with precise rules of segregation. Elsewhere Paul claims to have been the most ardent *Pharisee* of them all (Gal. 1^14).

6. Paul alludes to his past career as *persecutor of the church* sometimes to demonstrate the sovereignty of divine grace to the undeserving (1 Cor. 15^9-10), sometimes, as here, to give evidence of his first hand acquaintance with the Pharisaic position and his extreme zeal for the Law (cp. Gal. 1^13-14). In his Pharisaic days he had regarded the crucifixion as the just penalty imposed by the Law on one who had broken it and taught others to break it; Christ had died under the curse of Deuteronomy (Gal. 3^13; cp. Deut. 21^23; 28^15ff.), and his followers must not be allowed to contaminate the holiness of Israel by perpetuating his lawlessness. As a Christian he came to recognize that reverence for the Law, so far from leading him into the presence of God, had actually blinded him to that presence in the person of Jesus (2 Cor. 3^14–4^4). This explains the violence of his repudiation of the Law as a way of salvation and the violence of his onslaught here on those who persist in so regarding it. With all his talk of 'dogs', he is not so much attacking real contemporary enemies as the ghosts of his own past.

Nothing discredits the legal standards of the old life more in Paul's eyes than the memory that in those days he was held *blameless*. Taught by Christ, Paul has come to acknowledge the inadequacy of *righteousness under the law*. A legal code is bound to deal with overt actions rather than with character, to concentrate on the practicable and therefore on the minor pieties and duties, and to give a man the impression that his standing with God depends on his own merit (cp. Rom. 10^1-3).

7. Paul is here using book-keepers' language, and this is not made sufficiently clear by the RSV translation. All the advantages and merits which Paul the Pharisee entered on the credit side of his own balance sheet Paul the Christian enters on the debit side. It was not that Jewish privilege and Pharisaic virtue were worthless; they were a positive handicap to be overcome by the man who has learnt to live by grace alone. Paul is not here contradicting what he has said in Rom. 3^1-2, that it is a great advantage to be a Jew. There he argues that the possession of the Old Testament is an advantage, provided

that it is interpreted as 'the oracles of God', i.e. as the book of God's gracious promises, and not as a legal code of behaviour. Here he is talking about the supposed assets of those who interpreted the Old Testament legalistically.

8. *Indeed* is a somewhat colourless rendering of four words which give an impression of excited emphasis: 'yes, and more than that . . . ' Paul has not only written off the assets he once enjoyed. He can think of nothing else worth entering in the ledger alongside of the supreme profit of *knowing Christ Jesus my Lord*. This phrase has obvious affinities with the language of Ephesians and Colossians (Eph. 3^{19}; 1^{17}; 4^{23}; Col. 2^3; $1^{9,10}$; 2^2; 3^{10}), yet even in those other letters it has no precise parallel. 'The knowledge of God' is as near as the Old Testament ever comes to a definition of religion, and it covers not merely knowledge of God's truth, but a personal response of faith and obedience to God's self-revelation. Paul seems to have avoided this form of expression in his earlier letters, possibly because he had no particular occasion to use it, possibly because of the problems created in the churches by 'Gnostics' who prided themselves on some esoteric knowledge vouchsafed only to themselves (1 Cor. 8^{1-11}; $13^{2,8}$; 14^6; but see also Gal. 4^9). Here he takes up the Old Testament phrase and fills it with a specifically Christian content and with a peculiarly personal intensity (cp. Gal. 2^{20}; 6^{14}).

So far Paul has been speaking about two different points of view. Now he reminds his readers that, when he speaks of regarding his Jewish advantages as loss, this is no mere figure of speech. He has actually *suffered the loss* of them. It was a simple fact that as a Christian missionary he had forfeited all that he once valued, not to mention comfort, liberty, and now possibly life itself. The point was that, although this was real loss, it did not feel like loss in comparison with the new gain which outweighed it (cp. 2 Cor. 3^{10}). Everything he has surrendered may be dismissed as *refuse*, sheer waste.

in order that I may gain Christ. This clause must not be construed as though the loss were all present and the gain all future. In the next paragraph Paul goes on to speak of hopes as yet unrealised, but the immediate sequel shows that at this stage he is still thinking of present experience. He has rejected all other forms of profit because he now finds his true gain in Christ.

9. *be found in him.* The RSV has taken the verb as a true passive, and so has given the impression that the reference is to what will be discovered at the Last Judgment. But the passive form of this verb is regularly used intransitively with the sense 'turn out to be', 'prove to be', 'find oneself', or even (as in French) 'be present'. *in him* must carry the full weight of meaning of the Pauline 'in Christ', i.e. incorporated into union with Christ (cp. 2^5). Thus the sense required is: 'for the sake of . . . finding myself incorporate in him' (NEB).

The man in Christ possesses *righteousness*. Paul's treatment of this theme here is so condensed that we should be at a loss to interpret the verse if we did not have the whole of Galatians and Romans as a commentary on it. Incidentally, the perfunctory allusion to the great debates of an earlier period of his ministry is another cogent indication that the Philippian church was not now being troubled by Judaizers.

The adjective 'righteous', the noun 'righteousness', and the (in Hebrew and Greek) cognate verb 'justify', are not originally moral terms, but legal. In the Hebrew law court a judge, faced with two litigants, must 'justify' one and 'condemn' the other, i.e. give judgment for the one against the other. To 'justify' thus meant either 'to give a man his rights', 'to do him justice', or 'to declare a man in the right', 'to give a verdict in his favour'; and the verdict would not necessarily depend on the man's moral character. When these terms are used metaphorically in a religious setting, the question is: what must a man do if God is to declare that he is in the right and so give judgment in his favour? The Jewish answer was that he must obey the Law of Moses. Paul's answer, supported by such Old Testament texts as Ps. 143² and Gen. 15⁶, is that men are too sinful ever to be able to earn their justification by their own efforts, but that in any case what God really requires is faith. If a man has faith, he has offered to God the one thing he requires, and God declares him to be in the right. This is to possess by God's declarative act *the righteousness from God that depends on faith*. The trouble with righteousness *based on law* is that it is always self-righteousness (cp. Rom. 10¹⁻³). If I try to earn God's favourable verdict by my own goodness, I am aiming at *a righteousness of my own*, one which is my own achievement and which will give me a claim on God's recognition. But as long as I am doing this, I disqualify myself from the true righteousness, which is not based on merit. For *faith* is not an alternative way of earning God's favour: *faith* is the opposite of merit, an admission that I cannot earn God's approval, but can only accept his free offer of forgiveness, grace, and love. And since the offer is made in the life and above all in the death of Christ, true righteousness, the condition of being truly right with God, must come *through faith in Christ*.

Paul never regarded a doctrine of atonement as complete unless it was expressed in three tenses: it was a past fact, a present experience, and a future hope. It is remarkable how often all three appear together in his letters (e.g. Rom. 5¹⁻²). Though he occasionally uses *righteousness* when speaking of the ongoing experience of salvation (Eph. 6¹⁴), and even of the future hope (Gal. 5⁵), he normally associates the noun, the verb 'justify' always, with the initial act of faith: *righteousness* is the new status to which a man is admitted immediately on becoming a believer (Rom. 5¹⁹; 10¹⁰). So here Paul deals with the initial status in v. 9, with the continuous process in v. 10, and with its goal in v. 11.

10. All four clauses of this verse have to do with the continuous development of the Christian life. The RSV obscures this, and it is better to revert to the more literal and accurate RV: 'that I may know him, and the power of his resurrection, and the fellowship of his sufferings, becoming conformed unto his death.' At his conversion the believer finds himself united with Christ. This union is an objective fact, something God has done once for all, needing only to be accepted by faith. But once accepted, it must also become a fact of experience. The Christian must come to *know him* in whom he now lives, and what this involves is spelt out in the following clauses. The *resurrection, sufferings*, and *death* of Christ are not treated as episodes in the gospel story, nor as future experiences in which the Christian must one day share, but as forces present and active in the truly Christian life. Otherwise Paul would hardly have put *resurrection* first. He does so because he is thinking of the Christian's knowledge of Christ. From his own history Paul knew that a man must be convinced of Christ's *resurrection* before he could come to a proper estimate of his *sufferings* and *death*; and he must rise to the new life of God's new creation (2 Cor. 5^{17}; Col. 3^1) before he can learn the secret of Christ's *sufferings*. It was moreover the *resurrection* that had checked Paul in his zealous pursuit of legal righteousness and had persuaded him that this pursuit had made him an enemy of God.

It was Paul's belief that God had appointed Christ to be head of a new humanity, just as Adam was head of the old. He had made good his right to represent other men by identifying himself fully with them in their condition of sin and helplessness (Rom. 8^3; 2 Cor. 5^{21}; Phil. 2^7), so that they might be identified with him in his new life of goodness and glory (1 Cor. $15^{22,49}$). In his death and resurrection the old manhood had come to an end and the new had begun (2 Cor. 5^{14-17}). The Christian, then, is one who believes that in the representative dying and rising of Christ he himself has passed through the death and resurrection of the old Adam (Rom. 6^{4-8}; Eph. 2^{4-6}; Col. 3^{1-4}). But the implications of this faith have still to be lived out. He must consider himself dead to sin and alive to God (Rom. 6^{11}). He must put off all vestiges of the old life and put on the new (Eph. 4^{22-4}; Col. 3^{9-10}). He must allow the Spirit of God to renew his inner nature and transform him stage by stage into the likeness of Christ (2 Cor. 3^{18}; 4^{16}; Eph. 3^{14-21}). All this is included in getting to know *the power of his resurrection*.

An important part of this transformation is a new attitude to suffering. The RSV translation, *may share his sufferings*, gives the regrettable impression that Paul actually wanted to suffer, that he sought martyrdom. In fact, he never needed to go looking for trouble;

it came of its own accord, incidental to the discharge of his missionary duties. Κοινωνία here, as in 2¹, means more than sharing. Paul's aspiration is to know 'the fellowship of his sufferings', i.e. to find that the sufferings which come, unsought though not unexpected, in the course of his Christian service draw him ever closer to his Lord (cp. Col. 1²⁴). Suffering borne for Christ's sake brings with it strength and comfort from God (2 Cor. 1⁵), and enables the sufferer to observe, beyond what is seen and transient in his own life and the lives of others, that which is unseen and eternal (2 Cor. 4¹⁶⁻¹⁸). In this last context Paul also speaks of 'always carrying in the body the death of Jesus, so that the life of Jesus may also be manifested in our bodies' (2 Cor. 4¹⁰). This explains what he here means by 'becoming conformed to his death' (RSV *becoming like him in his death*). Christ's death, in which the powers of evil and destruction seemed finally to have triumphed over him, in fact carried him for ever beyond the possibility of their control (1 Cor. 2⁶⁻⁸; Col. 2²⁰; Rom. 6⁹). The Christian in his baptism has also passed through death into life, has died to the old order (Rom. 6⁵; Gal. 6¹⁴), and his whole life must be a process of letting the old die in order that the new may live.

11. *if possible.* In view of 1⁶, 1²¹⁻³, and 3²⁰⁻¹, and notwithstanding 1 Cor. 9²⁷, it would be absurd to suppose that Paul harboured any serious doubts about his eternal destiny. He puts his passionate longing in this hypothetical form solely because salvation is from start to finish the gift of God and he dare not presume on the divine mercy. The NEB 'if only' is better; and better still is Goodspeed's 'in hope of attaining'.

By *the resurrection from the dead* Paul means the resurrection of the body (1 Cor. 15³⁵ᶠᶠ·; 2 Cor. 5¹⁻¹¹; cp. Rom. 8²³; Phil. 3²¹), which he expected to take place at the Advent of Christ. The inner transformation to which he has alluded was a secret process, unseen except to the eyes of faith, and often belied by outward circumstance, especially by the liability of the physical body to suffering, decay, and death (2 Cor. 4⁷⁻¹⁸; Col. 3¹⁻⁴). The Jews and early Christians did not, like many of the Greeks, regard man as an immortal soul incarcerated in a mortal body and waiting eagerly to be released from it. To them the body was an integral part of the human personality, and they could not conceive of any worthwhile life after death except in bodily terms. Thus the body, together with the physical universe with which it is inseparably linked, must be included in the redemptive purposes of God. Paul did not hold this belief in any crass or naive form, for he declares that 'flesh and blood cannot inherit the kingdom of God' (1 Cor. 15⁵⁰). The physical nature must be transformed into a mode fit for the spiritual life to which it goes (1 Cor. 15⁵¹⁻³; 2 Cor. 5¹⁻⁴; Phil. 3²⁰⁻¹), just as Christ's body had already been transformed (1 Cor. 15¹²ᶠᶠ·). Not everyone would *attain* this goal, but only those to whose earthly lives it would be an appropriate climax.

3: 12–16 *The Race of Faith.*

It now occurs to Paul that his extended use of book-keeping terminology could be misunderstood. If his readers took what he has said about profit and loss too literally, they might suppose that at his conversion he had merely surrendered his Jewish assets for the more valuable asset of knowing Christ. In that case they would expect his Christian experience of union with Christ to give him an even greater sense of superiority than he had as a Pharisee. So he pauses for a moment in his argument to point out that he makes no claim to possess any assets that he can call his own or to have reached his goal. The language of the counting-house needs to be replaced by that of the athletic stadium. He presses ahead in hope of winning the race, since this was the purpose for which he had been won by Christ. The Christian race is a race of faith from start to finish, and it allows no room for any sense of achievement until it is over. The runner does not congratulate himself on the laps he has completed, but puts all his effort into those ahead, pressing on to the finish, where the prize which awaits him is God's summons to the life above (vv. 12–14). Such a view of life is the mark of a mature Christian. Provided they think of themselves in this way, the Philippians may be sure that, even if some of their opinions are erroneous, God will lead them to the truth. Only they must allow their conduct to be directed by a single standard, the common rule of faith (vv. 15–16).

12–14. This passage has been translated in a variety of ways because of the difficulty in determining where the metaphor of the race track begins. According to the RSV it does not begin until the middle of v. 13, and this may be correct. On the other hand, the verb διώκω (*I press on*) is undoubtedly part of the metaphor in v. 14, and there is a strong case for thinking that Paul must already have the race in mind when he first uses the verb in v. 12. Beare makes the metaphor start at the beginning of v. 12, and, since he takes the words *am already perfect* to be a reference to initiation into a mystery cult, he has to appeal to Paul's propensity for mixed metaphors. The most reasonable compromise is that v. 12ᵃ is a transition from the commercial metaphor of the last paragraph to the athletic metaphor, which begins at v. 12ᵇ.

12. The Greek has no word for *this*, and the absence of an object is probably significant. Paul is doing something more than disclaim the achievement of the aspirations he has just listed. He is denying that achievement itself has any place in the life of faith.

am already perfect. Paul uses the passive of τελειοῦν, which can have any of the following meanings: (a) 'to finish one's course'; (b) 'to grow up to maturity'; (c) 'to reach perfection'; (d) 'to die'; (e) 'to be initiated into a religious cult'. The adjective τέλειος is used in v. 15, where it appears to mean 'mature'; but this need not determine the sense of the verb here. In 4¹² Paul undoubtedly uses a technical term drawn from the vocabulary of the Greek mystery cults, and it is possible that he is doing the same here. One view is that he goes out of his way to make this particular disclaimer because he knows of a party in the church who regard their baptism as initiation into a state of final perfection to which nothing needs to be added (cp. 1 Cor. 4⁸ and perhaps 2 Tim. 2¹⁸). In that case, the use of τέλειος at v. 15 must be sarcastic. But we should not attribute to Paul a sense of superiority to those who considered themselves perfect, since this would constitute a kind of inverted self-righteousness. Lohmeyer, who discovered hidden references to martyrdom all through this epistle, thought that Paul was here referring to his coming death as initiation or perfecting. Ignatius, to be sure, says something very like this about the certain death to which he was travelling (*Eph.* iii. 1), but his preoccupation with martyrdom is quite unlike Paul's dispassionate acceptance; and in any case he uses a different verb (οὔπω ἀπήρτισμαι). Paul would hardly have felt it necessary to write to his friends that he had not yet suffered martyrdom. As for the other meanings, the choice will depend on our decision about the beginning of the race metaphor: if the metaphor begins only at v. 13ᵇ, we must choose (c); if it begins at 12ᵇ, we shall adopt (a).

to make it my own. The Greek here has a conditional clause, with very much the same effect as that in v. 11: 'I press ahead in hope of winning'. The clause which follows is introduced by a prepositional phrase (ἐφ᾽ ᾧ), which can be taken three ways.

(a) We can supply an antecedent: ' . . . in hope of winning that for which I was won by Christ.'

(b) The antecedent may be contained in the preceding verb: ' . . . in hope of winning the race, since for this purpose I was won by Christ.'

(c) 'Εφ᾽ ᾧ may mean simply 'because' (so RSV; cp Rom. 5¹²; 2 Cor. 5⁴; Phil. 4¹⁰).

All three renderings have their advocates. Pauline usage supports the third, but this does not in the present context give as good sense as the second.

The one thing of which Paul is unshakably convinced is that *Christ Jesus has made me his own.* All that God asks in response is faith. But

Paul knows how deep a hold pride has on the human heart, how dearly a man loves to have something to show for himself, how natural it is to slip into self-justification. For this reason faith can never be merely passivity. It takes an effort to live by faith instead of by merit, and it is this continuous effort that Paul here depicts as a race, never won until it is over.

13. In the AV and RV the words *I do* were printed in italics to show that there was nothing corresponding to them in the Greek. The effect of the almost ejaculatory *but one thing* is well expressed by the NEB: 'All I can say is this.' *what lies behind* is not the Jewish advantages enumerated above, but that part of the Christian race so far completed. The man of faith does not waste his energies worrying about the state of his own soul. He knows that his salvation is God's work, not his own (cp. 1^6; 2^{13}). He believes indeed that he is being gradually transformed into the likeness of Christ (2 Cor. 3^{18}), but this is a hidden process (Col. 3^{3-4}), hidden not least from him who undergoes it. His job is to press on to *what lies ahead*, the remainder of the race, confident that there he will meet the same grace that has marked the track behind him.

14. *the prize of the upward call* is a literalistic attempt to improve on the inaccurate 'high calling' of AV and RV, and it conjures up the unfortunate picture of a race track running for ever uphill. Ἄνω can mean 'upward', but in the New Testament it more commonly denotes what is in heaven in contrast with what is on earth (κάτω). The phrase is too condensed to admit of word for word translation. The genitive is a genitive of definition: the prize consists in God's invitation or call, and an 'above invitation' must be to a life which is to be lived above, i.e. in God's own eternal presence.

15. It is hard to know whether or not τέλειος (*mature*) is a deliberate or even a subconscious echo of the verb used in v. 12. Certainly Paul cannot be contradicting himself by assuming a perfection he has just denied. If the verbal link is intended, then the implication is that in a Christian the only perfection is the mature knowledge that he is not perfect. But Paul frequently repeats a word or uses cognate words in the same context with considerable shift of meaning; and, if this is the case here, then nothing is lost, and much confusion is avoided, by the use of different words in the English translation.

15–16. These verses are capable of two radically different interpretations, which may be paraphrased as follows.

(a) 'This point of view which I have been expressing is the mark of a mature Christian. If in any way you disagree with it, I do not ask you to accept it on my authority. It must be a matter of personal conviction, and convictions of this kind are never the product of argument, but always of divine illumination. We are all at different levels of understanding, and the one thing that matters is that every Christian should act in accordance with his own conscience, consistently with the level he has attained.'

(b) 'This point of view which I have been expressing is the mark of mature Christians like you and me. Granted this fundamental attitude of mind, you may be sure that, if there is anything about which you hold unsound opinions, God will lead you to see the truth about that as well. The main thing is that we must conduct our life together by that one standard we all share.'

The first of these has been adopted by most commentators, though many of them have shown some uneasiness about it. It has obvious attractions, particularly to our modern individualism. But it is open to grave objections, both theological and philological. (a) The context shows that there were limits to Paul's tolerance. His letters as a whole hardly leave us with the impression that every Christian is entitled to his own opinions, provided they are conscientiously held. (b) The idea of living by faith and not by merit, so far from being an optional extra to which mature Christians may or may not attain, is integral to Christianity as Paul understood it. (c) The emphasis of this epistle, to which it returns in v. 17, has been the common life of Christians, not their individual progress. As Beare points out, the notion 'that Christians are to be spiritual virtuosos, each pursuing his own inward development in keeping with his individual attainments' is quite out of keeping with Paul's concept of the church as a living organism. (d) The relative pronoun (ὅσος), which the RSV renders *those of us who*, is normally used by Paul inclusively rather than partitively, that is to say, he does not use it to distinguish some members of a group from others, but to include all those addressed. In Rom. 6³ and Gal. 3²⁷, for example, he is not distinguishing some Christians who have been baptized from others who have not; since all Christians have been baptized into Christ, it follows that all have been baptized into his death (have put on Christ). Similarly here the sense is: 'since we are all mature, let us maintain this mature way of thinking.' (e) Though the basic meaning of ἑτέρως is *otherwise*, it is frequently used in a pejorative sense, as in the English derivative 'heterodox' (cp. Rom. 7²³; 2 Cor. 11⁴; Gal. 1⁶). (f) If Paul had intended to say that others might disagree with the point of view he has expressed, we should have expected the clause to begin with 'but if' (εἰ δέ or ἀλλ' εἰ καί) or with 'even if' (εἰ καί) rather than 'and if' (cp. 1 Cor. 7²¹; 2 Cor. 4¹⁶; Phil. 2¹⁷; 2 Cor. 5¹⁶; 7⁸; 12¹¹). 'And if' (καί εἰ) is most naturally taken to introduce either another way of putting the same point (Rom. 11¹⁶) or a consequence which follows from the previous statement (1 Cor. 6²). (g) If the purpose of the divine revelation was to bring the otherwise-minded Christian into agreement with Paul's mature point of view, he would surely have written, 'To you also God will reveal this'. *That also* implies that what is revealed is something over and above the mature mind, which they already possess. (h) The verb στοιχεῖν, here translated *hold true*, is derived from a word meaning 'line' or 'row', and literally means 'to be drawn up in line'. Metaphorically it means either 'to keep in step with others', 'to follow in someone else's steps', or, more generally, 'to conform'. It would be an odd word to use of Christians each pursuing his independent course at the dictates of his own conscience. This point is all the stronger when we consider the phrase as a whole, τῷ αὐτῷ στοιχεῖν, which is so reminiscent of τὸ αὐτὸ φρονεῖν ('have a common mind') in 2² that it is most naturally taken to mean 'have a common rule of behaviour'. If this is the right meaning, it forms a healthy corrective to a possible misconstruction of Paul's athletic metaphor. By the image of a race Paul has no desire to arouse competitive feelings. This is not the kind of race in which one man's success is another's failure. The only kind of victory is the team's triumph over the hazards of the track, and all who finish the course win the prize.

3: 17–4: 1 *Citizens of Heaven.*

Paul has laid bare his inmost heart to his friends, because he knows that they need a pattern of faith to imitate. Earlier he called them to imitate Christ as the model for their common life. Now, with that same common life in mind, he bids them to imitate him and those of their own number whose lives are modelled on his. Christ they never saw, and Paul they are not likely to see again. They need a visible standard to help them to distinguish true faith from counterfeit. In some churches, though happily not Philippi, there are men who claim to be Christain without giving the cross the place of central importance in their faith. They talk glibly enough of their goal, of their service to God, of the glory that is theirs; and all the time their minds are bounded by the standards and horizons of this transient world. The only goal that awaits them is perdition, the only God they serve is their own self-esteem; and, if they could see what they call their glory in its true light, they would recognize it as disgrace (vv. 17–19). By contrast the true Christian is one who knows himself here and now to be enrolled as a citizen of the heavenly commonwealth, who acknowledges the primary claim which that citizenship makes on his loyalty, but who knows also that the transformation which will make him fit for the heavenly city must be Christ's work and not his own, and that it will not be complete until Christ returns to finish the task of bringing the whole universe under his authority (vv. 20–1). Nothing less than this is the faith in which Paul encourages his friends to stand firm (v. 1).

17. *join in imitating me.* Paul often instructs his converts to imitate him (1 Cor. 4¹⁶; 11¹; 1 Thess. 1⁶; 2 Thess. 3⁷⁻⁹), and he does this without self-consciousness, because in this way they will be imitating Christ. Here the imitation has two special features: it is not his general conduct they are to copy, but his faith, the life of faith into which he has thrown himself with the wholehearted commitment of an athlete; and they are to be co-imitators (συνμιμηταί), i.e. their imitation of Paul, as of Christ, is to govern their corporate life. On the great play that Paul makes with compounds of συν- see T. R. Glover, *Paul of Tarsus*, pp. 178–9. If there are those in the church who find it hard to imitate an absent Paul, they have a pattern nearer at hand in those members of their own company who have modelled their lives on his.

18–19. There are three reasons for thinking that Paul is here describing a class of Christians: to denote their way of life he repeats the verb περιπατεῖν (*live*) which he used in the previous verse of the commendable examples of faith in Philippi; he would hardly be reduced to tears by the misrepresentation of the gospel on the part of unbelievers; and they would not be called *enemies of the cross of Christ* unless they at least claimed to be Christian (cp. 1 Cor. 1¹⁷; Gal. 6¹²). This means that they cannot be identified with the 'dogs' of v. 2, whom we saw to be unconverted Jews. Paul does not appear to believe that such persons are to be found in Philippi. He has *often told* his friends that they exist elsewhere and is now reminding them, partly to point a contrast with the true faith he has been depicting, partly to drive home the need for a standard by which to judge.

Paul's tears may well be due to a combined feeling of responsibility and frustration, because it is his teaching that has been distorted. The aberrant Christians have found his preaching of Christ crucified repugnant, and have constructed for themselves a Christianity without a *cross*. What this means is explained in the following clauses. Unfortunately for us they contain abuse rather than accurate description, and it is hardly surprising that scholars have held a wide diversity of opinions about them. The Philippians would be under no such disability, since Paul had *often told* them this cautionary tale when he was with them. If we find this passage tantalizing (cp. 2 Thess. 2⁵), that is the penalty for reading private correspondence.

Most commentators have seized on the clause *their god is the belly* (κοιλία) as the most explicit. Some have seen in it a straightforward attack on gluttony or other forms of self-indulgence, on those who *glory* in a perverted liberty; but would sensualists have appeared to Paul as *enemies of the cross*? Others have detected a subtle reference to Judaizing Christians who insisted on keeping the levitical food laws; but it is safe to say that this interpretation would not have occurred to anyone unless he was convinced on other grounds that 3²ff· was a warning against the insidious attacks of Judaizers. A more fruitful line of thought is suggested by Rom. 16¹⁷⁻¹⁸, where those who foment quarrels and make life difficult for their fellow Christians are said to be ministering to their own κοιλία, which in that context must mean 'self-esteem'. This is in keeping with the usage of the Septuagint, where this word frequently denotes the affections, the mind, the innermost heart, the person (e.g. Job 15³⁵; Lam. 1²⁰). We are reminded that Paul uses σάρξ ('flesh') to denote the whole psycho-physical life of unredeemed man and includes quarrelling, bad temper, envy, selfish ambition, and jealousy among the sins of the flesh (Gal. 5¹⁹⁻²⁰). The flesh, in short, is one of the terms Paul uses to denote the old, earthbound humanity from which Christians have been rescued into the new humanity of Christ; it is the equivalent of the natural man (1 Cor. 2¹⁴), the old manhood (Rom. 6⁶), the first Adam (1 Cor. 15⁴⁷). 'The mind of flesh is death' (Rom. 8⁶), because its outlook is limited by the interests and possibilities of the present transient world order, which stands under God's annihilating judgment. Thus when Paul speaks of men *with minds set on earthly things*, he is not himself advocating an otherwordly religion. The contrast is between the old, earthbound life of self-seeking and self-justification and the new humanity of Christ, open to the gracious and transforming influences of heaven. Both face the prospect of mortality, but for the one it is *destruction*, for the other a confident expectation that what is mortal will be swallowed up in life (v. 20; cp. 1 Cor. 15⁵³⁻⁴; 2 Cor. 5⁴). What separates the old from the new is *the cross of Christ*. Christ so identified himself with sinful men that, when he died and rose, they died and rose vicariously in him (2 Cor. 5¹⁴⁻¹⁵; Rom. 6¹⁻¹¹). *enemies of the cross* are those who, by failing to accept the death of the old life, the κοιλία, disqualify themselves from the new.

20. The emphasis in this verse is on the personal pronoun (*our*): 'we, by contrast, are citizens of heaven' (NEB). The image of the heavenly *commonwealth*, which Paul has already invoked at 1²⁷, would appeal to the Philippians, whose city was a Roman colony. As a Roman citizen writing to Roman citizens he could equally well have said, 'our commonwealth is in Rome'. Rome had given the full franchise of the imperial city to towns and individuals in the provinces in order that they might represent and spread in their neighbourhood the Roman way of life, its laws, customs, and culture, until the whole heterogeneous mass of the empire should be united in sentiment, outlook, and loyalty as well as in political and military fact. Paul pictures the

world as an empire over which Christ rules de jure, though not yet de facto. Each local church is a colony of heaven, its members enjoying full citizenship of the heavenly city (cp. Gal. 4[26]; Eph. 2[19]), but charged with the responsibility of bringing the world to acknowledge the sovereignty of Christ. Neither the Roman colonist nor the Christian depended for the meaning, character, and purpose of his life on the ethos of his alien environment, nor did he allow that environment to determine the quality of his behaviour.

Paul does not call Jesus *Saviour* in his earlier letters. With the possible exception of Eph. 5[23], this is the earliest Christian use of the title. It is found ten times in the Pastoral Epistles, five times in 2 Peter, four times in Luke–Acts, and once each in the Gospel and First Epistle of John, and in Jude. It is, however, far from obvious whether any secure inference is to be drawn from these facts. We cannot say that the term was avoided in primitive Christianity because of its associations with the Greek mystery religions or with the Roman imperial cult,[20] since this inhibition would have applied equally to Κύριος ('Lord'), and would have had even greater force towards the end of the century as the church came into more frequent contact and conflict with paganism.

21. The belief about life after death here expressed in summary form is more fully worked out in 1 Cor. 15[35-55] and 2 Cor. 3[18]–5[17]. Paul held that, when Christ left the tomb, his physical body was transformed into a spiritual body (here called *his glorious body*), just as a seed planted in the soil dies and is given a new body. A similar transformation must be undergone by the Christian, but in his case it comes only as the climax of a long process of change (see notes of vv. 10–11). Even when the inner man is being renewed daily, the outer man may be visibly subject to decay (2 Cor. 4[16]). Some modern readers would have been better pleased if at this point Paul had been prepared to allow the outer husk to drop away and leave the inner self unhampered by its weakness. But the Jew did not think of man as an immortal soul entombed for a time in a mortal body. To him a man's body was himself. If there is to be life everlasting, this mortal, *lowly body* must be changed as Christ's had been.

When Paul wrote his first letter, he gave no indication where the resurrection life was to be lived; Christians, whether they died or survived to the coming of Christ, would be caught up to meet him in the air (1 Thess. 4[17]). In this his last letter he gives the impression that the life everlasting is to be lived on a transformed earth. The reason is that in the interim he had grappled with the problem of the relation

[20]For references see W. F. Arndt and F. W. Gingrich, *A Greek–English Lexicon of the New Testament and Other early Christian Literature.*

of man's physical body to the physical uniersve of which it is a part, and had come to the conclusion that the resurrection or redemption of the body was unthinkable apart from the transfiguration of the cosmos as a whole (Rom. 8^{18-25}). This explains why here the transformation of the *lowly body* is said to be achieved *by the power which enables him even to subject all things to himself*. Paul is quoting the same verse of Ps. 8 as he has already quoted in Rom. 8^{20} (cp. 1 Cor. 15^{26}; Eph. 1^{22}). It was God's intention that the universe should be subject to man. When man sinned he forfeited that authority, and the universe, bereft of its due control, fell victim to frustration, and could be liberated only when man resumed his proper place as son of God. Thus Christ, in fulfilling man's destiny, was at the same time making the universe *subject . . . to himself*. Here, as in Eph. 1, the resurrection of the body is not seen as an isolated event, but as the last act in the drama of cosmic redemption. The one difference is that in Ephesians the power at work is ascribed to God, here to Christ.

1. It is easy for us to forget that this last chapter, in which Paul has admitted the reader to the intimacy of his own personal religion, began as an excuse for a repeated command to rejoice. But Paul himself has not forgotten his pastoral purpose. He reverts not to 3^1 but to 1^{27}. They are to *stand firm thus*. All that he has written in the previous chapter is to be taken as a commentary on what it means to *stand firm* in the life of faith, which has *joy* for its most conspicuous characteristic.

4: 2-9 *Final Instructions.*

The letter moves rapidly, almost disjointedly to its close. First we are given a glimpse of the reason why Paul has concentrated on the theme of unity. Two women, obviously important and influential members of the church, have been quarrelling and must be reconciled (vv. 2-3). For the church at large there are some practical reminders of what it means to be a Christian (vv. 4-9).

2-3. Nothing more is known of *Euodia* and *Syntyche* than we are told in these verses. What we do know is that women occupied a more prominent position in Macedonian society than in other parts of the Graeco–Roman world. *laboured side by side with* is a rather jejune rendering of a word which means 'shared my athletic contest'; Paul's mind is still on the stadium (cp. 3^{13-14}), though presumably not this time on the foot-race. The phrase here translated *agree* has been used before at 2^2, and this suggests that, when Paul wrote the more general injunction, he already had this quarrel in mind. If the two women had been members of Paul's team of fellow workers, it is no wonder that their quarrel should have repercussions throughout the church. In spite of many efforts to identify the *true yokefellow*, he still maintains his incognito, unless indeed Syzygus ('yokefellow') is a proper name, and Paul is telling him to live up to it by acting as mediator. *Clement* is a Roman name, of which there must have been many in this Roman city. For *the book of life*, cp. Exod. 32³²; Ps. 69²⁸; 139¹⁶; Dan. 12¹; Luke 10²⁰; Rev. 3⁵; 13⁸; 17⁸; 20¹²⁻¹⁵. Philippi, like other cities, must have possessed a civic register containing the names of its citizens; and *the book of life* is the citizens' roll of the heavenly commonwealth.

4. See note on 3¹.

5. *forbearance*, like 'moderation' (AV), is altogether too negative and passive a word to do justice to the many-sided Greek, τὸ ἐπιεικές. The NEB comes much nearer with 'magnanimity'. This is one of those untranslatable ethical terms (cp. the English 'gentleman'), which, instead of denoting a particular virtue, have come through the cumulative process of tradition to embrace a whole quality of life. Matthew Arnold regarded ἐπιείκεια as the one distinctively Greek attitude to be taken up into Christianity and translated it 'sweet reasonableness'. According to Aristotle, it meant 'equity' as opposed to strict justice, the generous treatment of others which does not insist on the letter of the law and is therefore the highest form of justice (*Eth. Nic.* 1137ᵇ11). But he also used the cognate adjective to denote the educated, cultured classes (*Pol.* 1308ᵇ27). In the New Testament the meaning of the word is best judged by the company it keeps (1 Tim. 3³; Tit. 3²; Jas. 3¹⁷; 1 Pet. 2¹⁸). It is that considerate courtesy and respect for the integrity of others which prompts a man not to be for ever standing on his rights; and it is pre-eminently the character of Jesus (2 Cor. 10¹). This is the impression which Christians must give to *all men*, i.e. to the outside world.

The Lord is at hand. The commonly accepted understanding of these words has been well expressed by Beare. 'Christians are to live "like men who are awaiting their Master" (Luke xii. 36); and their conduct and character are determined by that expectation and not by the hostility of the world in which they live. *Near* is certainly to be taken in this temporal sense; the Apostle is not speaking of the nearness of the Lord in his abiding presence with us, but of the imminence of his coming to establish his kingdom.' This view is not, however, free from linguistic or theological difficulty. The Greek ἐγγύς, like the English 'near', can be used either spatially or temporally; in the one case it means 'in the vicinity', in the other 'in the immediate future'. But in the second, temporal sense it is always a time or an event that is near, not a person. If Paul had wanted to say that Christ was coming soon, there were ways of saying this without solecism or ambiguity. But are we so sure that this is what he intended? He undoubtedly believed in an imminent Advent, if by imminent we mean one that might

happen at any time. The decisive act of God had already occurred
the death of Jesus and the subsequent eschatological events of
resurrection and gift of the Spirit. Christians were therefore living in
the 'last days' and must live under the shadow of the end. But there is
no reason to suppose that he ever believed in an end which must hap-
pen by a given date, even if he were ignorant of the warnings of Jesus
against such speculation (Mark 13^{32}; Acts 1^7). On the other hand he
must have been aware that the words he uses here are a quotation from
the Old Testament, where they refer to the presence of God with his
faithful worshippers (e.g. Ps. 33(34)^{18}; 118(119)^{151}). Already in his
earliest epistle he has made it plain that those who have once known
the abiding presence of the living Lord need not be concerned whether
the Advent comes soon or late (1 Thess. 5$^{1-10}$).

6. *anxiety* is an attempt to carry the burden of the future oneself, *prayer* is
leaving it in the safe hands of God. *Thanksgiving* for past benefits is the
surest road to confidence in future ones. This verse is one of many
indications in the epistle that Paul was familiar with the teaching of
Jesus (cp. Matt. 6$^{25ff.}$).[21] The use of three synonyms (*prayer, supplica-
tion, requests*) in a single sentence is one of the points which links the
style of this letter to that of Ephesians (cp. Eph. 6^{18}).

7. the peace is said to be God's peace, but not merely because he gives it;
it is the tranquillity of his own eternal being. *which passes all under-
standing* (lit. 'surpasses all thought') may mean that it is a mystery
beyond comprehension. But there is more probably a glance back at
the previous verse; however much a man may ask in prayer, what God
gives is infinitely more, surpassing all that the mind can conceive (cp.
Eph. 3^{20}). *keep* is a military metaphor: God's peace will keep guard
over the heart, turning it into a fortress immune to the assaults of care
and fear.

8. *Finally.* Or 'and now' (see note on 3^1).

In Rom. 7$^{7-25}$ Paul has analysed the experience of the man who
tries to live by law and finds that the prohibitions with which his
mind is filled operate by the power of suggestion to provoke the very
activities they forbid. Here he describes the opposite. The Philippians
are not merely to *think about these things*; the word Paul uses is a
stronger one, 'let your minds dwell on' *these things*. Their minds are to
be so filled with what is admirable that there is no room for evil
thoughts. The remarkable fact, however, is that the list contains
nothing that is specifically Christian. The first six (true, noble, just,

[21]For further parallels, see A. M. Hunter, *Paul and His Predecessors*,
pp. 52–61; W. D. Davies, *Paul and Rabbinic Judaism*, pp. 136–41.
For a more detailed discussion of Paul's use of two of the sayings
of Jesus, see D. L. Dungan, *The Sayings of Jesus in the Churches of
Paul*.

pure, endearing, attractive) might have been taken from any Stoic primer of moral instruction. The seventh (ἀρετή) is the typically Greek term for moral *excellence*, which Paul uses only here. And the eighth, *worthy of praise*, denotes all that men hold in high esteem. In short Christians are to be appreciative of the moral standards of their pagan neighbours and ready to learn from them. God is not the God of Jews and Christians only.

9. The last word nevertheless lies with distinctively Christian teaching *learned* as a lesson, *received* as a tradition, *heard* in Paul's preaching, and *seen* in his example.

4: 10–23 *The Present from Philippi.*

Paul has left to the end the most delicate part of his letter and his main reason for writing it, his thanks for a gift of money. He has already referred to it twice (1^5; 2^{25-30}), but more must be said. If the task appears to embarrass him, it is because this is a situation in which it would be all too easy to say the wrong thing. He knows that they cannot really afford the money, but he cannot tell them so openly without seeming ungracious. He knows that love and concern naturally express themselves in presents, and how hard it is to give anything to a man whose wants are few. If he belittles his need, they may think him ungrateful. If he overdoes the gratitude, they may suspect him to be in greater need than he is and blame themselves for not having sent help sooner (vv. 10–13). With careful sensitivity he steers his way through the pitfalls, reminding his friends of their past generosity, and rejoicing in their continuing affection (vv. 14–18). He leaves it to God to repay his debt (vv. 19–20). The letter ends with the usual greetings and blessing (vv. 21–3).

10. It is difficult to read the words *now at length* without the feeling that Paul might have written more graciously and thus saved himself the trouble of correcting a possible misunderstanding in the following sentence. Michael has made the attractive and convincing suggestion that these words were a quotation from the covering letter which accompanied the gift of money. The Philippians had written apologetically because there had been such a long interval between this gift and the previous one. Paul replies, in effect: 'You talk about "now at long last"; but I know that you have been caring all along and only lacked means.' This is not the only place in Paul's correspondence

where the sense is improved by the introduction of quotation marks (cp. 1 Cor. 8¹⁻⁴).

revived. The word Paul uses is a vivid metaphor: 'you have given fresh blossom to your care for me.' It is also one of four words or phrases in this short paragraph which occur also in the closing chapters of Ecclesiasticus. One cannot help wondering whether this book had been included in Paul's recent reading of the Greek Scriptures.²²

you had no opportunity is probably a polite way of saying 'You lacked the means'. The fact is that for their most recent gift they had created the opportunity by sending Epaphroditus. They were a poor church and had given beyond their resources for several years to contribute an adequate sum to the collection which Paul organized for the church of Jerusalem (2 Cor. 8²⁻⁴).

11. The word translated *content* (αὐτάρκης) was a popular one among Greek philosophers, particularly in the ethical systems of Aristotle, the Stoics, and the Epicureans. But there is no need to assume that Paul was familiar with any of these schools. The word was in common use in everyday speech, denoting the self-supporting man, the man who is his own master (cp. Ecclus. 5¹; 11²⁴; 40¹⁸). We know how particular Paul was to earn his own living and not to be dependent on others (1 Cor. 4¹²; 9¹⁵⁻¹⁸; 2 Cor. 11⁷⁻⁹; Acts 20³⁴; 1 Thess. 2⁴; 2 Thess. 3⁸). Here he is speaking of a larger independence, in which all his wants are supplied by God.

12. *I have learned the secret.* These five English words represent one word in Greek, a technical term taken from the vocabulary of the mystery religions: 'I have been initiated', or, as Beare felicitously puts it, 'I have become adept'. But the word is all Paul borrows. He has no interest in arcane rites, nor is he an ascetic, seeking rigours for their own sake or promoting his own spiritual development by self-imposed discipline (cp. Col. 2²⁰⁻³). The only discipline he believes in is that which comes to him direct from God, the hardship incidental to the pursuit of his calling. This and this alone was the scene of his initiation; and it has taught him how to cope not only with *want* but with *plenty*, no doubt the harder lesson of the two.

14. *to share my trouble.* He values the money not for itself but for the sympathy it conveys (cp. vv. 17–18).

15. Paul addresses them by the Latinized form of the name *Philippians*, rather than the ordinary Greek form, perhaps out of deference to their civic pride in their colonial status. It is his custom to prefer official Roman place names to local ones. Here, as at 1⁵, Paul refuses to think

²² Ἀναθάλλω (v. 10; cp. Ecclus. 46¹²; 49¹⁰; 50¹⁰), αὐτάρκης (v. 11; cp. Ecclus. 40¹⁸), δόσις καὶ λῆμψις (v. 15; cp. Ecclus. 41¹⁹; 42⁷), ὀσμὴ εὐωδίας (v. 18; cp. Ecclus. 50¹⁵).

of the early gifts of money from Philippi merely as personal presents to himself, but speaks of them, in an almost jocular use of commercial terms, as an investment in his missionary enterprise, which made them his partners, sharing both the outlay and the profit (*giving and receiving*). It is odd that he should describe this period as *the beginning of the gospel*. We must either suppose that he is writing from the point of view of the Philippians, or, better, take the phrase closely with what follows: 'in the early days of my missionary work after my departure

16. from Macedonia.' If that is what he intends, he rapidly corrects himself, recollecting that the first two instalments arrived while he was still *in Thessalonica*.

17–18. The commercial metaphor continues: 'Please do not think I set great store by the remittance; what I do set store by is the interest mounting up in your account. But here is my receipt: paid in full and overpaid. I am well supplied . . . ' 'Aπέχω (*I have received*) is the word regularly written on the bottom of a Greek receipt. With one of his characteristic switches of metaphor Paul suddenly turns to the language of sacrifice.

19. *my God*. This is the second time Paul has spoken of God in this personal way (cp. 1³). It is peculiarly appropriate here. Paul himself cannot do for the Philippians what they have done for him. His God will do it for him.

21–22. *Greet every saint*. The church meeting is charged with the duty of conveying a separate personal greeting to each of its members. This is the one exception to the general rule that Christians are saints only in the plural, and the exception is more apparent than real (cp. Eph. 1¹). Paul distinguishes between *the brethren who are with me* and *all the saints*, the former presumably being his colleagues, the latter the members of the church in Rome. *Caesar's household* does not mean the emperor's family circle, but the establishment of slaves and freedmen employed in the imperial civil service. Some of them would have had contacts in Philippi through being engaged on government missions.

THE LETTER TO

THE COLOSSIANS

INTRODUCTION

1. AUTHORSHIP AND INTEGRITY

Like Ephesians, Colossians claims to be by Paul. Unlike
Ephesians, it is a real letter, full of references to persons and
places, written to a particular church to deal with a specific
problem, and containing clear cross-references to the undoubtedly genuine letter to Philemon. Thus the prima facie case for
authenticity is strong. It is true that we cannot with any confidence claim, as we can for Ephesians, that this letter was
known and used by Christian writers of the early second
century. There are phrases in Barnabas (xii. 7), Ignatius (*Eph.*
x. 2; *Trall.* v. 2; *Smyrn.* i. 2), Polycarp (x. 1), and Justin (*Apol.*
lxxxv, xcvi) which could be echoes of Colossians; but none of
them is at all certain, and in any case they tell us nothing about
authorship. The earliest real evidence comes from Marcion
(c. A.D. 140), who included Colossians in his canon of Pauline
letters, from Irenaeus, who cites it as a letter of Paul (*Adv. Haer.*
III. xiv. 1), and from the Muratorian Canon. There is, however, one weighty argument by which we may compensate for
this lack of early attestation. Colossians bears a striking resemblance to Ephesians. One explanation, which in spite of all its
difficulties still remains the most probable, is that both are by
Paul. Certainly if we accept Ephesians as a Pauline letter, a

fortiori we shall accept Colossians. If we do not accept Ephesians, then it must have been written by an imitator who knew Colossians and believed it to be by Paul. One way or the other the Pauline authorship of Colossians receives solid support.

Doubt was first cast on the authenticity of the letter in the nineteenth century, and for reasons which no modern scholar would regard as adequate: the absence of many distinctively Pauline words and ideas, the presence of words and ideas not found in the other letters, and the supposed similarity of the 'heresy' attacked in it to the Gnostic systems of the second century. The first two points are no argument at all, since similar lists can be compiled for all the other letters, and some difference of vocabulary is to be expected when an author is dealing with a radically new theme. The exact nature of the false teaching at Colossae must be investigated more fully later. Here it is enough to note three points:

(a) there were antecedents to Gnosticism in both pagan and Jewish religion prior to the rise of Christianity;

(b) the differences between the teaching of Paul's Colossian opponents and that of Basilides or Valentinus are more obvious than the similarities; and

(c) the similarities are readily accounted for by the fact that the second century Gnostics knew both Colossians and Ephesians.

The only valid argument against the Pauline authorship of Colossians is the argument from style. Considerable tracts of the letter are written in a style indistinguishable from that of Ephesians and quite different from the concise, debating style, of Romans and Galatians. Here are the same long sentences (one of them longer than any in Ephesians), compounded of final, participial, and relative clauses, together with a multiplicity of genitival constructions and prepositional phrases. No one may use the argument from style against Ephesians without acknowledging that it applies with equal force against Colossians. The weakness of this argument is that it does not apply equally to the whole of Colossians, parts of which have by any criteria the authentic ring of Pauline composition. For this reason three scholars have held the view that the author of Ephesians made some extensive interpolations in a brief, genuine epistle of Paul to Colossae.[1] Most scholars, however, have judged this theory improbable, partly because of its complexity, partly because it does not really explain the facts. Close correspondence between Ephesians and Colossians is not confined to the 'interpolations', nor are the divergences between the two letters, which have made scholars like Goodspeed and Mitton think that they must have been written by different authors, confined to the supposedly original letter of Paul. Moreover, once the 'interpolations' are removed, whichever of the three lists we adopt, the residual letter is so void of content as to leave us wondering why it ever needed to be written, let alone preserved. There is no evidence that this hypothetical letter was ever known to anyone except its hypothetical interpolator. If it is possible to believe that the author of Ephesians had any hand in the writing of Colossians, there is no serious reason for denying that that author was Paul himself.[2]

2. THE CHURCHES OF THE LYCUS VALLEY

Colossae lay in the valley of the River Lycus (the modern Curuksucay) at a point where it plunges into a narrow gorge and not many miles above its confluence with the Meander (three miles NNW from the modern Chonas). Ten miles downstream to the west, on a plateau to the south of the river, stood Laodicea (Col. 2[1]; 4[13-16]). Six miles north of Laodicea on the

[1] H. J. Holtzmann, *Kritik der Epheser- und Kolosser-briefe* (1872); C. Masson, *L'Épitre de Saint Paul aux Colossians* (1950); and P. N. Harrison, *Pastorals and Paulines* (1964). All three writers adhere to the theory of interpolation, but their analyses show wide discrepancies of detail.

[2] In a reply to Holtzmann H. von Soden pointed out that Colossians has many noteworthy resemblances of language, style, and thought to Philippians (see the ICC commentary by T. K. Abbott, p. lviii). For a full defence of Pauline authorship, see E. Percy, *Die Probleme der Kolosser und Epheserbriefe* (1946)

other side of the river was Hierapolis (Col. 4¹³). From ancient times to the present day this valley has provided the easiest route through the mountains of Phrygia. Travellers from Greece or Italy to Syria and Mesopotamia could reach it either from Ephesus up the valley of the Meander (Strabo xiv. 663) or from Troas via Pergamum, Sardis, and the valley of the Cogamus.

The oldest of these three towns was Colossae, and its glory lay all in the past. According to Herodotus (vii. 30), it was a large city when Xerxes passed through it in 481 B.C. on his expedition against Greece. Eighty years later, when Cyrus arrived there from Sardis, it was still prosperous and large (Xen. *Anab.* I. ii. 6). But by the time of Strabo (xii. 8), it had sunk to the status of a township (πόλισμα). As Lightfoot has said, 'without doubt Colossae was the least important church to which any epistle of St. Paul is addressed.'

The decline of Colossae was probably caused by the rise of Laodicea. Here, on the site of an earlier settlement called Diospolis or Rheas (Pliny, *Nat. Hist.* v. 105), Antiochus II (261–246 B.C.) founded a new city and named it after his queen. It grew rapidly to become an important commercial and industrial centre, famous for its banks (Cic. *Ep. ad Fam.* iii. 5; *ad Att.* v. 15), for its textiles manufactured from the glossy-black wool of the local sheep (Strabo xii. 578), and for its medical school (Galen, *De san. tuend.* vi. 439). In A.D. 60, when the whole district was devastated by one of the severe earthquakes to which it has always been liable, Laodicea was rich enough to restore the damage without imperial aid (Tac. *Ann.* xiv. 27).

Hierapolis, as its name indicates, owed its initial importance to religion. Its hot mineral springs and a cave filled with poisonous gases had long been the centre of a Phrygian cult of the Great Goddess. On this site Eumenes II of Pergamum (197–160 B.C.) founded a city, which in due course came to share the commercial interests and prosperity of the district.

After the death of Alexander the Great (323 B.C.), the Lycus valley, together with most of Asia Minor, came under the rule of the Seleucid kings of Antioch, and one of them, Antiochus III (223–187 B.C.) settled, a large number of Jews in the area (Jos. *Ant.* XII. iii. 4; cp. Cic. *Pro Flacc.* 68). In 190 B.C. this part of SW Phrygia was ceded to Eumenes II of Pergamum, one of whose successors, Attalus III, bequeathed his whole kingdom to Rome, so that on his death in 133 B.C. it became the Roman province of Asia.[3]

Nothing is known of the beginnings of Christianity in these three towns except what can be gleaned from Paul's letter. He himself never visited any of them (Col. 2¹). On one journey he appears to have been travelling with Silas and Timothy along the great trade route, which would have brought him through Colossae and Laodicea on the way to Ephesus, but they were 'forbidden by the Holy Spirit to speak the word in Asia' (Acts 16⁶). In describing Paul's next journey Luke uses a vague expression which probably means that he reached Ephesus by the higher route down the valley of the Cayster (Acts 19¹). The gospel must have been brought to the Lycus valley by friends and colleagues of Paul whom he had met and converted during his three-year stay in Ephesus (Acts 19¹⁰). The most important of these was Epaphras, a native of Colossae (Col. 4¹²), whom Paul describes as his own representative and credits with the foundation of the church in his home town (Col. 1⁷), and also with a pastoral care for the other two churches (4¹³). The slave Onesimus also belonged to Colossae (4¹⁹), and therefore so also, we may infer, did his master Philemon, who was another convert of Paul and had a church meeting in his house (Philem. 2, 19), and whose son Archippus held some sort of office in the church (Col. 4¹⁷). It is probable, though not certain, that Paul was also personally acquainted with Nymphas, in whose house a (the) church met at Laodicea (Col 4¹⁵).

Although he is unknown by sight to the majority of their members, Paul clearly regards these three churches as his churches. He agonizes over them and assumes that they will

[3]For a fuller account of these places, see W. M. Ramsay, *The Cities and Bishoprics of Phrygia*, i. pp. 32–121, 208–13; and D. Magie, *Roman Rule in Asia Minor*, i, pp. 126–8, 985–6.

look to him as their real founder. He writes this letter because Epaphras has recently come to visit him and has brought a somewhat disquieting report of events in Colossae. It has often been assumed, particularly by the advocates of an Ephesian imprisonment (see pp. 3–5), that the situation was serious enough for Epaphras to make a special journey to consult the imprisoned apostle. But this is not the impression made by the letter itself. Paul is confident that the church in Colossae is sound and loyal, and he reacts to the news of strange speculations there with none of the passionate urgency of his letter to Galatia. Epaphras, having delivered his report, seems in no hurry to return home; the reply is to be carried by Tychicus, and Epaphras sends his greetings. It is more probable therefore that Epaphras was travelling to Rome on business and took the opportunity of consulting his old friend and father in God about a bothersome problem (see also the note on 4^{13}). At about the same time Paul has had a further contact with Colossae through the runaway slave, Onesimus (Col. 4^9). But Onesimus is not likely to have known much about the church in his home town never having been a member of it (Philem. 10).

3. THE SITUATION IN COLOSSAE

The news brought by Epaphras was that the simpler members of the church were being dazzled and misled by a more sophisticated member or clique (2^8), who had questioned their qualifications for membership of the church (2^{16-18}), and had dictated to them a strict regimen of ascetical practices (2^{20-3}). It has long been a scholarly convention to refer to this troublesome teaching as 'the Colossian heresy', and to describe it as 'an incipient form of Gnosticism'. Both of these designations are loose, almost to the point of anachronism. Heresy implies the existence of a well-established orthodoxy, and it was to be more than a century before the church even began to draw such a distinction. As Beare has said, 'even the great Gnostic schools of the second century are called heretical only in relation to the standards of orthodoxy which were established in the very effort to discredit them.'[4] Gnosticism is a term properly applied to the theosophical systems of such second century teachers as Valentinus and Basilides. But in a secondary sense it has come to be loosely used to denote any anticipation of these systems whether in Graeco-oriental religion or in the syncretistic fringes of Judaism. The result is that any interest in the corporate or cosmic aspects of religious belief, any wrestling with the problem of evil on a world scale, any claim to special, not to say esoteric, knowledge, almost any use of the word γνῶσις ('knowledge'), is liable to be labelled Gnostic. The danger of such double usage is that the early antecedents of Gnosticism are likely to be interpreted in the light of the end product, and that where one element of Gnosticism is detected others are likely to be assumed.

The only safe procedure is to start with the evidence of Colossians itself, without any presuppositions drawn from other sources. But this is not as easy as it sounds. Because Colossians is a real letter, it takes for granted much that we should like to have been told. Paul had no need to describe the teaching he attacks, because his readers already knew it at first hand (cp. 2 Thess. 2[5]). He had only to make cryptic allusions to it, and the Colossians would recognize at once what he was talking about. To add to our difficulties, we cannot be sure either of the extent or of the accuracy of Paul's allusions. Some scholars have conjectured (in defence of the Pauline authorship of the letter) that all the unusual words in it were taken over by Paul from the vocabulary of his opponents. The word πλήρωμα ('fulness'), for example, is one of the technical terms of Valentinian teaching and could therefore be ascribed also to an earlier form of Gnosticism. But it is at least as likely that Valentinus derived his terminology from Colossians, especially as the word occurs inother Pauline epistles in senses which have no connexion with Gnosticism. Again, it is commonly assumed that the expression 'angel-worship' (2[18]) is a reliable clue. But Paul was quite

[4] *The Interpreter's Bible*, xi, p. 137.

capable of resorting to pejorative and emotive language in debate (cp. Phil. $3^{2,19}$), and, since we are allowed to hear only one side of the argument, it is possible that his opponents would have resented this term as a misrepresentation of their 'philosophy', much as a Roman Catholic might have repudiated a Protestant description of the Mass in the days before the Ecumenical Movement. Josephus attributed to the Essenes the practice of praying to the sun (*B. J.* II. viii. 5). Frankel's theory that this was deliberate disparagement, designed to suit the taste of heathen readers, was rejected by Lightfoot, who insisted on taking Josephus at his face value.[5] But Frankel was right. We now know from the fuller evidence of Qumran what was the truth underlying Josephus's caricature: the Essenes had a solar calendar, and one of their quarrels with Jerusalem was that the festivals celebrated according to a lunar calendar were not subject to the true law of God inherent in the order of nature. With this illustration before us, the question we must ask is: what beliefs and practices had the Colossian 'philosophers' adopted that Paul could stigmatize as 'angel-worship' without any hint that he thought them idolatrous?

For our reconstruction we must rely on five items.

(a) The primary concern of the 'philosophers' was with morality. They were appalled by the prevalence of sensuality and tried to guard against it by a strict asceticism (2^{20-3}). This is the one non-Jewish element in their system. Any asceticism which is not merely tactical springs from a dualism which regards matter as inherently evil and therefore tries to suppress bodily impulses and passions.

(b) They tried to find a warrant for their asceticism in the ceremonial rules of the Old Tessament. This accounts for the references to circumcision, festivals, new moons, and sabbaths. If the connexion is not at once obvious to us, it must be remembered that we are not dealing with what the Old Testament really means, but with the rigours that might be detected in it by a pagan coming to it for the first time, particularly if he

[5] *St. Paul's Epistles to the Colossians and to Philemon*, pp. 354ff.

took 'his stand on visions' and allowed that kind of inspiration to control his exegesis (2^{13-18}).

(c) They believed that Christ was a true revelation of God with authority over part of human experience and conduct, but that other aspects of life must be controlled by other authorities with an equal claim to derive from God. This may be inferred from Paul's insistence that, although other forms of authority exist, they are all subordinate to Christ, who alone is the full and sufficient revelation of God (1^{15-23}).

(d) They were an exclusive clique, priding themselves on their own insight, and ready to 'disqualify' those who did not share it (2^{18}).

(e) They called their beliefs a 'philosophy' (2^{8}).

The last point has been largely disregarded by those who have spoken so confidently of a Gnostic heresy and have sought its origins in Graeco-oriental religion. Yet the parallels with other ancient philosophical systems are interesting and instructive. All philosophy in the Hellenistic age could be described as morality in quest of a rational basis. Ever since the conquests of Alexander the Great had shaken the fabric of society beyond the possibility of repair, men had been looking for a new principle to regulate their lives. Both Epicurus and Zeno, the founder of Stoicism, had started with the problem of evil. To Epicurus the one enemy of happiness was fear, which he believed could be avoided by the quiet life ($\dot{a}\tau\alpha\rho\alpha\xi\dot{\iota}\alpha$); and he adopted the atomic philosophy of Leucippus and Democratus because, if randomness is the sole cause of existence and the soul does not survive death, there can be nothing to fear either from the gods or from life after death. Zeno taught that desire was the cause of all evil and that the good life could be attained by suppressing the emotions. He found his intellectual support in the philosophy of Heraclitus, who by introspection had discovered in himself a *logos* (rational faculty) which he took to be one with the *logos* (rationality) of the universe around him. Armed with this notion the Stoics proclaimed that the good life was life lived 'according to nature', by which they did not mean doing what comes naturally, but rather allowing the *logos* within to be in harmony with the universal *logos*. Before the Christian era Stoicism had been reinforced by the advent of astrology from the east. For ancient astrology was the belief that the rule of law evinced in the orderly motions of the heavenly bodies had a controlling influence on the lives of men and nations. The planets themselves in particular were world-rulers, readily identifiable with the gods and goddesses of the Olympian pantheon, whose names they bear to this day. Thus astrology transformed both the Stoic philosophy and popular religion into a belief in universal law.

It would be going beyond the evidence to say that the Colossian 'philosophy' was an amalgam of Stoic and Jewish ideas and practices, though even that would be closer to the truth than any loose talk about Gnosticism. What we can safely say is that it grew out of the general intellectual ferment of the Graeco-oriental world, that its chief concern was not with speculation but with conduct, and that it developed by using the Old Testament as a philosophical textbook, somewhat after the same fashion as Epicurus had done with the writings of the atomic physicists and the Stoics had done with Heraclitus.

This strange mushroom growth would have been singularly unimportant and would have disappeared without leaving any trace in the annals of human thought, if it had not provoked Paul into writing his fullest statement of the cosmic implications of the gospel and of the universal sovereignty of Christ.

ANALYSIS

I	**1: 1–2**	Address.
2	**1: 3–12**	Thanksgiving.
3	**1:13–23**	The Pre-eminence of Christ.
4	**1: 24–2: 5**	Paul's Ministry.
5	**2: 6–15**	An Answer to False Teaching: (a) the Victory of Christ.

6	**2: 16–23**	An Answer to False Teaching: (b) the Irrelevance of Legalism.
7	**3: 1–4**	An Answer to False Teaching: (c) the True Source of New Life.
8	**3: 5–17**	The Old Life and the New
9	**3: 18–4: 1**	The Christian Family
10	**4: 2–6**	Final Instructions.
11	**4: 7–18**	Messages and Greetings.

COMMENTARY

1: 1–2 *Address.*

In form and much of its content the greeting is the same as the opening greeting of Ephesians, and the notes there should be consulted. The only differences are: the inclusion of the name of Timothy (on which see Phil. 1¹); the address to a particular church; the description of the Colossians as 'brethren'; and the omission of the name of Christ from the end of the grace.

2. Paul frequently uses the adjective ἅγιοι (*saints*) as a noun to denote members of the church, holy because they belong to Christ; and the RSV has assumed that he is doing so here. But when two adjectives are joined by a single definite article, it is harsh to treat the first as a noun. In Eph. 1² the two adjectives are both used as nouns. Here both are adjectives, qualifying *brethren*. This letter is addressed 'to the dedicated and believing brotherhood at Colossae, incorporate in Christ.'

Lightfoot's suggestion that *faithful* here 'hints at the defection' of some members of the church and so has the effect of directing the letter to 'the true and steadfast members' exaggerates the seriousness of the trouble at Colossae and is not borne out by the letter as a whole, which is addressed precisely to those who 'were shaken in their allegiance' by the strange new 'philosophy' to which they have been subjected.

brethren is Paul's favourite designation for his fellow Christians, and he uses it in every one of his letters. One reason why he seems so little interested in the organization of the church is that he thinks of it as a family. A family, like a body, has a natural, organic unity, which does not need to be organized.

from God our Father. This is the only one of Paul's letters in which the name of Christ is not joined to that of God in the opening grace. The omission cannot be theologically significant in view of the high Christology that is to follow. We should therefore take it as a salutary warning against reading too much into apparent irregularities in Pauline usage. Cp. also the unusual form of expression in v. 3.

1: 3–12 *Thanksgiving.*

As in all his other letters except Galatians, Paul begins with thanksgiving. In this way he can tell his readers how pleased he is with them, and yet protect them from smugness by a reminder that their Christian faith and life are the product of God's unmerited grace. He has received continuous and encouraging reports from his friends, who can vouch that the Colossian church is making steady progress in faith and brotherly love, and so giving clear evidence that it has treasure laid up in heaven. His latest report, from their founder Epaphras, has confirmed all that he has heard before (vv. 3–8). It is because he has received this good news of successful missionary enterprise among people he has never visited that Paul is impelled to pray for their further progress. The first requirement for any Christian is the renewal of the mind (cp. Rom. 12^2; Col. 3^{10}), which carries with it a growing recognition of the will of God (cp. Rom. 1^{28}; 10^2; Phil. 1^9). Obedience to truth already recognized is the first condition not only for Christian behaviour but also for further insight into God's will. But they will need strength from God, strength he has shown himself well able to supply, if they are to remain serene in face of the trials imposed upon them by difficult circumstances and difficult people, and to live up to all that God has done for the Gentiles in giving them equal rights with his ancient people the Jews in his newly established realm of light (vv. 9–12).

3. *We always thank God.* Paul's use of the first person plural is still under debate. Does he always use it as a true plural, i.e. of himself and at least one other person (here Timothy), or does he ever use the epistolary plural, referring to himself alone? There are passages where a switch from plural to singular might seem to imply a deliberate distinction (Col. 1^{23}; 4^3; 1 Thess. 2^{18}), and others in which it does not

(Col. 1²⁸⁻⁹). If we read through 1 Thessalonians, we begin with the impression that 'we' designates Paul, Silvanus, and Timothy, only to find at 3¹ ('we were willing to be left behind at Athens alone') that it cannot refer to anyone other than Paul. It is quite likely that the question we are asking was one Paul himself never troubled to ask, so that he could slip naturally from the one sense to the other, only occasionally reverting to the singular for clarity or emphasis. In the present context, if Timothy is included, this is a matter of courtesy, and the real subject of the sentence, as v. 7 demonstrates, is Paul.

4. *we have heard.* In v. 8 Paul mentions the recent report he has received from Epaphras, and it is possible that this is the only news of Colossae he has had. But, since he had many friends in the churches of the Lycus valley, this is unlikely, and the emphatic 'always' in v. 3 must mean more than 'since Epaphras arrived'. He has been thanking God for the church at Colossae ever since he first heard of it.

4–5. The familiar triad of *faith*, *love*, and *hope* is found so often in the New Testament, and not only in the letters of Paul, that it must have belonged to the earliest, pre-Pauline tradition of catechetical teaching (Rom. 5¹⁻⁵; 1 Cor. 13¹³; Gal. 5⁵⁻⁶; Eph. 4²⁻⁵; 1 Thess. 1³; 5⁸; Heb. 6¹⁰⁻¹²; 10²²⁻⁴; 1 Pet. 1³⁻⁸,²¹⁻²). Here however it appears with two differences: *hope* is not here the subjective attitude of expectation, but the thing hoped for, the objective treasure *laid up . . . in heaven* (cp. Rom. 8²⁴; Tit. 2¹³; Heb. 6¹⁸); and it could not therefore be linked with *faith* and *love* in simple co-ordination. The actual connexion between the three is far from clear. We can dismiss the idea that Paul is attributing to the Colossians a mercenary motive, congratulating them on having shown *faith* and *love because of* (i.e. for the sake of gaining) *the hope*. We could take *because of the hope* closely with the main verb, treating the intervening clause as a parenthesis: 'we always thank God . . . because of the hope . . . ' But this is syntactically awkward and would break up the triad of Christian graces. The best solution is to understand *the hope* as the source, rather than the motive, of the *faith* and *love*: the faith and love 'both spring from the hope stored up for you in heaven' (NEB). Christian *faith* is the belief that God has raised Jesus to new and eternal life in which believers are offered a share. The mutual *love* of Christians is one of the clearest tokens that this new life is being appropriated (Rom. 5⁵; 1 Cor. 12³¹; Gal. 5²²). Faith in God and love for one another are thus already a proleptic experience of the life everlasting. In making *faith* and *love* dependent on the future *hope* Paul is not contradicting what he has said in 1 Cor. 13¹³. There hope is the subjective attitude, and the argument is that, when faith gives place to sight and hope to the thing hoped for, love will remain.

The words *you have heard before* represent a single Greek word (προηκούσατε). But before what? Most commentators have followed

Lightfoot in seeing here a reference to the false teaching reported by Epaphras and contrasted by Paul with *the word of the truth*. They heard the truth before they were exposed to the falsehood. But this is to overload the verb, which in classical Greek always means 'to hear something in advance', i.e. before seeing it or before it happens. It never means 'to hear one thing before another'. Thus, if we insist on the strict sense of the verb, Paul could only mean that the Colossians had heard of the Christian hope before its fulfilment; and this seems too obvious to be worth saying. It is more likely therefore that the verb is being used, like many other words in hellenistic Greek, in a slightly weakened sense: 'you first heard' (cp. the analogous use of προελπίζειν in Eph. 1¹²). This interpretation becomes inescapable if, as seems probable, λόγος *(word)* here means 'the act of speech' rather than 'the thing said': 'of this you first heard when the gospel truth was spoken to you.'

6. Paul offers two testimonies to the truth of the gospel, universality and effectiveness. *in the whole world* seems to us an exaggeration, only slightly modified in the NEB version, 'the whole world over'. But this is a note which Paul frequently strikes (Rom. 1⁸; 10¹⁸; 2 Cor. 2¹⁴; Col. 1²³; 1 Thess. 1⁸). He is of course well aware that there are parts of the world, such as Spain, where the name of Christ has not yet been heard (Rom. 15²⁰⁻⁴). But he is also justifiably impressed by the rapid march and widespread acceptance of the gospel. He is even more impressed by its effects, *bearing fruit and growing*. Moule has pointed out that here, as in Mark's parable of the Sower, fruit-bearing precedes growth. But Paul's metaphor is different from Mark's, because he is thinking of a tree, which bears fruit at the end of one season and puts forth new spurs for the next. In the same way the gospel bears fruit in the conduct of believers and subsequently spreads through the winning of new converts.

They had *understood the grace of God in truth*, i.e. recognized the gospel for what it truly is, a gospel of grace. Paul can give no higher approval than this, for *grace* is the very heart of his preaching. Grace is God's unconditional love and mercy, which needs neither to be earned nor deserved, only accepted. The Christian life and all that it comprises, the right of access to God, membership in his family, growth in love, wisdom, and holiness, the hopes of eternal bliss, all depend on grace alone. 'It depends not on man's will or exertion, but upon God's mercy' (Rom. 9¹⁶). Men are indeed justified on the grounds of their faith, but faith is nothing more than the recognition and acceptance of grace (Rom. 4¹⁶). The reason for the passionate anxiety of Paul's letter to the Galatians is his fear that they have 'fallen away from grace' (Gal. 5⁴). The one thing that matters is that grace shall be allowed to be grace, and not transformed into merit (Rom. 11⁶). Whatever else has gone wrong in Colossae, on this score at least Paul has no anxiety.

7. *Epaphras* seems to have been the evangelist of all three churches of the Lycus valley (4¹³). Paul calls him *fellow servant*, using a word which emphasizes their common allegiance to the one master and the common responsibility entrusted to them by him (σύνδουλος, cp. Phil. 1¹). T. R. Glover has pointed out how much of Paul's character is revealed by his fondness for compounds of συν. 'The dearest of all ties for Paul is to find men sharing things with him' (*Paul of Tarsus*, p. 180). Among his friends he mentions fourteen fellow workers, four fellow prisoners-of-war, two fellow soldiers, two fellow slaves, and one yokefellow. He does not treat Epaphras as an assistant, but as a colleague. It might seem that this statement needs some qualification in view of the following sentence. The reading adopted by the RSV is undoubtedly the correct one (*on our behalf*), and it certainly implies that in his work as an evangelist and pastor Epaphras has acted as Paul's representative. There is ample evidence, too, that Paul regarded himself as the one apostle of the Gentiles, commissioned by Christ to present to God the offering of the Gentiles' faith (Rom. 15¹⁶: cp. also the notes on Eph. 1¹; 3¹⁻³). But it does not therefore follow that he had a hierarchical view of the Christian ministry. *Epaphras* was a *minister of Christ*, acting directly under Christ's authority, not under Paul's. Paul would have liked to evangelize the whole world in person, if that had been possible. In the case of Colossae he acknowledges that it is unnecessary; his colleague Epaphras has done it for him.

8. The report brought by Epaphras was for the most part encouraging. Beare has suggested that what he brought was some tokens of their *love* towards Paul himself. But since the prayer for their continuing growth which follows is explicitly based on Epaphras's report, it is more likely that he brought further evidence of the mutual love already mentioned in v. 4. It was *love in the Spirit*, i.e. more than human affection, supernatural, God-given love.

9. *And so.* The connexion of thought is considerably stronger in the Greek than this mild rendering suggests (cp. Eph. 1¹⁵; 1 Thess. 2¹³; 3⁵): 'this is the reason why . . . ' The piling up of three nearly synonymous terms connoting intellectual processes, and of four in 2², has been taken as evidence that Paul was attacking a form of 'Gnostic' teaching on its own territory. Gnosticism is the name given to any religious movement which claimed to impart an esoteric knowledge (γνῶσις) of specially revealed divine truth, by mastering which the soul could make good its escape from the trammels of an evil mundane existence into the supernatural world which was its true home. If Paul is indeed countering such a doctrine, his answer is that Christian gnosis belongs equally to all members of the church, that it is revealed in the person of Christ, and especially in his death and resurrection, and that it has more to do with the ethics of the present world than with the secrets of the next. But against this interpretation it should be noted:

(a) that similar prayers are found in the other three imprisonment letters (Eph. 1¹⁷; Phil. 1⁹; Philem. 6), and that all four words occur regularly in the earlier letters;

(b) that only one of these words is used in the section of this letter which explicitly deals with the false teaching at Colossae (2⁴⁻²³); and

(c) that the word here (and at 2²) translated *knowledge* is not γνῶσις but ἐπίγνωσις. It is true that these words can be used with little or no distinction. According to Lightfoot, the compound form denotes 'a larger and more thorough knowledge'. But strictly speaking ἐπίγνωσις means 'insight', 'recognition', 'acknowledgment', and any of these senses would fit splendidly in the present context. It makes a considerable difference to the theology of the letter which rendering we choose. If we speak of *knowledge of* God's *will*, we imply the existence of a constant corpus of divine truth, waiting to be known; and ethical education will than consist in increasing understanding of unchanging principles. If on the other hand we speak of 'insight' into God's *will*, or of 'recognition' of it, we are declaring our belief in a dynamic purpose which has to be understood afresh in relation to each new circumstance or decision. Now Paul was inexorably opposed to any attempt, either by Jewish law or by pagan philosophy, to reduce God's *will* to a set of rules. For him God's *will* was embodied in a person, and Christian ethics consisted in the development of a mature judgment which could bring 'the mind of Christ' to bear on each new situation (1 Cor. 2¹⁶; cp. Phil. 2⁵). It is important too that the element of acknowledgment should not be left out. In the spiritual realm there is no knowledge without commitment.

10 *fully pleasing to him*. Paul uses a noun (AV 'unto all pleasing') which in classical Greek had the bad sense of 'obsequiousness'. In later Greek inscriptions it occurs with the complimentary sense of popularity or divine favour well deserved. Paul agrees with the classical writers that conduct designed to gain human approval is ignoble (3²²; cp. Gal. 1¹⁰; 1 Thess. 2⁴; Eph. 6⁶), but only because the gaining of God's approval is the whole duty of man (Rom. 8⁸; 12¹⁻²; 14¹⁸; 1 Cor. 7³²; 2 Cor. 5⁹; Eph. 5¹⁰; Phil. 4¹⁸).

The order of the participles, *bearing fruit* and *increasing*, shows that the image in Paul's mind, here as at v. 6, is that of a vine or fruit tree, which shows its health and vigour in two distinct ways, by producing a harvest and then by continuing to put forth new shoots in readiness for the next crop. Insight into God's will bears fruit in conduct and then gives rise to a fresh growth of insight.

11. The meaning of this verse is highly compressed, and, if we did not have the parallel in Eph. 1¹⁹⁻²⁰ to guide us, we might be at a loss to know what Paul meant by *his glorious might*. For 'glory' is a term widely employed in the Old Testament to convey any impressive aspect of God's character, any manifestation of his power or wisdom,

and sometimes even the divine presence itself. But in Ephesians Paul writes explicitly of the power by which God raised Christ from the dead and indicates that this same power is at the disposal of Christ's followers. 'Christ was raised from the dead by the glory of the Father' (Rom. 6⁴), and from the same source Christians may expect to be *strengthened* for their task of knowing and pleasing God.

This tacit link between the glory of God and the resurrection helps to explain the remarkable transition from glory to *endurance and patience*. 'Endurance' (ὑπομονή) is the refusal to be daunted by hard times, 'patience' (μακροθυμία) the refusal to be upset by perverse people. The Christian's growth to spiritual maturity must take place in a world antagonistic both to his faith and to his good works. *Joy* is one of the distinctively Christian qualities (Gal. 5²²; Phil. 1¹⁸; 2¹⁷; 3¹; 4⁴), the more so as it is constantly linked in the New Testament with hardship and suffering.

12. The manuscript evidence is fairly evenly balanced between the reading of the RSV text (*us*) and that of the margin (*you*). These two Greek pronouns were regularly confused (cp. v. 7), which is hardly surprising seeing that in the first century A.D. they were already pronounced exactly alike. But the internal evidence of this letter and the parallel in Ephesians are together decisive in favour of the margin. This is Paul the Jew addressing himself to Gentile readers. It follows that *the saints*, here as in Eph. 1¹⁸ and 2¹⁹, must mean Jewish Christians. God's promise had been first made to the Jewish nation (Rom. 9⁴⁻⁵). Even with the coming of Christ and the breaking down of national barriers, the gospel was still 'to the Jew first and also to the Greek' (Rom. 1¹⁶). Only through Paul and his missionary colleagues had God at last *qualified* the Gentiles *to share* in privileges which were basically Jewish.

inheritance is an unfortunate translation for κλῆρος, particularly as the phrase taken as a whole, *the inheritance of the saints in light*, inevitably carries overtones of the life everlasting which are totally absent from the present context. Κλῆρος means 'lot' or 'what is assigned or allotted', and it is the word used in the Septuagint for the allocation of land in Palestine among the twelve tribes of Israel. By the use of this word Paul draws a comparison between the old Israel entering Canaan, with each tribe allotted its territory in the promised land, and the new Israel entering the kingdom of Christ, the realm of *light*. Gentile Christians are to thank God that they have been declared fit for an equal share in this territory, first occupied by their Jewish brothers.

1: 13–23 *The Pre-eminence of Christ.*

In his prayer Paul has described the entry of the Gentiles into the church in terms reminiscent of Israel's entrance into

Canaan. The Exodus, together with its sequel in the giving of the law and the settlement of the tribes in their new home, lay at the heart of the Old Testament religion. Accordingly, many of the prophets, in predicting the glorious new age of the Messiah, had thought of it as beginning with a new Exodus. The early Christians thus had in the story of Israel's national origins a ready source of colourful language with which to express their conviction that the new age had begun. Paul now proceeds to explore this comparison further. As formerly God had rescued the Hebrew people from oppression in Egypt, so now he has rescued the new Israel from the dark powers which dominate the present world order and has settled them in the kingdom of Christ. The difference is that their emancipation has not been from physical slavery or political tyranny, but from sin (vv. 13–14). This does not mean, however, that what Christ has done for men is devoid of outward, political, and even cosmic implications. He is the very centre and crown of the creation, because he is man as God from the beginning designed man to be. God created man to be his own image, reflecting his own character and responding to his love, and intended that he should hold pre-eminence over the rest of creation (v. 15). All that God has made, not only the earthly and visible but the invisible realm of supernatural powers, belongs to man's world and must be understood in relation to man and his destiny. Christ's supremacy is there absolute and universal. He is the embodiment of that purpose of God which underlies the whole creation, and so he supplies the principle of coherence and meaning in the universe (vv. 16–17). These staggering assertions can be made about the place of the man Jesus in creation because in the experience of the church he holds precisely this place of supremacy in God's new creation. He is head over those who through his death and resurrection are incorporated into unity with him, and he is the source of their new life; and all this is only the beginning of the process by which God is establishing him in complete pre-eminence over the universe. God always intended that his heavenly wisdom should find a home in man, and so in Christ God himself in all his fulness chose to dwell, so that through Christ's vicarious death he could bring about the reconciliation of the whole rebellious universe to himself. (vv. 18–20). The first and most striking evidence of this is in the experience of the Gentile Christians themselves. Formerly alienated from God both in their thinking and consequently also in their conduct, they have now been reconciled to God through Christ's death and can stand fearless and unashamed in his presence, so long as they remain constant in their faith. And this they may feel encouraged to do by the knowledge that their experience has been shared by others all over the world (vv. 21–3).

13. If the new life to which the Colossians have been admitted is 'light' (v. 12), then the old life from which they have been rescued is the territory where *darkness* reigns. There is nothing specifically Gnostic about this contrast, though the Gnostics used it. 'Light' and 'darkness' are universal symbols for truth and falsehood, good and evil, and are regularly so used in the Old Testament. In the dark men cannot see things as they truly are and cannot see where they are going. *Darkness* is thus the ethical condition of the whole world apart from Christ (Rom. 13^{12}; 2 Cor. 6^{14}; Eph. $5^{8,11}$); but it is also something more, a sinister tyrant which has held men under its *dominion* (cp. Eph. 6^{12}). Darkness is the character of those principalities and powers which are to be listed in v. 16, and which must have played a central part in the Colossian 'philosophy'. But now there is no need for men to go in fear of these dark powers, let alone to pay them homage. Their writ still runs in the non-Christian world, but Christians are no longer their helpless victims. As God once took Israel out of Egypt and made them settlers in Palestine, so now he has taken his people out of the old dark order and made them settlers in *the kingdom of his beloved Son*. The life we lead is so intimately bound up with that of the surrounding society that no new life is possible unless we are *transferred* to a new setting. For the first Christians this transfer must have been more obvious than it is today when secular society is permeated by centuries of Christian influence. There are few explicit references in the New Testament to *the kingdom of* Christ (Matt. 13^{41}; 1 Cor. 15^{24-8}); but it is everywhere assumed in the belief, based on Ps. 110^{1}, that he is seated at God's right hand. From the moment of his exaltation he has begun to reign, and that reign must continue until all hostile forces in the universe are subject to him. Until then *the dominion of darkness* can still do a great deal of damage. Only it cannot control the life of the Christian or interfere with his relationship to God.

14. In case his readers are tempted to take the Exodus imagery too literally, Paul adds that the Christian's deliverance is a spiritual one, *the forgiveness of sins*. The forces of evil affect a man's life in a variety of ways, but they control it only in so far as he gives them his assent (Rom. 6[16]). In Rom. 5–7 Paul has analysed in great detail the condition of the man who tries to live by a moral code, only to find that even the code itself becomes a means by which sin compels him to do what he knows to be wrong. Not until he begins to live instead by God's free grace and mercy is the control broken. The cross is the proof that God has accepted him (Rom. 5[8]), and that no power in the universe can separate him from God's love (Rom. 8[38-9]).

15–20. There is a theory, which constantly reappears in a new form, that these verses were not composed by the author of Colossians. E. Norden[6] and M. Dibelius (pp. 10ff.) have argued that the passage consists of formulae devised in the hellenistic Jewish synagogue in praise of the divine Word or Wisdom; C. Masson that it was a pre-Pauline hymn, into which the author of Ephesians interpolated v. 18[a]; E. Käsemann[7] that it was a Gnostic hymn celebrating the authority of the World Ruler over the powers of the cosmos. On this prevalent but Protean theory the following points should be noted.

(a) As with the 'hymn' in Phil. 2[6-11], poetic form is achieved only by the excision of words which do not fit, on the grounds that they are a gloss by the final editor. In other respects the case for hymnic structure is much weaker here than in Philippians. Lohmeyer's popular theory concerning Phil. 2[6-11] initiated an enthusiastic sifting of the epistles for early hymns and formulae, much of which has been more ingenious than convincing. What we find in the New Testament is a great deal of evidence for a stock of common ideas, common methods of using the Old Testament, and common vocabulary, but no evidence at all for the use of an identical form of words by any two writers or by any one writer on two occasions. Beare, for example, has drawn attention to a correspondence between Col. 1[15-20] and Heb. 1[1-4] in the sequence of ideas they contain; but the wording of the two passages is so different that he rightly restricts himself to the inference that they were built up out of a common stock of credal material.

(b) The exalted claims here made for Christ are not exactly paralleled in any of the earlier letters of Paul. But each of the Pauline letters contains some theological ideas which are peculiar to it, and the theology of this passage is in some ways, as we shall see, distinctively Pauline.

(c) Even if we were to accept the hymn theory, we should still have

[6] *Agnostos Theos*, pp. 252ff.

[7] 'Eine urchristliche Taufliturgie', *Festschrift Rudolf Bultmann*, pp. 133ff.

to say that the meaning of the passage in Colossians is what the author of the letter (Paul) intended it to mean. Speculations about the previous function of the hymn may have some interest for the study of Christian origins, but they are totally irrelevant to the exegesis of Colossians. For this reason these verses must not be excised from the context in which they stand. The thought of the passage as a whole begins with redemption and returns to redemption. This fact helps us to solve the biggest problem of all: how could claims of this magnitude be made about a man who had died little more than thirty years ago, and who was remembered as a personal friend by men and women still living when the letter was written? The answer is that Paul comes to Christ's place in creation through his place in the new creation (Col. 3^{10}; cf. 2 Cor. 5^{17}; Gal. 6^{15}; Eph. 2^{15}). In the life, death, and resurrection of Christ God the Creator had been active, not merely repairing the ravages of the Fall, but bringing into existence, and that for the first time, that manhood in his own image which it had always been his plan to create. In Christ therefore Paul finds the secret not only of man's redemption but of his creation; and since man was destined by God to be lord of the universe, this is the secret also of the whole creation.

(d) An alternative theory, much more plausible than that of a pre-Pauline hymn, has been advanced by C. F. Burney.[8] He has suggested that Paul was here adapting to Christian use a rabbinic midrash on Gen. 1^1, 'in the beginning ($b^e reshith$) God created', and Prov. 8^{22}, 'the Lord begat me as the beginning (*reshith*) of his way, the antecedent of his works, of old' (Burney's translation). The equation Wisdom = *reshith* in the second text led to the substitution of the one for the other in the first. The full meaning of the opening words of Genesis was then exploited by giving three meanings to the preposition *b*-('in','by', and 'for') and four meanings to *reshith* ('beginning', 'sum-total', 'head', 'first-fruits'). Thus the rabbis could say that God created the world 'in', 'by', and 'for' Wisdom, and that Wisdom was the 'first-born of all creation', its 'sum-total', 'head', and 'source'. The attractiveness of this hypothesis is that it neatly accounts for all the complexities of the passage we are discussing. And since in rabbinic teaching Wisdom and Torah had long been equated, the passage would then form an exact parallel to those other passages where Paul takes a quotation from the Old Testament in which the rabbis had detected a covert reference to the Torah, and claims that in reality the reference is to Christ (cp. 1 Cor. 10^{1-4} and notes on Eph. 4^{7-11}).

15. The two titles here ascribed to Christ raise a number of intricate and interlocking problems. Is Paul speaking of the pre-existent or of the incarnate Christ? Is the first title, *the image of the invisible God*, drawn

[8]'Christ as the ΑΡΧΗ of Creation', *Journal of Theological Studies*, xxvii (1925–6), pp. 160ff.

from the biblical story of the creation of man, or is Christ being identified with the personified Wisdom, which in Wisd. 7²⁶ is called 'the image of God's goodness' (cp. Phil. *Leg. Alleg.* i. 43; *de Conf.* 97)? Does *first-born of all creation* mean that Christ is included in the creation, or does it express his priority to and supremacy over the creation? The traditional answer to these questions, that this is one of the three New Testament examples of Wisdom or Logos Christology (cp. John 1¹⁻¹⁴; Heb. 1¹⁻⁴), is superbly presented by Lightfoot. He argues that it is not because he is man that Christ is *the image* of God, but because he is the eternal pattern of which man was the copy; that Philo repeatedly calls the Logos both *the image* of God and *the first-born* (though with a different Greek word); that in Ps. 89²⁷ *first-born* is a title of sovereignty rather than of primogeniture; that all the early Fathers correctly referred these titles 'to the Eternal Word and not to the Incarnate Christ'; that no other view does justice to the background of the term in the speculations of Alexandrian Judaism; and that the only (and impossible) alternative is that the theme of the whole passage is not creation as we normally understand it, but the new, spiritual creation in Christ. In spite of the immense weight of erudition and authority behind it, this view is not free from difficulties.

(a) The Christ to whom these titles are attributed is the Christ through whom Christians have received their redemption and into whose kingdom they have been transferred, i.e. the crucified and exalted Lord.

(b) Lightfoot's distinction between being the image of God and being made in the image of God is not borne out by Pauline usage. Man is the image of God (1 Cor. 11⁷); and in the one other place where Christ is called the image of God (2 Cor. 4⁴), it is clearly the Christ of the gospel story and not a pre-existent figure.

(c) In the first of these titles there is an implied contrast, as Lightfoot himself points out, between the visible *image* and *the invisible God*. He who is *the image* both represents and reveals God, which hardly fits the precosmic existence of the eternal Word.

(d) *First-born* was a title given by divine election to Israel (Exod. 4²²), and in a derivative sense to Israel's anointed king. Ps. 89²⁷ does not speak of eternal nature, but of divine appointment: 'I will make him the first-born, the highest of the kings of the earth.' Thus Lightfoot is right in saying that to be *first-born* is a matter of status and sovereignty, with no necessary connotation of temporal priority. But he does not carry his own argument far enough. Christ too is *first-born* by divine appointment. Cp. Rom. 1⁴, where Christ is said to have been 'designated Son of God in power ... by his resurrection from the dead'; and Rom. 8²⁹, where Christ as head of the new creation becomes what he always was in the predestining plan of God, 'first-born among many brethren'. Similarly, when Paul uses the word *first-born* for the second time in v. 18 of the present passage, it unmistakably denotes a status to which Christ attained by his resurrection.

(e) Lightfoot did not adequately ponder what pre-existence could have meant in the monotheistic Judaism to which he appealed. What, for example, is meant by the personified Wisdom in Prov. 8, Ecclus. 24, or Wisd. 7? It oscillates between being an attribute of God (a picturesque way of saying 'God in his wisdom') and the divine plan for human life which is incidentally the ground plan of the universe, capable of being identified with the Torah (Ecclus. 24[7-12,23]). In this second sense we are repeatedly told that Wisdom was created by God (Prov. 8[22]; Ecclus. 24[8]; Wisd. 6[22]). Philo's Logos, too, for all the grandiloquent terms used to describe it, was created. In *De Opificio Mundi* he relates the two creation stories of Gen. 1–2 to Plato's two worlds: God first created the ideal world of perfect forms, which Philo equates with the Logos, and then produced a copy of it in physical materials. The process is compared to the activity of an architect who, before building a city of wood and stone, has the plan of it complete in his mind. Thus the Logos, in so far as it can be said to pre-exist, exists as a plan in the mind of God. The rabbis also used to discuss which pre-existent things were actually created and which existed only in the predestining counsels of God (*Bereshith Rabba* 1; cp. in the Babylonian Talmud *Pes.* 54[a]; *Ned.* 39[b]).

(f) Whether or not we agree with Burney's theory of an adapted midrash, there can be little doubt that the personified Wisdom is somewhere in the background of this passage. But we may well doubt whether Lightfoot was correct in supposing it to lie in the foreground. For later in this letter Paul reminds his readers that they have already put on the new manhood which is being constantly renewed 'after the image of its creator' (3[10]). It is improbable that he would have used the word 'image' twice in so brief a compass without intending a connexion between the two. To this we may add the evidence of Ephesians, which is either Paul's own fuller treatment of the same theme or the earliest commentary on Colossians, written by one who thoroughly understood Paul's mind. There, in the parallel passage (1[20-3]), the cosmic supremacy of Christ is not based on his pre-existence but on his manhood; and the argument is clinched by a quotation from Ps. 8, the psalm of man's universal lordship. The main thread of Paul's thought, then, is the manhood of Christ. But there is a simple and sufficient reason why this is not incompatible with a subsidiary reference to Wisdom. Wisdom is a personified attribute of God, but an attribute which God always intended to communicate to men (Prov. 8[4,31]; Ecclus. 24[8]; Wisd. 7[27]). In her most exalted guise, she never ceases to be a way of life. The ideal man, therefore, was bound to be one in whom Wisdom made her home, and whose life had thus become a perfect mirror *of the invisible God*; and this is precisely the justification which Paul offers in v. 19 for the claims he has made for Christ.

16. This statement that *in him* (i.e. in the historic Christ) *all things were created* is a highly compressed one, whose meaning becomes clear only when we reduce it to its component elements. God so designed the universe that it was to achieve its proper meaning and unity only under the authority of man (Gen. 1²⁸; Ps. 8⁶). But this purpose was not to be implemented at once; it was 'to be put into effect when the time was ripe' (Eph. 1¹⁰), when Christ had lived human life as God intended it, and had become God's image in a measure which was never true of Adam. Only in unity with 'the proper man' could the universe be brought to its destined coherence. For one who believes in predestination it is but a small step from this to saying that the universe was created *in him*; and the step was facilitated by the further notion that Christ embodied the divine Wisdom.

For the idea of *heaven* as a part of the created universe, see the notes on Eph. 1³,¹⁰. There is no contrast here between the perfection of *heaven* and the imperfection of *earth*, between eternity and time, between good and evil. *Heaven* and *earth* belong inseparably together as two complementary aspects of man's environment. Earth is the scene of people and things, the *visible*, physical entities. Heaven is the scene of forces which are none the less real for being *invisible*. The list which follows shows clearly enough which *invisible* realities Paul has primarily in mind. He may conceivably have had a mental picture of *thrones*, *dominions*, *principalities*, and *authorities* as angels. But a mental picture is not the same thing as a concept. All that matters is that their names disclose what they represent. They stand for all the various forms of power and authority which pervade the corporate life of man.

About these spiritual forces Paul has some important things to say. First, they *were created* and so are part of the good world brought into existence by God. Man is, as Aristotle put it (*Pol.* 1253ᵃ3), 'a naturally political animal', constitutionally designed to live in organized societies. Thus the creation of man logically entailed the creation of all those structures of power and authority which are integral to the orderly, civilized life of man in society (cp. Rom. 13¹). But they do not exist in their own right. They are created to subserve the true ends of man; and, since those ends are all summed up in Christ, it can be said that they were created *through him and for him*. All human authority is ultimately derived from God and carries the indelible stamp of its origin, even when it is exercised in defiance of God's will. That it could be so exercised was, and is, self-evident; and Paul himself needed no other reminder of this than his own imprisonment. Through the contamination of human sin all the invisible powers are to a greater or lesser extent alienated from God, and therefore from their proper functioning in the divine scheme of things, and need to be restored (cp. v. 20).

This strong emphasis on the superiority of Christ over the powers probably means that he was accorded a much more limited position in the Colossian 'philosophy'. It would appear that Paul's opponents accepted Christ and claimed to be Christians, but held that there were considerable tracts of human behaviour which could not be subsumed under his rule, but must continue to be governed by other manifestations of divine authority. If this be so, then their nearest modern counterparts are those theologians and philosophers who have insisted that the ethics of the gospel cannot be applied to the corporate life of society.

17. Note the tense of the verb (*is*), ignored by too many commentators. We are not told that Christ existed before the world began, but that he *is before all things*. In other words, this is not a statement about remote antiquity, but about the absolute and universal priority of Christ. It is notoriously difficult for us creatures of space and time to say anything about eternity without misleadingly clothing it in temporal or spatial imagery. Appearing in the midst of time, Christ so fully represents and reveals the divine purpose and wisdom that only the language of eternity can do him justice. Similarly, in the Fourth Gospel (8^{58}), it is the man Jesus who claims, 'Before Abraham was I am', because he has fully accepted that which God has decreed, the identification of the Logos with manhood in his own person.

Advocates of the Logos Christology have no difficulty in explaining how in Christ *all things hold together*. In the philosophy of Heraclitus, which was taken over in large part by the Stoics, the Logos was, one might almost say, the chemical formula of the universe. It could be identified with 'the harmony of tension as in bow or lyre' (Fr. 45 ap. Hippol. *Refut.* ix. 9), which held together the warring elements of the physical world. In the same vein Philo describes the Logos as the 'bond' of the universe (*de Profug.* 20; *de Plant.* 2; *Q.R.D.H.* 38). A similar idea occurs in Ecclus 43^{26}, which is probably quite uninfluenced by Greek philosophical teaching. Lightfoot is so carried away by this theme that he instances the law of gravity as an expression of the mind of Christ. It is dubious, however, whether Paul's mind is much dwelling on the physical structure of the world. His concern is that Christ should be seen to be the principle of cohesion in man's world, and specifically in the sphere of the spiritual powers (cp. Eph. 1^{10}; 3^{10}).

18. The connexion of this verse with what precedes may be established in two different ways, corresponding to the two possible interpretations of v. 15. If, with Lightfoot, we hold that the subject of v. 15 is the pre-existent Logos, then we must say that at this point Paul turns from Christ's sovereignty over the natural order of the physical creation

to his sovereignty over the spiritual order of the new creation. 'As He *is* first with respect to the Universe, so it was ordained that He should *become* first with respect to the Church as well. The γένηται here answers in a manner to the ἔστιν of ver. 17.' But this view is open to two crippling objections.

(a) In v. 20 we are told that the universe needed to be reconciled to God through the cross of Christ. Prior to the crucifixion, then, it could hardly be said, without qualification, to be under Christ's sovereignty.

(b) Between the ἔστιν (is) of v. 17 and the γένηται (become) of v. 18[b] there intervenes the ἔστιν of v. 18[a]. What Paul says is almost the exact opposite of what Lightfoot wants him to say. Christ *is the head* over the church, in order that he may become head over everything else. The alternative view, then, is that the subject of v. 15 is the historic Christ; that vv. 16–17 deal with the status he holds in God's eternal decree; and that vv. 18–19 are the point at which these stupendous claims are anchored in history. What Christ is de jure in God's decree, he must become de facto; and the resurrection, by which he has become head of the church, is the beginning of the process.

On Christ as *head of the body*, see Eph. 4[15]; 5[23]; and on the curious idea that this is not a metaphor, see E. Best, *One Body in Christ*, pp. 98–101. The last word in the verse, *pre-eminent*, shows that *head* here carries its usual connotation of supremacy. But *head*, *beginning*, and *first-born* are variations on a single Hebrew root (see above pp. 77–8; cp. Eph. 4[15]), and this strongly suggests that the three are to be taken as near synonyms, with the primary sense of source or origin. Christ's death and resurrection are the source of new life to others, the means by which they are incorporated into the life of the church. But this is only the *beginning* of a unity which is to embrace the whole universe.

19. The RSV has simplified the problem of this verse by inserting the words *of God*, which have no counterpart in the Greek. Πλήρωμα (*fulness*) was a technical term in the Gnostic system of the Valentinians for the totality of aeons or spiritual beings which they believed to provide an indispensable link between the immaterial and unknowable God and the physical world. It might therefore seem a plausible conjecture that the Colossian 'Gnostics' were already using this term to denote the hierarchy of spiritual powers in which they were finding some place for Christ, and that Paul was borrowing their language to refute their case. This explanation, however, after a long run of popularity, should now be finally discarded. Though it would fit the present context where πλήρωμα is used absolutely, it would not fit 2[9] or any of the passages where the word occurs in Ephesians. The word is common enough in a variety of non-technical senses in the Septuagint and in the New Testament. It is much more likely that the Valentinians borrowed the term from Paul, since they are known to have

quoted (or misquoted) in support of their own speculations the verses from Colossians and Ephesians in which it is found. The correct explanation, which underlies the RSV rendering, is clearly enough indicated by the syntax of the sentence. Though the subject of the sentence, *all the fulness*, is in the neuter, the participle 'making peace' is in the masculine, which proves that the subject is a person, i.e. that *all the fulness* is a periphrasis for God, meaning 'God in all his fulness'. It is true that this particular periphrasis is not attested in Jewish writings, but there are many analogies, e.g. the Name, the Great Glory, the Shekinah (lit. the Dwelling), not to mention the Holy Spirit.[9]

Paul makes an even higher claim for Christ than his argument requires. What we have been led to expect is that Christ's appointment by God to a position of sovereignty over the whole cosmos is reasonable and credible because in him the divine Wisdom made her home. But Wisdom is only one among the many attributes of God, and Paul sets no limits to the splendour of Christ. It was God's will that in him not Wisdom alone but the complete Godhead should find permanent residence (cp. 2[9]). Thus in this verse we have the final justification for the interpretation we have given to this passage as a whole. All that has been said in vv. 15–18 can be said of the historical Jesus; *for in him the complete being of God came to dwell.*

20. In two respects Paul here goes beyond what we find elsewhere in his writings.

(a) In his earlier letters he uses the word *reconcile* of the new relationship established by the cross between man and God (Rom. 5[10-11]; 11[15]; 2 Cor. 5[18-20]). Sin made men enemies of God, fighting against his true purpose for them, and the cross removed the barricade of misunderstanding and hostility. Even when he spoke of the reconciliation of the world (Rom. 11[15]; 2 Cor. 5[19]), the context shows that he had in mind the world-wide efficacy of the gospel for the needs of men. This present verse includes all this and more besides. God's plan covers the reconciliation of *all things*, not only *on earth* but *in heaven*; and we can infer from v. 16 that this means the principalities and powers.

(b) Again, in the earlier letters the effect of the cross on the spiritual

[9]See G. Münderlein, 'Die Erwahlung durch das Pleroma', *New Testament Studies*, viii (1962), pp. 264–76. He cites in support of this interpretation the Targum on Ps. 68[17] ('See, on Mount Sinai, humble as it is, the Word of the Lord has chosen to allow the Shekinah to dwell') and the Targum on Isa. 42[1] ('My chosen in whom my Word takes pleasure, I will put my Holy Spirit on him'). It can hardly be sheer coincidence that this verse of Ps. 68 immediately precedes that quoted and made the basis of midrashic exegesis in Eph. 4[7-11].

powers is to reduce them to impotence and subjection (1 Cor. 2⁶⁻⁸; 15²⁴⁻⁶). Now, without abandoning the idea that they need to be defeated (2¹⁵), Paul has come to believe also in their reconciliation to God. This is because they preside over the corporate, organized life of human society, and man's salvation cannot be complete until they have been restored to the place assigned to them in the Creator's design for the ordered life of man. Those who are alienated from God, whether men or powers, are alienated also from one another. The wars and hatreds which divide mankind at the earthly level have their counterpart on the heavenly plane in the clash of violent forces which are greater than the sum of their individual human parts. Only through reconciliation to God can *peace* be restored at both levels of worldly existence.

21. All this talk of cosmic peace might seem like castles in the air if it were not that at one point reconciliation has already become a fact of experience. Paul's Gentile readers have come to recognize that in their previous pagan existence they were *estranged* from God, *hostile* in the way they thought as well as in the way they acted. Now they have

22. been *reconciled*, given access to his presence and brought into harmony with his character and will, not by their own effort or reform, but by Christ's death: *his body of flesh* was the point at which he wholly identified himself with sinful men (Rom. 8³; 2 Cor. 5²¹; Gal. 3¹³), even to dying the accursed death of a criminal. In this way the barrier of sin and hostility was surmounted from God's side.

The RSV has taken ἄμωμος in its basic etymological sense of *blameless*. But in the vocabulary of the hellenistic synagogue this word had acquired the meaning 'unblemished', almost certainly because of the similarity of sound between the Greek μῶμος ('blame') and the Hebrew *mûm* ('blemish'). An animal offered in sacrifice must be unblemished, and it is as a sacrificial metaphor that the word is most commonly used in the New Testament (Eph. 1⁴; 5²⁷; Heb. 9¹⁴; 1 Pet. 1¹⁹; Rev. 14⁵). Most of the other words in this clause have a sacrificial ring about them (*present, holy, before him*), and it is best taken as a sustained metaphor. When a man offered an animal in sacrifice, he laid his hand on it in order to identify himself with his offering and to express his aspirations to be himself holy and unblemished. Paul's thought then is that Christ has offered himself to God as the perfect sacrifice, and that Christians must in their turn identify themselves with his sacrificial self-giving. Made one with him in *his body of flesh*, they are also to be one with him in his body which is the church, there to share with him the quality of his new resurrection life.

23. God's initial act of reconciliation is complete in the death and resurrection of Christ, and their part has been to accept it in faith. God can now be trusted to finish his work in them (cp. Phil. 1⁶), *provided that* they *continue in the faith*, i.e. in the attitude of faith in which they

have begun. This faith is a persistent clinging to *the gospel*, which is defined for them in three ways: it is the one they were taught when they first became Christians; the one which has now been preached all over the world (for *to every creature* read 'in the whole creation'); and it is the one which Paul himself was commissioned by Christ to preach.

1: 24-2: 5 *Paul's Ministry.*

Paul has been expounding the place of the Gentile churches in God's master plan for the world. The reconciliation of the world to God, begun in the cross, is being continued in the church, and particularly in the making of peace between Jew and Gentile. In this process Paul himself has played a leading part by his insistence that Christianity has transcended the old racial and religious divisions. It might, however, appear that his imprisonment not only curtailed his apostolic activities but cast doubt on their validity and impugned his understanding of God's purpose. But he himself sees his sufferings in an entirely different light. The cross has demonstrated that reconciliation is a costly business. Wherever the gospel of reconciliation is preached there is a price to be paid in suffering. Paul has been glad to draw off on to himself something of the full tally of suffering which would otherwise have been borne by the churches, and he regards this as an integral part of his ministry. From the dawn of history to the present God's plan for the world has been kept secret, but now it is at last disclosed. At its heart is the indwelling Christ, miraculously uniting in his own person men out of all nations, and so giving solid grounds for confidence in a glorious future for them, and through them for the world (vv. 24-7).

There is nothing esoteric about this gospel Paul has preached; it is for all, and all are capable of the maturity required to grasp it. For the indwelling Christ is recognized precisely when his power is at work to supplement the weak resources of men (vv. 28-9). Even in prison Paul is still in the thick of the struggle, still extending his missionary reach by wrestling with the anxieties, problems, and needs of those he has never met. He wants them to be in good heart, to experience the unity of love, and so to reach a full assurance that Christ himself is

God's secret plan, the man in whom are all the hidden treasures of God's truth. Nobody must be allowed to deceive them into any less exalted view of Christ. That could never happen in Paul's presence, and present he will be, in spirit at least, to safeguard their faith (vv. 1–5).

24. From the momentary recollection of his call to the ministry Paul returns to the *Now* of his imprisonment, which he treats as a natural corollary to apostolic mission (cp. Phil. 1¹²⁻¹⁴). The theme of joy in face of suffering is common throughout the New Testament (e.g. Matt. 5¹²; Acts 5⁴¹; Heb. 10³⁴). It is enough for the servant that he be treated as his master (Matt. 10²⁴⁻⁶). Christ lives on in *the church* and makes its sufferings his own, so that suffering borne for the gospel can be the deepest form of fellowship with him (Phil. 1²⁹⁻³⁰; 3⁸⁻¹⁰; cp. Rom. 8¹⁷; 1 Pet. 4¹³; 5⁹; Rev. 1⁹). Here, however, Paul does not emphasize the spiritual benefits of suffering to himself but its effect on others. In the most obvious way his suffering was *for your sake*; he was in prison because he had insisted on the ending of Jewish privilege and the admission of Gentiles to the people of God on equal terms with Jews (see notes on Eph. 3¹). But here he implies something more. The double compound verb he uses ($\dot{a}\nu\tau a\nu a\pi\lambda\eta\rho\hat{\omega}$) suggests that he suffers not only on their account but in some sense in their stead. The RSV translation (*complete*) misses this and also gives an impression of finality, quite absent from the Greek, as though, once Paul has suffered, no deficiency remains. But what does Paul mean by *what is lacking in Christ's afflictions*? He cannot mean that the redeeming work of Christ on the cross was incomplete and needed to be supplemented by the suffering of his followers. He believed that Christ had died once for all (Rom. 6¹⁰), and the next paragraph of this letter is one of his most forceful statements of this theme. In any case he never uses the word 'affliction' ($\theta\lambda\hat{\imath}\psi\iota s$) of the crucifixion. He is thinking rather of what Christ continues to suffer in *his body, the church* (cp. Matt. 25⁴⁵; Acts 9⁴). In this corporate sense of the word 'Christ' (cp. 1 Cor. 1¹³; 12¹²; Phil. 2¹,⁵), *Christ's afflictions* will not be complete until the final victory over evil is won. Someone must carry the burden, and the strong may take over the share of the weak (Gal. 6²). Paul is glad that he has been able to do enough of the heavy lifting to spare his churches some of their load. It is almost as if he is thinking of a fixed quota of suffering to be endured, so that the more he can attract to himself the less will remain for others. 'I am glad to suffer on your account. I make my contribution to the mounting tally of what Christ must still endure by drawing to my own person what would otherwise have fallen to his body, the church.'

It is unlikely that he intends any vivid contrast between *my flesh* and *his body*. The commonest use of the word 'flesh' in Paul's letters is as a synonym for the old, unredeemed human nature (see Eph. 2³). He also uses it occasionally simply to denote human weakness and exposure to pain (e.g. 2 Cor. 4¹¹; 12⁷), and this may be the sense intended here (NEB 'my poor human flesh'). But it should be noted that the *body* too can suffer and would have had to carry its own load if Paul had not intervened. So it may well be that *in my flesh* means little more than 'in my person' (cp. Eph. 5²⁹⁻³¹).

25–26. *the divine office* is a somewhat florid rendering of a phrase which means 'the task assigned by God'. The RSV has apparently been influenced by Lohmeyer's contention that οἰκονομία here has a double meaning: 'office' and 'divine plan'. 'Paul was entrusted with the office of minister in order to give effect to the divine plan.' This is a correct summary of what Paul is saying, but in this context the idea of a divine plan is contributed by *the word of God* and *the mystery*, not by οἰκονομία, which Paul never uses in that sense (see Eph. 1¹⁰). *to make . . . fully known* (πληρῶσαι) is the simple form of the verb which appeared as a double compound in the last verse. It is one of the characteristics of Paul's style to pursue in this way the variations of a verbal root (cp. 1 Cor. 11²⁹⁻³²). Here it is no mere play on words, for through his sufferings he is able to communicate something of the power of the gospel. There is a close parallel in Acts 20²⁷: 'I did not shrink from declaring to you the whole counsel of God.' On the meaning of *mystery*, see Eph. 1⁹.

for ages and generations (lit. 'from the aeons and from the generations'). Aeons was the term chosen by the Valentinians for those emanations from the Divine which in their system constituted a mediating hierarchy of angelic powers between God and the material world. The RSVmg, *from angels and men*, assumes that this Gnostic term was already in use at Colossae. According to 1 Cor. 2⁶⁻⁸, God's plan was concealed from 'the rulers of this world', the spiritual powers which conspired to crucify Christ. But the RSV text is much to be preferred.

It is not quite clear what is the referent of *saints*. In general it means Christians. But Paul sometimes restricts its range to the Jewish Christians (1¹²; cp. Eph. 1¹⁸; 2¹⁹), or even to the mother church in Jerusalem (e.g. 1 Cor. 16¹). In the parallel passage in Eph. 3²⁻⁶, the revelation that Gentiles were intended to be equal partners in the church is said to have been made to the 'holy apostles and prophets', and in some special fashion to Paul himself. The revelation must have come to the church at a time when it was still predominantly, if not entirely, Jewish. But Paul is concerned here with the content of the revelation, not with the manner of its coming or the identity of its recipients, and we may therefore be satisfied with the general sense of *saints*.

27. This metaphorical use of *riches* is typically Pauline. Christ has opened

the door for him to an inexhaustible treasure of goodness (Rom. 2⁴), glory (Rom. 9²³; Eph. 1¹⁸; 3¹⁶; Phil. 4¹⁹), wisdom (Rom. 11³³), and grace (Eph. 1⁷; 2⁷), and every time he explores it he finds something new to take his breath away.

Paul uses the word *glory* and its cognates more than eighty times and in contexts which cover every aspect of his theology. God is 'the Father of glory' (Eph. 1¹⁷), all-glorious in himself and the sole source of glory. He had manifested to Israel the splendour of his presence (Rom. 9⁴), but the old covenant had now been eclipsed by the new (2 Cor. 3⁷⁻¹¹). God's glory had taken on a new depth of meaning since it had been seen in Christ (2 Cor. 4⁶), and particularly in his resurrection (Rom. 6⁴). God had created mankind to be his 'image and glory', i.e. the reflection of his own character (1 Cor. 11⁷), but through their refusal to acknowledge their dependence on him (Rom. 1²¹⁻³), they had forfeited that derivative splendour (Rom. 3²³). In Christ the divine likeness had been restored (2 Cor. 4⁴), and therein lay *the hope of glory* for others (Rom. 5²). Those who by faith were united with him were already acting as mirrors to his glory and undergoing a hidden transfiguration (2 Cor. 3¹⁸), which would reach its culmination only with the return of Christ (Col. 3⁴). That would be the signal for the redemption of the physical body, transformed like Christ's own body into a body of glory (Phil. 3²¹). Thus the two uses of the word in the present verse span between them the whole range of Paul's thought, from the rich overflow of the *glory* that is God's own being to the vision of a world transfigured by the divine presence. But the centre of the picture is occupied by *Christ*. In his sharing of the divine purpose of love and mercy, in his readiness to be identified with sinful men, to live their life and die their death, and in his rising to be head of the new humanity, Paul finds the brightest jewels in God's treasury of *glory* and the guarantee of his hopes for the future. The *mystery* is *Christ in you* (cp. Rom. 8¹⁰; 2 Cor. 13⁵; Gal. 4¹⁹), and, greatest wonder of all, it is to be proclaimed by Jews *among the Gentiles*. If the indwelling Christ can transcend the deepest social, political, and religious divisions which split mankind, no limits can be set to his ultimate accomplishment.

28. The triple repetition of *every man* emphasizes the universality of the gospel and suggests that somebody in Colossae has been making exclusive claims (cp. 1 John 2²⁰). To become *mature* is not reserved for the elite, but is within the grasp of all. Paul believed in serving God with his intelligence (1 Cor. 14¹⁵), but he also knew from experience that his capacity for apprehending the deepest spiritual truths was at its highest in times of weakness (1 Cor. 2³⁻⁴; 2 Cor. 12⁹), and that the simple can frequently grasp what is hidden from the wise (1 Cor. 1²⁶⁻⁹; cp. Luke 10²¹).

29. Paul himself is the best example of the mystery of the indwelling

Christ. The *toil* is Paul's, but *the energy* is Christ's. He is most himself when least reliant on his own resources (cp. Phil. 2¹²; 2 Cor.12¹⁰). *striving* is one of his many athletic metaphors, which is picked up in the following verse; even prison cannot keep him out of the athletic contest.

1. No other sentence in Paul's letters speaks more eloquently than this of the scope of his affection and interest, not even in his constant references to his wide circle of intimate friends. It was natural that he should be anxious over the churches he had founded (2 Cor. 11²⁸), which had countless guides but only one father (1 Cor. 4¹⁵), and that in moments of stress he should long for the directness of personal contact, when so much may be conveyed by the changing inflections of the voice (Gal. 4²⁰). Twice he tells us that his pastoral care subjected him to unbearable tension (1 Thess. 3¹; 2 Cor. 2¹²⁻¹⁴). Yet, as though he did not have enough worries to occupy him, he must also agonize over those he has never met. The extension of his exertions to *all who have not seen my face* shows that he is not at this point concentrating on the problem reported by Epaphras. This disposes of the conjecture that he mentions *Laodicea* but not Hierapolis because the trouble in Colossae had spread to the one but not yet to the other.

2. *assured understanding* (lit. 'the conviction of understanding'). The RSV has elided the two words, but it is better to keep more closely to the Greek: 'the conviction which comes from understanding.' Paul is praying that the experience of being united in love will give them enough understanding to be the basis of a settled conviction, and that this in turn will lead to a grasp of God's larger purpose. On *knowledge*, see 1⁹.

   Here, as in 1²⁷, the *mystery* is *Christ*, but the emphasis has changed. There it was Christ in you, here God in Christ. The Christ who lives on in the church is himself the embodiment of God's wisdom, and it is that indwelling wisdom which dictates his giving of himself to believers.

3. All the powers and activities formerly attributed to the personified Wisdom of God must now be attributed to Christ. This is another way of saying what has been said at 1¹⁹, that God in his full wisdom has chosen to dwell in him. When Paul says that *the treasures of wisdom* are *hid* in Christ, he does not mean that they are concealed from human understanding. They are there to be seen, but it requires the gift of understanding to see them.

4. The RSV rightly takes *this* to refer to what precedes. Others have thought it to be prospective: 'what I mean is this; let no one . . . ' In that case this verse would become the beginning of the new paragraph. But v. 5 seems to belong with v. 1. *delude . . . beguiling speech.* The Greek words imply a parade of rational ideas made plausible by specious but unsound argument.

5. *with you in spirit.* Cp. 1 Cor. 5$^{3-5}$.

The NEB is probably correct in taking *good order* and *firmness* as military metaphors: 'your orderly array and the firm front which your faith in Christ presents.' Whatever danger there may be at Colossae from sophisticated perversion of the gospel, Paul has confidence in the spiritual defences of the church.

2: 6–15 *An Answer to False Teaching : (a) the Victory of Christ.*

When the Colossians received the Christian missionary tradition about the life and teaching of Jesus, they at the same time received Christ as their Lord and committed themselves to live under his authority. They must remain true to all they were then taught. This is the only protection against the humbug which is being offered to them in the guise of a philosophy, purporting to have immemorial tradition behind it, and at the same time to do justice to the realities of spiritual power in the world. The one thing that matters is to take seriously the supreme reality, that the complete being of God is revealed in Christ, and that in his person the completeness to which Christians are called is already an accomplished fact. What they possess in him does not need to be supplemented from any other source, since all other forms of authority are subordinated to his (vv. 6–10). The unredeemed human nature of the past and the old world order to which it belonged were admittedly governed by powers other than Christ, and Christ had had to submit to them. But in his death he had stripped off the old existence over which they claimed control, and by his resurrection he has entered on a new life in which he holds universal and unqualified sovereignty. Baptism is a symbolic re-enactment of his death and resurrection. In contrast to circumcision with its token surrender of a portion of the body, baptism involves the total surrender of the old sinful personality in order that it may be replaced by the new manhood of Christ (vv. 11–12). The Colossians know from the experience of forgiveness that they have passed from the dead state of their former paganism to new life. The moral law under which they had lived had pronounced a death sentence on their breaches of it, which their own consciences had signed, but God had taken the death warrant and nailed it to the cross of Christ. The spiritual authorities standing behind the moral and criminal law were proved by the crucifixion to misrepresent the will of God which they were supposed to serve, and were thus robbed of their power to thwart God's purpose (vv. 13–15).

6. *received*. The verb παραλαμβάνω and its correlative παραδίδωμι are regularly used by Paul of the receiving and handing on of oral tradition (e.g. 1 Cor. 15³). It is probable that the two words had already become technical terms in the vocabulary of hellenistic Judaism, corresponding to the Hebrew *qibbel* and *masar*, for the handing down of the oral law, which scribal legend traced back to Moses (*Pirke Aboth* i. 1). In all the other Pauline passages they refer to the transmission of the gospel or of an outline of ethical instruction. This normal usage is assumed here, but subordinated to the new idea that what the missionaries had passed on to their converts was *Christ* himself.

7. *rooted and built up*. There is not only the characteristic change of metaphor here (cp. Eph. 3¹⁷), but a change of tense from perfect to present which the RSV has not attempted to reproduce. They have already taken root in the Christian tradition which is Christ himself, and are now in the process of being *built up* in their unity with Christ and consolidated *in the faith*.

8. *makes a prey*. As he opens his attack on the false teachers, Paul uses a rare word which means 'kidnap'. The picture is not of a marauding beast seizing its victim, but of a slave-trader making a raid (cp. Amos 1⁶). The Colossian Christians have been rescued from the tyranny of the old regime and settled in the kingdom of Christ (1¹³), and the danger is that the old ideas under a new guise should catch them off their guard and carry them back to slavery (cp. Gal. 4⁹). Paul has no quarrel with *philosophy* in general, but with a particular system which had dignified itself with this name. If he is suspicious of 'the wisdom of this world', it is not because it is wisdom but because it is worldly (1 Cor. 1²⁰⁻¹). So we should probably print *philosophy* in inverted commas and take the following καί (*and*) as explicative: 'by "*philosophy*" which is really *empty deceit*'. Man-made *tradition* is contrasted with the true tradition of v. 6; so it is not the fact of transmission but the purely human origin that Paul repudiates. The same phrase was used by Jesus in his criticism of the Pharisees (Mark 7⁷), where the point is that they are content to learn rules by rote without any real knowledge of the God from whom those rules purport to come. It is possible that Paul is here echoing the teaching of Jesus, of which he had a very full knowledge. But his readers could hardly be expected to pick up so delicate a cross-reference, and *human tradition* does not of itself mean 'rules learnt by rote'. It is more likely that the self-styled

'philosophers' had attempted to authenticate their teaching by an appeal to its antiquity.

the elemental spirits of the universe is the most probable meaning of τὰ στοιχεῖα τοῦ κόσμου, and it has the support of the majority of modern scholars; but it is not the only possible translation, nor is it wholly free from difficulty. Στοιχεῖον is derived from a verb which means 'to be in line' (cp. Phil. 3¹⁶), and its basic meaning is 'a member of a series', 'component', 'element'. It is used of the letters of the alphabet, the elements of the physical world, the fundamental principles of logic, mathematics, etc., and of the heavenly bodies, particularly those which constitute a series, such as the zodiacal signs or the seven planets. The question to be decided here and in Gal. 4³·⁹ is whether Paul is talking about something elementary or something elemental, about 'the elementary instruction belonging to this (materialistic) world' or 'the elemental powers which control the present world order'. In favour of 'elementary' it has been argued: that the context has to do with instruction (*human tradition*); that of the rules mentioned in the sequel only those relating to the ritual calendar can be obviously linked with the controlling authority of the heavenly powers, yet the στοιχεῖα are more closely associated in the argument with ascetical practices (vv. 20–1); and that this sense is attested in Heb. 5¹², whereas the evidence for the sense 'elemental powers' is all later than the New Testament. The case for the majority view is however much stronger.
(a) The phrase used in AV and RV, 'the rudiments of the world', is linguistically awkward (no proper analogy is provided by 'the wisdom of this world'); and the same awkwardness would attach to the Greek so interpreted.
(b) 'Elementary' in English carries a pejorative tone which is not carried by τὰ στοιχεῖα. The Greek word does not mean 'rudiments' or 'elementary beginnings' but 'the fundamentals'; and it would be hard to apply this sense to the present context.
(c) The contrast between *according to the* στοιχεῖα and *according to Christ* signifies that they are being regarded as rivals to Christ, competing with him for man's allegiance.
(d) The parallel passage in Galatians leaves little doubt that there Paul thinks of the στοιχεῖα as personal beings, identifiable on the one hand with the angelic mediators of the Jewish law and on the other hand with the pagan gods. Jew and Gentile alike have been slaves to the στοιχεῖα. In the case of the Gentiles, this was 'bondage to beings that by nature are no gods'. But if, after becoming Christians, they insist on obedience to the Jewish law or any part of it, they are turning back again 'to the weak and beggarly elemental spirits whose slaves you want to be once more.' Incidentally, this passage proves that this term was not adopted by Paul for polemical purposes from the vocabulary of the Colossian opponents. The conclusion to be drawn from all

this is that, notwithstanding the lack of attestation from writings earlier than the New Testament, στοιχεῖα was already being used in the religious syncretism of the first century, in which astrology played so important a part, to denote the astral powers which were believed to influence the destiny of mankind. From the earliest period of Old Testament history the Hebrew people had been familiar with the idea that the heavenly bodies were spiritual beings (e.g. Judg. 5[20]), and this was one of the ingredients in the Jewish doctrine of principalities and powers (see on Eph. 1[10]). Thus *elemental spirits* is yet another designation for the heavenly powers enumerated in 1[16] and 2[15]. The Colossian 'philosophy' required men to do homage to these powers and to accept their authority over at least some areas of human behaviour.

9. The general thrust of this verse is clear enough. It repeats 1[19] without its ambiguities. There is no need for men to spread their allegiance among a variety of manifestations of divine authority, since God's nature and purpose are seen complete in Christ. But opinion is still divided on the interpretation of *bodily*. There are four possibilities, each with its enthusiastic supporters:
(a) 'in bodily form', i.e. incarnate;
(b) 'embodied', i.e. in the corporate life of the church;
(c) 'in organic unity', and not diffused throughout a hierarchy of powers;
(d) 'in solid reality'. In spite of the powerful advocacy of Lightfoot and some qualified support from Moule, (a) must be dismissed. In Pauline theology incarnation was not a process of filling but of self-emptying, and Christ's supremacy over the powers comes only with the resurrection; and the present tense of the verb here indicates that Paul is thinking of Christ as he now is. (b) has a superficial attractiveness, but, as Moule points out, it puts far too much weight on to a single adverb and turns it into an obscure anticipation of what is said more fully and clearly in the next verse. (c) fits admirably with the hypothesis that Paul had taken the term *fulness* from the vocabulary of his opponents, but is not wholly dependent on it, since the Colossian 'philosophy', whatever its details, must have treated Christ as one of many heavenly powers through whom the Godhead was mediated to man. Lohmeyer connects *bodily* in this third sense with 'head' in v. 10: 'the only reason why the fulness dwells bodily in him is that he has become head of a body, i.e. Lord of the reconciled universe.' But Paul does not use the word 'body' of the universe, and the *fulness of deity* is something more than the lordship over the universe which it entails.
(d) would be open to the same objections as (a) if we supposed that Paul was combatting some sort of docetic Christology, such as was later associated with Gnosticism. But there is no difficulty if we interpret

this verse in the light of v. 17, where σῶμα ('body') is used to denote the solid reality of the new age in contrast with the shadowy anticipations of it in the legal systems of the age that is past.

10. The *fulness of life* which is God's design for men is precisely that exemplified in Christ, and *in him*, i.e. in union with his representative and inclusive manhood, Christians can be said to possess it already. As personal experience they still have to appropriate it in a lifelong process (1⁹; cp. Eph. 3¹⁹; 4¹⁰), and Paul can be very scornful of those who imagine that the possession of all things in Christ absolves them from the need for continual growth (1 Cor. 4⁸; cp. Phil. 3¹²⁻¹⁴). But there is no fear that the Colossians will misunderstand his realized eschatology in this way. Theirs is the opposite danger of assuming that completeness is beyond their grasp unless their Christian beliefs and practices are supplemented by belief in a variety of spiritual powers and a strict discipline of ritual and ascetic observance. Paul does not deny the existence of these powers, but he insists that all are subordinate to Christ and can therefore add nothing to his authority. The metaphorical use of *head* here in no way justifies the assertion of Lohmeyer and others that Paul thinks of the cosmic powers as a body, organically united under Christ's rule. He holds his supremacy over them by divine appointment, not yet by their recognition (1 Cor. 15²⁴⁻⁵). Only the church is ever described as his body, and only through the church is the cosmos to be brought into unity with him (Eph. 1¹⁰; 3¹⁰).

11–12. All that is required for the development of Paul's theme is found in v. 12. Christ's love for sinful men enabled him so to identify himself with them that he died and rose again as their representative. Where men accept this identification by *faith in the working of God*, i.e. faith that in Christ God himself has been working out his own plan of salvation, they are brought into a vital and effective union with him. This is expressed in the sacrament of *baptism*. The water is the symbol of the divine judgment, and immersion in it is the voluntary acceptance of that death which is God's sentence upon sin (Rom. 6²³). But since Christ died that very same death (Rom. 6¹⁰), baptism is also a symbolic union with him in his death and resurrection (Rom. 6³⁻⁵; 2 Cor. 5¹⁴). The old nature dies, to be replaced by the new manhood of the risen Lord. Thus the baptized person no longer lives in that old order over which the principalities and powers hold sway, nor does he owe them any continuing allegiance. By faith he has accepted a solidarity with Christ which carries with it a share in his supremacy over all other representatives of spiritual authority.

Why then does Paul complicate his argument by the obscure and difficult reference to *circumcision* in v. 11? The commonly agreed answer, and no doubt the correct one, is that the 'philosophers' were insisting on it as the one true initiation. Paul's reply to them is that the true *circumcision* is not literal but metaphorical (*made without hands*), not the removal of flesh from the body, but the surrender of the impenitent heart (cp. Rom. 2^{28-9}; Eph. 2^{11}; Phil. 3^3). But this is only the beginning of our difficulties. Does *the body of flesh* mean 'the physical body' (as in 1^{22}) or 'the sinful, unredeemed nature' (as in v. 18; cp. Eph. 2^3; Phil. 3^3); and does *the circumcision of Christ* mean baptism considered as the Christian equivalent of the Jewish rite, or does it mean Christ's own death regarded as a vicarious circumcision? Literally, of course, *putting off the body of flesh* cannot apply to the living. Accordingly, C. A. A. Scott[10] put forward the theory that v. 11, like v. 10, deals with what happened inclusively in the person of Jesus, and that the transition to what has happened in the individual experience of believers comes at v. 12. The true circumcision of Christians took place when Christ on their behalf underwent the spiritual counterpart of circumcision in stripping off his physical body. This view has the double advantage of giving to *body of flesh* the same significance as it has in 1^{22} and of laying the foundation for a plausible explanation of v. 15. In divesting himself of his body Christ at the same time divested himself of the principalities and powers in control of the world to which that body belonged. To all this, however, there are serious objections, linguistic and theological.

(a) The reference at 1^{22} is determined by the possessive pronoun ('his body of flesh'), but here, in the absence of any possessive pronoun or noun, it goes without saying that *the body of flesh* belongs to the subject of the clause, i.e. believers.

(b) The connexion between v. 11 and v. 12 is closer in the Greek than in the English of the RSV. In the Greek, *buried* is an aorist participle dependent on the main verb *you were circumcised*, and must refer to action prior to or contemporaneous with it. The two verses together speak of the union of believers with Christ in his death, burial, and, resurrection; and logic combines with syntax in demanding that the reference should be the same throughout.

(c) The idea of stripping off the physical body at death is no doubt congenial to some modern conceptions of life after death, but it flatly contradicts Paul's theology of resurrection. Christ did not escape the jurisdiction of the world-rulers by leaving his physical body in their clutches, like the young man escaping from the guards in Gethsemane, nor is this the hope that Paul offers to his converts. His assurance that 'we shall be changed' (1 Cor. 15^{52}), that we shall be 'further clothed, so that what is mortal may be swallowed up in life' (2 Cor. 5^4), that Christ 'will change our lowly body to be like his glorious body' (Phil. 3^{21}), is grounded in the conviction that this had already happened to Christ at his resurrection. What Christians are required to strip off is not their physical bodies, but 'the old nature with its practices' (3^9),

[10]*Christianity according to St. Paul*, p. 36; cp. J. A. T. Robinson, *The Body*, p. 46.

and this they do at baptism. The sphere in which the world-rulers exercise their authority is not the physical universe, as contrasted with some disembodied, spiritual existence, but the old world order corrupted by sin, as contrasted with the world which God has designed and is bringing into being through the reconciling power of Christ. We return therefore to what, after all, is the natural and straight-forward meaning of these verses. The Colossians are to take no notice of any demand that they should be circumcised. True *circumcision* is not minor physical surgery, but major spiritual surgery, the excision of the old Adam; and this they have undergone in the Christian substitute for *circumcision*, which is *baptism*.

12. It is commonly said that only Colossians and Ephesians speak of Christians as already *raised* with Christ, whereas in the other letters their resurrection remains a hope for the future (e.g. 2 Cor. 4[14]; Phil. 3[11]). The chief evidence for this contention is found in Rom. 6[5]: 'if we have been united with him in a death like his, we shall certainly be united with him in a resurrection like his.' But the future tense can be used of logical as well as chronological relationships (if A is true, then B will also be true); and the context leaves no room for doubt that this is an example of the logical future: if baptism is rightly regarded as a symbolic union with Christ in his death, then it follows that it will also be a symbolic union with him in his resurrection. For how could Christians be expected to 'walk in newness of life' (Rom. 6[4]), to conduct their lives on the assumption that they are 'dead to sin and alive to God in Christ Jesus' (ibid. 6[9]), to behave 'as men who have been brought from death to life' (ibid. 6[13]), if baptism had in fact left them dead and buried, with no hope of resurrection before the last trumpet? In all three letters union with Christ in death and resurrection is an objective reality offered and accepted in baptism, with consequences to be worked out in Christian experience and behaviour, and with an assurance of ultimate confirmation in the redemption of the body.

13-15. The RSV has assumed that *God* is the subject throughout, and this is probably correct. But no subject is expressed in the Greek, and it has been held that Christ is the subject of all or some of the verbs.

13. On *dead in trespasses*, see Eph. 2[1]. *the uncircumcision of your flesh* must be understood on two levels at once. They were physically uncircumcised, and Paul could hardly have used such an expression in writing to Gentiles without intending some allusion to this. But this in itself contributed nothing to their spiritual deadness. They were, after all, in the same physical condition now that they had received 'the circumcision of Christ' (v. 11) and God had *made* them *alive together with him*. Physical *uncircumcision* was significant only as a symbol of alienation from God and from his covenant of grace (Eph. 2[11-12]). The circumcised Jew might be morally as uncircumcised as the Gentile, yet his circumcision was still an advantage, because with it he had been

'entrusted with the oracles of God' (Rom. 2^{28}–3^3). The Jewish and Gentile Christians alike (note the change of pronoun from *you* to *us*) had been *forgiven*, but for the Gentile this has been a more remarkable event, in that it had come to him unheralded. The connexion between new life and forgiveness is an important one. Whether a man is morally and spiritually dead or alive depends on his relationship with God, the one source of life; and the relationship, once severed by sin, can be restored only by forgiveness (cp. 1^4).

14. A *bond* ($\chi\epsilon\iota\rho\delta\gamma\rho\alpha\phi\text{o}\nu$) is a promissory note in the hand-writing of the signatory, possibly containing a penalty clause (see e.g. Job 5^3; Philem. 19). The idea is that the Jews had signed a contract to obey the law, and in their case the penalty for breach of contract was death (Deut. 27^{14-26}; 30^{15-20}). Paul assumes that the Gentiles were by conscience committed to a similar obligation to the moral law in so far as they understood it (cp. Rom. 2^{14-15}). Since the obligation had never been discharged, *the bond* remained outstanding *against us*, with a constant threat that the penalty clause should be invoked. The RSV has understood the difficult dative $\tau\text{o}\hat{\iota}\text{s}$ $\delta\delta\gamma\mu\alpha\sigma\iota\nu$ (*with its legal demands*) in the light of the parallel in Eph. 2^{15}. But there the dative is governed by a preposition ($\dot{\epsilon}\nu$), and it is the law itself which is said to be set out in legal regulations, not as here the human undertaking to obey the law. It is better to take the dative phrase with *bond*, which in the Greek it immediately follows, and to translate: 'our undischarged commitment to the decrees of the law, which stood as an accusation against us.' This *bond*, which was in effect a death warrant, signed by the conscience of the accused, God first *cancelled* and then *set aside*, i.e. in a double demonstration of its nullity the document was first erased and then eliminated. When a man was crucified, it was the practice to nail a placard to the cross, stating the charge against him (John 19^{19-20}; Luke 23^{38}; Mark 15^{26}; Matt. 27^{37}). Pilate was responsible for *nailing . . . to the cross* the ostensible charge against Jesus, but over it God nailed the real charge, the comprehensive guilt of mankind. There is a universal quality about the sins which conspired to put Jesus on the cross, in which successive generations have seen the mirror of their own; and also about the forgiveness with which he absorbed all that the world's wickedness could do to himself and to God, and put it out of circulation.

15. The RSV takes God to be the subject of the sentence, and it cannot be denied that the result makes excellent sense. On *principalities and powers*, see note on Eph. 1^{10}. Paul believed that these powers, like their human agents, had acted in good faith in bringing about the crucifixion, but in ignorance of the true purpose of God (1 Cor. 2^{6-8}). The Roman authorities were responsible for the maintenance of public order, to which the activities of Jesus seemed a threat; and the Jewish authorities were charged with the administration of their law,

which they believed to be of divine origin, and which Jesus seemed to undermine. Jesus was sentenced to death as a criminal by the combined action of the highest religion and the best government the world had till then known. By crucifying him who subsequently proved to be God's own Son, the powers showed that they had totally misrepresented God's will. In the cross therefore, which appeared to be the exercise of their authority, God in fact *disarmed* them, stripped them of their authority. In the cross he had *made a public example of them*, exposing them as usurpers who had tried to make their limited authority absolute and had succeeded only in making it demonic. In the cross he had reduced the powers to submission, like a Roman emperor celebrating his victories in the field by leading his conquered enemies in his triumphal procession.

The only question is whether this excellent sense can be got from the Greek. The verb translated *disarmed* is in the middle voice, which properly ought to be reflexive: it is used again at 3⁹, where it means 'to divest oneself', and the corresponding noun has just been used in v. 11 for the 'putting off' of the old nature. There is thus a strong case for saying that the subject must be Christ, who on the cross divested himself either of 'the powers of evil which had clung like a Nessus robe about His humanity' (Lightfoot), or of the fleshly body over which those powers claimed a right (see notes on v. 11). The two objections to this interpretation are that it requires an unwarranted change of subject, and that it involves an intolerable mixture of metaphors. Paul is not wholly averse to mixed metaphors (e.g. Eph. 4¹⁴), but could he really have depicted Christ celebrating a triumph over a cast off suit of clothes? Most commentators have found it easier to believe that he was here using the middle voice with an active meaning, as not infrequently happens in hellenistic Greek; and this view is at least as old as Hilary and Jerome.

2: 16–23 *An Answer to False Teaching: (b) the Irrelevance of Legalism.*

Paul's chief objection to the 'philosophy' did not lie in its intellectual speculations but in its practical consequences, and to these he now turns. Unfortunately this is one of the most obscure paragraphs he ever wrote, containing a number of phrases which have defeated all attempts at elucidation and have reduced the commentator to guesswork. One possible explanation of this obscurity is that Paul from time to time quotes the jargon of those he is criticizing. The general sense however is clear enough. A fastidious clique has adopted a strict regimen, including ascetic rules with regard to eating and drinking and the observance of a ritual calendar, and is taking the rest of the church to task for laxness in these matters (v. 16). This asceticism is the product of an exaggerated and puritanical form of Judaism; and Paul dismisses it, along with the legalistic system from which it springs, as a shadowy anticipation of the solid reality which was to come in Christ. The Colossians must not let themselves be disqualified from running in the Christian race by self-appointed umpires who have the gall to lay down rules of their own about fasting. Such legalism is tantamount to worshipping the angelic mediators and guardians of the law, whatever visionary experiences may be claimed in support of it; and it thus detracts from the sole supremacy of Christ, from which alone the church derives its vitality and unity (vv. 17–19). The death of Christ, in which believers have a participating interest, has already carried them beyond the control of the old order and its presiding authorities, and they ought not to allow their conduct to be dictated from that source. Rules of abstinence are merely human in origin and concern merely transient things. In a sensual world, where the damage done by unrestrained passion is all too obvious, any repressive regime can gain a cheap reputation for spirituality. But, for all its show of sophistication, it is bound to be ineffective against the urges of man's lower nature (vv. 20–3).

16. Colossae was not the only place where Christians had scruples about *food and drink* or about the observance of holy days (cp. Rom. 14^1–15^{13}; 1 Cor. 8–10). Paul himself did not share such scruples and regarded them as a sign of immaturity. In writing to Corinth and Rome he insisted that in such matters everyone must be free to follow his own conviction, with the proviso that 'the strong' (those like himself without scruples) must go out of their way to avoid offending the tender conscience of 'the weak' or scrupulous (Rom. 15^1; 1 Cor. 8^{9-13}). The difference at Colossae was that there the scrupulous were threatening to impose their rigid principles on the rest of the church.

The regulations listed are mainly of Jewish origin, though some allowance must be made for pagan influence. Only the Jews kept the *sabbath*, so it is likely that *festival* and *new moon* also have their primary reference to the Jewish calendar. The levitical code had much to say on *questions of food*, clean and unclean, but not about *drink*. But within

Israel there had always been small groups, such as the Nazirites and the Rechabites, who for religious motives abstained from intoxicants. On the other hand, v. 21 strongly indicates that the restrictions here envisaged went beyond anything required in the Jewish law, and were part of an ascetic programme foreign to the Jewish mentality. Such asceticism usually arises from a dualistic view of life which despises the material world and in particular the human body. It is easy to give the impression that this set of rules was an amalgam of incompatibles, yet to its advocates it must have seemed a coherent system. Paul treats it as an offshoot of Judaism, but it was probably put together by Gentile Christians who looked to the Old Testament to provide the justification for their ascetic principles.

There is an obvious connexion between the principalities and powers and the keeping of holy days. According to Gen. 1^{14-16}, God created the heavenly bodies to regulate the calendar, with sun and moon ruling over day and night. This was a way of saying that the festal year with all its sacrificial rites was based on the laws of nature. One of the quarrels between Qumran and Jerusalem was that Jerusalem persistently adhered to the old lunar year, whereas the covenanters of Qumran held that only a solar calendar was 'God's time'. Along some such lines as these the Colossian clique must have argued that conduct too must be made to conform to nature and its controlling powers.

17. Those who possess *the substance* can dispense with the *shadow*. The RSV translation, *what is to come*, cannot be correct, since, if the fulfilment lay still in the future, the *shadow* would not yet be superseded. It is because the solid reality has come in *Christ* that the old legalism is now seen to be 'a shadow of what was to come' (for this sense of $\mu\epsilon\lambda\lambda\omega$ cp. Rom. 5^{14}; and cp. also Heb. 9^{11} with 10^{1}). The levitical laws of purity offered only a token holiness. The Jewish festal year, with all its priestly and liturgical apparatus, hinting in advance at an atonement it had no power to effect, was but the messianic age casting its shadow before it. The sabbath in particular had long been celebrated as an anticipation of the age to come.

18. *disqualify*. The RSV rightly derives this rare compound verb (cp. the simple form used in 3^{15}) from the word for umpire ($\beta\rho\alpha\beta\epsilon\dot{\nu}s$) and not, as did the AV, from the word for prize ($\beta\rho\alpha\beta\epsilon\hat{\iota}ov$). *insisting on* is a Hebraism, common enough in the Septuagint, but without parallel in the New Testament. The word translated self-abasement (lit. 'humility') is used again in 3^{12} in a list of virtues, where it is translated 'lowliness'. Here it seems to be a technical term for fasting, the normal way in the Old Testament for a man to humble himself before God (e.g. 1 Sam. 7^{6}). Most of the commentators have taken the words *worship of angels* at their face value and have ascribed to the Colossians an elaborate angelology. Lightfoot observes that the phrase is linked to the previous one by the single preposition which governs both and concludes that

'there was an officious parade of humility in selecting these lower beings as intercessors, rather than appealing directly to the throne of grace.' But could Paul have failed to denounce as idolatry any cult which made an open profession of such worship? Another possibility, and a more plausible one, is that 'angel-worship' is Paul's contemptuous dismissal of their practices. In their veneration for the most stringent rules that can be derived from the Old Testament they are really directing their worship to the angels through whom the law was given (Acts 7⁵³; Gal. 3¹⁹; Heb. 2²) and not, as they imagine, to God. Strong confirmation of this view is to be found in Galatians, the only other letter in which Paul uses the expression 'elemental spirits of the world' (see above on 2⁸). In Galatia the opposition had been persuading the churches to proceed beyond Paul's teaching to 'advanced Christianity' by adopting some at least of the provisions of the Jewish law, and there is no reason to suppose that in presenting their case they had mentioned angels or elemental spirits. It is Paul who points out that the Gentile converts had once worshipped the elementals in the guise of pagan gods (not that they were real gods), and that the course they proposed to take would make them slaves again to the same masters as before (Gal. 4³⁻¹⁰).

taking his stand on visions is as good a guess as any at the meaning of three words which have so baffled the commentators that many have resorted to conjectural emendation. The difficulty is that this rendering does not exactly fit any of the attested meanings of the verb. On the other hand, the attested meanings yield no tolerable sense.[11]

The worst feature of any system which puts an emphasis either on rigorous rules or on spiritual experiences is that it engenders too good a conceit of themselves in its devotees (cp. Mark 12³⁸⁻⁹; Luke 11⁴³).They claim a superiority of mind, but in Paul's opinion their pride merely shows that they still have a *sensuous mind* (lit. 'a mind of the flesh'; cp. Rom. 8⁷; 1 Cor. 3¹ᶠᶠ·), a mentality bounded by the horizons of the old, corrupt existence.

19. This verse is closely parallel to Eph. 4¹⁶, yet with one significant difference. There the body is supplied with joints and here it is supplied *through its joints and ligaments*. Those who believe that Paul wrote Colossians but not Ephesians have argued that this is a glaring example of the misunderstanding of the original by the copyist; but

[11]The verb is used: (1) of a god frequenting a sacred spot; (2) of a person setting foot on sacred ground; (3) of a person entering into possession of a property or inheritance, or metaphorically of a historian taking possession of his period (2 Macc. 2³⁰); and (4) of official envoys to an oracle being admitted, after initiatory rites, to the oracular shrine. For an entertaining list of emendations, see Bruce.

the variation cannot credibly be ascribed to incompetence. As Lightfoot points out, it is adequately explained by the different aims of the two letters, the one emphasizing 'the vital connexion with the Head', the other 'the unity in diversity among the members'. Apart from this the two passages are in close agreement. In both the thought develops not so much from anatomical knowledge as from a word-play, basically Hebrew but intelligible in Greek, on the literal and metaphorical senses of *head* (see notes on Eph. 4^{16} and Col. 1^{18}). The literal head of the body is also its ruler, beginning, and source of vitality. This being so, *nourished* is too narrow a translation. The head is not conceived as the source of the body's supply simply because food is ingested through the mouth; we should at least have to add air through the nostrils and light through the eye (Matt. 6^{22}; Luke 11^{34}). The argument is that to put oneself under the rule of authorities other than Christ is to cut oneself off from the one source of supply on which both the unity and the growth of the church depend. The theory of Dibelius and others that *the whole body* here is the universe rather than the church has nothing to commend it (cp. v. 10).

20. It has already been established (vv. 11–12) that Christ's death was a vicarious, corporate death. He died as the representative of all mankind, and therefore in him all mankind died (2 Cor. 5^{14}). Death, in which the world-rulers appeared to assert their control over him, in fact carried him for ever beyond their grasp, and with him in principle all mankind (1 Cor. 2^{6-8}; Rom. 6^9). In baptism the believer accepts this death as a representative event undergone in his name and so makes it his own, committing himself to the affirmation that his old life has come to an end with Christ on the cross. But the corollary to this is that *with Christ* he has *died to the elemental spirits*. The preposition here translated *to* (ἀπό) really means 'from', i.e. 'out of the control of'. The Christian still lives in *the world* which those spiritual forces dominate, but he does not *belong* to it, and is therefore under no obligation to take their orders. Paul is using the word *world* in the sense which we associate with the adjective 'worldly'.

21. The RSV rightly places these rules in quotation marks. Possibly they were actually part of the Colossian manifesto. More probably Paul is ridiculing his opponents by attributing to them a total withdrawal from all worldly contacts: 'Don't handle that, don't taste this, don't touch anything!' If you pursue to its logical conclusion the notion that holiness consists in avoiding contamination, you can only end in avoiding everything.

22. Elsewhere Paul has demonstrated that prohibitions can never produce genuine morality (Rom. $7^{7ff.}$). Here he makes another point, which he couches in two different ways. (a) Rules of asceticism so concentrate the attention on *things which all perish* (cp. 1 Cor. 6^{13}) that they perpetuate man's bondage to the transient world of materialism and

sensuality from which they profess to offer an escape. (b) The rules are merely *human precepts and doctrines*, i.e. inherited customs and traditions slavishly and uncritically adopted from the past. These words are a quotation from Isa. 29[13], where the prophet complains that Israel's religion is not a personal knowledge of God but a set of conventional formulae learned by rote (cp. Mark 7[7]).

23. 'Εθελοθρησκία (*rigour of devotion*) occurs nowhere else in Greek literature, and Moulton and Milligan may well be correct in thinking that Paul has coined the word on the analogy of existing compounds. Whether this is so or not, the stress is not on rigour but on the voluntary nature of the observances, or possibly on the tenacity with which they are maintained. The world always respects *devotion* beyond the line of duty.

The Greek of the last clause is notoriously difficult, but the RSV gives good sense and is much to be preferred to any of the alternatives that have been proposed. The advocates of asceticism insist that it is the only way to check *the indulgence of the flesh*. Paul's reply is that it does not work. Two of his reasons have been given in v. 22, and a third is implied in v. 18. Whatever his opponents may have meant by 'the flesh', for Paul it covered a great deal more than sensuality. The works of the flesh listed in Gal. 5[19-21] include several which we should categorize as sins of the spirit. Arrogance, self-esteem, pride are all characteristics of the fleshly mind, and any code of behaviour which fosters them is a form of self-indulgence.

3: 1-4 *An Answer to False Teaching: (c) the True Source of New Life.*
Christianity offers a more radical and effective solution to man's ethical and spiritual problems than an ascetical legalism. It allows the old human nature, with its unruly passions and bad conscience, to die, nailed to the cross of Christ, so that it may be raised with him to a new life. The new life already exists as an objective reality in the unseen, heavenly realm where Christ now shares his Father's throne, and believers possess it only by that faith which unites them with him. Their acceptance of it at baptism carries with it the obligation to live as citizens of this new world, allowing it a controlling place in their thinking, instead of concentrating on the old life from which they have been rescued (vv. 1–3). In this way their lives will be gradually transformed by a process they themselves cannot observe, until at the coming of Christ they are seen to share the splendour of his new manhood (v. 4).

1–2. In these verses there is a distinction between *things . . . above* and *things . . . on earth* which may readily be misunderstood. Paul is not recommending either an otherwordly religion or a vague spirituality which never comes down to earth (see Eph. 1³; Phil. 3¹⁹). As in the Fourth Gospel, 'above' and 'below', 'heaven' and 'earth', denote two co-existent planes of human life. The *earth* is a synonym for 'the world' (2²⁰) or for 'the dominion of darkness' (1¹³). Heaven, the realm of *the things that are above*, is the kingdom of God's Son into which believers have already been transferred (1¹³; cp. Eph. 2⁴⁻⁶). When the Jews looked forward to God's coming act of deliverance and the establishment of his kingdom, they contrasted 'this age' with 'the age to come' It was one of the distinguishing marks of the gospel that 'the age to come' had arrived with Christ, and, to prove their point from Scripture, evangelists would cite Ps. 110¹, claiming that the Messianic king was now *seated at the right hand of God*. Yet they could not deny that 'this age' still continued to run its course, however confident they might be that its time was running out (1 Cor. 7³¹; 1 John 2¹⁷). They were living in two ages at once. But the idea of two overlapping ages makes havoc of temporal imagery, as the student of New Testament eschatology soon discovers. It was much easier to use spatial imagery and think of themselves as citizens of two worlds (cp. Phil. 3²⁰). Thus to *seek the things that are above* is to give Christ an allegiance which takes precedence over all earthly loyalties. His ends are to be their ends; and it follows that the means by which those ends are attained must be his means.

Set your minds. The present imperative signifies continuing action: 'let your minds dwell on things above' (cp. Phil. 4⁸). Their *minds* are to be filled with ideas inspired by the regnant Christ, their thinking so controlled and determined by his mind (Phil. 2⁵; cp. 1 Cor. 2¹⁶) as to leave no room for the influence of a worldly mentality.

3. The best commentary on this verse is Paul's own exposition of the theme in 2 Cor. 3¹⁸–5¹⁷. His critics in Corinth have used his battered physical condition to undermine his authority, hinting that he could not be a real apostle, since God would take better care of his messengers. Paul's answer is that they are basing their judgment only on what is seen and transient (2 Cor. 4¹⁸). He himself had once judged Christ by that same outward and worldly standard; but since his conversion, when he saw beneath the curse of the law on the condemned criminal the glory of the Son of God, he had never been able to look at any man in the same superficial fashion (ibid. 5¹⁶). The Christian life is a process in which, through constant fellowship with the risen Christ and through the operation of his Spirit, the believer is transformed into his likeness, from one stage of glory to another (ibid. 3¹⁸). But it is a secret process, invisible both to the outsider and to the believer himself, known only to faith. To protect that faith from the

encroachments of pride, which would turn spiritual renewal into a human achievement instead of accepting it as a gift of grace, God has provided that the process should be concealed within an 'earthenware vessel', a perishable body subject to pain and decay (ibid. 4⁷; cp. 12⁷⁻⁹). Those whose eyes are not on the seen and transient, but on the unseen and eternal, can detect beneath the decay of the outer nature an inner life which is being daily renewed (ibid. 4¹⁶⁻¹⁸). It is this *life* which is here said to be *hid with Christ in God*. There is perhaps also an echo of 2³: like the treasures of God's wisdom, God's master plan for the world, the hidden life is hidden in Christ; and the words *in God* are an added reassurance that this life is secure 'beyond the reach of harm', without the need for the spurious guarantees of a do-it-yourself-kit philosophy.

4. For greater emphasis Paul repeats what he has just said in a new form (cp. the variation of a theme in Rom. 8⁹⁻¹⁰). 'Your life' now becomes *our life*, and instead of being 'hid with Christ' it is identified with *Christ* himself (cp. Phil. 1²¹; Gal. 2²⁰). Paul has several words which he uses, singly or in combination, of the final coming of Christ: 'advent' (παρουσία), 'appearing' (ἐπιφάνεια), 'revelation' (ἀποκάλυψις). Here he uses the verb *appears*, as in the parallel passage 2 Cor. 4¹⁰⁻¹¹, to emphasize the point that what will be openly demonstrated at the end is what faith has known all along to exist in hidden form.

3: 5-17 *The Old Life and the New.*

Paul has now completed his refutation of the 'philosophy' current at Colossae. He has paid his opponents a compliment by assuming that they are genuinely concerned with moral standards, but he has reminded them that man's moral needs are too grave to be satisfied by any system of rules which endeavours merely to regulate the old life and control its unruly impulses. In their baptism Christians have accepted a more radical creed, that the old life has been put to death, nailed to the cross of Christ, and that they have been admitted to the new life of the risen Lord. But if this faith is to be credible their outward, visible conduct must conform to the realities of the new life of faith. The old life is dead; they must let it die. The indicative of faith must be matched by the imperative of ethics. This shift from indicative to imperative is characteristic of Paul (cp. Rom. 12¹; Eph. 4¹⁷) and is not to be explained by any appeal to the familiar tension between the ideal and the actual. To Paul the union of the believer with his Lord was the supreme reality, but it was a reality of status, not yet fully worked out in experience. Believers were like immigrants to a new country, not yet completely habituated to its ways of life. They had accepted citizenship in a new world and must learn to live in it.

The Colossians, then, are to kill off all that remains of the old life, especially all forms of gross and ruthless self-seeking, which draws upon itself a disastrous retribution. Paul does not suggest that such behaviour was to be found among the Colossian Christians, but it was, after all, only a few years since their conduct had been determined by the pagan ethos in which they had lived. Next in importance to the sins characteristic of paganism are the sins of the tongue which threaten the unity of the fellowship. Deceit, disruptive as it is of mutual trust, is incompatible with the life of the renewed humanity, in which there is no place for divisions based on race, privilege, language, culture, or social status, because union with Christ puts all on an equal footing (vv. 5-11).

Christians have discarded the old nature and have adopted instead a new style of dress. They must wear as their new garments the graces suited to their standing as God's chosen people. The distinctive quality of the new life is mutual forbearance and forgiveness, modelled on the example of Christ. The bond which holds all other virtues together and completes them by making them wholesome and attractive is love. The ruling principle of their common life must be that peace which Christ has brought to the whole warring universe, since it is the church's calling to be the place where that peace is most clearly in evidence, nourished by the gospel, by their mutual instruction, and by their common worship (vv. 12-17).

The Epistles of Paul, the Pastoral Epistles, Hebrews, James, and 1 Peter, all contain passages of ethical instruction which have many points in common. They tend to be written in a simpler style than that of the letter in which they are found (e.g. Rom. 12$^{6-21}$; 1 Thess. 4$^{1-12}$; Heb. 13$^{1-9}$), they cover largely the same ground, and they share a small vocabulary of catchwords which serve as a summary of their teaching. Such similarities used to be explained as a product of literary borrowing—later writers had copied from Paul. It is now generally agreed that they are evidence for the existence of a common oral tradition of catechetical teaching in the missionary outreach of the church (see on Eph. 4²⁵ and 5²¹).

5. *Put to death.* By some ironical twist this verb in its Latin form, 'mortify', came in the course of Christian moral theology to be associated with those very ascetical rigours which Paul is here repudiating. He is not advocating mortification of the flesh, but extermination of the old way of life. Rom. 6¹¹ shows that this chiefly calls for a new attitude of mind: 'you must consider yourselves dead to sin.' It is *what is earthly in you* that must die: not the body with its instincts and emotions, but the ignoble habits to which it has been inured. Πλεονεξία is more than *covetousness*; it is the arrogant and ruthless assumption that all other persons and things exist for one's own benefit. It is tantamount to *idolatry*, because it puts self-interest in the place of God.

6. On *the wrath of God*, see note on Eph. 5⁶. The RSV has been inconsistent in translating the same verb as a present tense there ('comes') and as a virtual future here (*is coming*). Paul believed in a future day of retribution, which he calls 'the day of wrath' (Rom. 2⁵) or 'the wrath to come' (1 Thess. 1¹⁰). But he also believed that this ultimate judgment was anticipated in the course of history in a variety of ways. The civil magistrate is 'the servant of God to execute his wrath on the wrongdoer' (Rom. 13⁴). 'God's wrath' had already come upon the Jewish nation in the form of political disaster (1 Thess. 2¹⁶). In a more general fashion 'the wrath of God' is seen in open operation in the moral decline which is the entail of rebellion against God (Rom. 1¹⁸). Probably both here and in Ephesians it is this third manifestation of the *wrath* that is intended, and so the verb should be translated as a true present.

7. On walked, see Eph. 2². The distinction between *walked* and *lived* is that between outward conduct and the established attitudes and sentiments from which such conduct springs.

8. The phrase *from your mouth* belongs with the verb, not just with the last noun in the list; all five vices are forms of intemperate speech.

9–10. *put off . . . put on.* The occasion referred to is baptism. But it is quite gratuitous to evacuate the metaphor of its power by conjecturing that the primitive rite of baptism included a literal change of clothes. The metaphorical use of these verbs is at least as old as Aristophanes (*Eccles.* 288), has its Hebrew parallel in the Old Testament (e.g. Job 29¹⁴; Isa. 61¹⁰), and is found in New Testament contexts which have no relation to baptism (e.g. 1 Cor. 15⁵⁴; 1 Thess. 5⁸). Paul has already said in Gal. 3²⁷ that all who have been baptized into Christ 'have put on Christ'. Here he adds two further points. (1) This new manhood which Christ both represents and communicates is *after the image of its creator*. Though he quotes from Gen. 1²⁷, he is not referring to man's original creation in the image of God. God's purpose of creating man in his own image is not fulfilled in the old, earthbound nature of Adam, but only in *the new nature* of Christ (cp. Eph. 4²⁴). (2) The creation of the new humanity is an ongoing process: it *is* constantly *being renewed*. This is not to say that the Christian, recreated at baptism, is thereafter in constant need of repair, though there may be some truth even in that. It is rather that his transformation is a gradual change 'from one degree of glory to another' (2 Cor. 3¹⁸; cp. 4¹⁶). Moreover, although every man must himself take the active and deliberate step of putting on *the new nature*, it is not the product of his own moral effort, but the creative handiwork of God.

The scope of Paul's thought has been somewhat restricted in the RSV by the use of the word *nature* where the Greek has 'man' (ἄνθρωπος). When we use the word 'man', we may mean an individual or representative human being, or we may mean the human nature he shares with others, his manhood, or we may mean the total human society to which he belongs, humanity, mankind. The RSV rendering has singled out the second of these senses. But whether he is thinking of Adam and the old humanity or of Christ and the new, Paul's mind moves freely from one sense to another without interruption. Thus here the new man is Christ, but Christ seen as the representative of a new manhood and as the embodiment of a new mankind. It is the third sense which provides the transition to the following verse. *renewed in knowledge* also gives the wrong impression. What is intended is that the renewal will lead to ever enhanced capacities for understanding God and his purpose, and this is admirably conveyed by the NEB: 'constantly renewed . . . and brought to know God.'

11. Anyone who is joined to Christ is joined also to all others who have a share in the new humanity. We are not asked to envisage a monochrome society, whose members are devoid of individual qualities, but one in which such differences are no longer grounds for discrimination or division. Cp. Gal. 3²⁸, where the three contrasting pairs include male and female. In neither passage does Paul attempt to cover all the divisions which split ancient society. He is writing from experience of those divisions which he has seen transcended in the fellowship of the church. Both *barbarian* and *Scythian* were pejorative terms used by the Greeks. A *barbarian* was someone who did not speak Greek. In classical times the word was used mostly of the Persians and therefore carried no implication of lack of culture. The nearest English equivalent is 'foreigner'. A *Scythian*, on the other hand, was a wild man from the trackless wildernesses of the north (Aesch. *Prom. Vinct.* 2; Arist. *Acharn.* 704; Jos. *c. Apion* ii. 37). Herodotus devotes a considerable excursus (iv. 1–117) to a description of Scythia, which he locates between the Carpathians and the Don, and of its inhabitants whom he believed to be immigrants from Asia. After the conquests of

Alexander, however, the term came to be used more widely to denote any of the mongol peoples of northern Asia.

Christ is all, and in all. One has only to consider the character and career of Paul to see that he was not interested in any mystical absorption into the person of Christ. His concern is with the ethical demands of the Christian faith. Loyalty to Christ as head of the new humanity is to take precedence over all divisive ties.

12. Christians are *God's chosen ones, holy and beloved*. All these terms are Old Testament designations of Israel, and together they constitute a claim that the church is the new people of God. After all that has been said about a new humanity, it might seem an anticlimax to speak instead of a new Israel. But the transition was a natural one for anyone brought up on the Old Testament. In Genesis the call of Abraham is God's answer to the fall of man, and Israel is called into existence in order to fulfil man's destiny.

The graces of the new humanity are those which make for harmony in the common life. *Meekness* (πραΰτης) has been well defined by Moule as 'willingness to make concessions'.

13. Paul is too much of a realist to imagine that the renewal he has been describing will produce faultless men and women. The characteristic of Christians is not that they never do anything wrong, but that they know how to deal with faults and complaints by mutual forbearance and forgiveness.

14. *love* is described as 'the bond of perfectness'. The RSV has taken this to be a Hebraism: 'the perfect bond', *which binds everything together in perfect harmony*. If we take the genitive as an ordinary descriptive genitive, the meaning will be 'the bond which completes' (NEB 'to bind all together and complete the whole'). The point will then be that each virtue, pursued for its own sake, may become one-sided and distorted. Love not only maintains the balance, but brings each of the other virtues to its perfection.

15. *rule*. The RSV has eliminated one of Paul's colourful athletic metaphors: the reference here is to an umpire or arbiter, whose ruling will settle conflicts of motive or principle. Paul would have been the last to say that a Christian must keep out of trouble and do anything for a quiet life; *the peace of Christ* is that which he intends for his church, *the one body*. It is the very nature of their calling to maintain its harmonious welfare.

16. On public worship in the Pauline churches, see Eph. 5¹⁹.

17. Cp. 1 Cor. 10³¹.

3: 18–4: 1 *The Christian Family.*

Paul's treatment of household duties is less full here than in Ephesians, except that slaves receive the same detailed attention, perhaps because the case of Onesimus was uppermost in his mind. The modern readers may feel a sense of disappointment that Paul's lofty ethical principles should prove to be reducible to such humdrum instructions, and may find it hard to square this passage with the sweeping declaration that in Christ 'there is neither slave nor free, there is neither male nor female' (Gal. 3[28]). The mistake is to suppose that Paul is enunciating laws to govern Christian society for all time. Has he not constantly proclaimed himself the enemy of all such unbending legalism? And has he not in the previous paragraph spoken of a constant renewal of the Christian which should lead him into ever deeper appreciation of God's nature and will? Paul is a man of the mid first century advising his contemporaries how best they may apply their new faith to the social conditions of their day, and specifically to the family as they knew it. Jew and Gentile alike assumed that the head of a household would wield an authority which others were bound to obey. Paul does not openly challenge this assumption, but he modifies both the authority and its acceptance by the Christian principle of mutual love and deference, so that both are transformed.

Husbands, fathers, and masters are reminded that they have duties as well as rights, and that they must earn the respect accorded to them. Wives, children, and slaves are taught to ennoble their submission to authority by treating it as part of the service they owe to Christ.

18. Cp. the fuller treatment in Eph. 5[22-33]. Note that the word used for the attitude of wives is different from that used for children: wives are to *be subject*, children to 'obey'; the wife is to respect her husband's position as head of the household, but without any implication of inferiority. It must be remembered too that, although Paul may have a Christian family primarily in mind, some of the wives addressed would be married to pagan husbands, and some husbands to pagan wives (cp. 1 Cor. 7[12-16]; 1 Pet. 3[1-6]).

19. This verse and v. 21 show where Paul's heart lay. The danger of domestic discipline is that it should be *harsh*. Authority must be authoritative without being authoritarian. If a wife is asked to submit, it is to her husband's *love*, not to his tyranny. It is interesting to compare

Paul with Jesus ben Sira, who, in spite of his mellow wisdom, alway sees everything from the point of view of the husband and father (Ecclus. 25–6; 30$^{1-13}$; 42$^{9-14}$).

20. *this pleases the Lord*. The Greek has 'this is pleasing in the Lord', and the RSV has ignored the preposition. 'In the Lord' must have the same force here as at v. 18, i.e. obedience to *parents* is not only pleasing (sc. to God), but is also a Christian duty.

21. Paul is not commonly regarded as an expert in child psychology, but, where Jesus ben Sira cannot see beyond the menace of the spoilt child, Paul is sensitive to the child's need for encouragement. In this he is true to his own memories of the ineffectiveness of a regimen of Don'ts (Rom. 7$^{7ff.}$). But he may also still have in mind the Colossian 'philosophy' and its exasperating rigours.

22–25. Cp. Eph. 6$^{5-8}$. Apart from variations in the order of the phrases, the main differences are:

(a) it is clearer here than in Ephesians that slaves are to serve their masters without being afraid of them, reserving their fear for *the Lord*;

(b) the *reward* they are to receive is here defined as *the inheritance*, i.e. life everlasting in the presence of God;

(c) in Ephesians it is the master who is reminded that God shows *no partiality*, here it is the slave. In the one case, the master is not to think that God is influenced by social position; in the other, the slave is not to trade on the fact that men treat him as an irresponsible chattel. On the dishonesty of slaves, see Philem. 18.

1. Paul has been quite unjustly criticized for not even hinting at a change of system. The church was a tiny minority in a pagan empire, whose policies it had no immediate prospect of influencing. Futhermore, the emancipated slave would not necessarily have been the better off for losing his economic security. It is the more remarkable that this verse contains the ultimate charter of social equality. Before their common *Master* slave and freeman stand on the same footing.

4: 2–6 *Final Instructions.*

The ethical section of the letter closes with some remarks about the attitude of Christians to outsiders. At first sight there seems to be a strange contrast between the passive role assigned to the ordinary Christian enjoying his full liberty and the active task of evangelism which the apostle reserves for himself, even in prison. But the contrast is more apparent than real. For prayer is a watchful readiness for opportunities, just as Paul himself is always looking for an extension of his own restricted efficacy. Time is precious and must be used to give a good impression of the Christian religion. Every word they speak to outsiders must reflect the grace and vitality of the gospel.

2. The command to be *watchful* was a regular theme of the primitive catechism (1 Cor. 16³; Eph. 6¹⁸; 1 Thess. 5⁶; 1 Pet. 5⁸; Rev. 3²⁻³; 16¹⁵), derived from the teaching of Jesus (Mark 13³³⁻⁷; Matt. 24⁴²), and carrying no doubt poignant memories of Gethsemane (Mark 14³⁴,³⁸). In view of the modern tendency to associate this wakefulness with an expectation of an imminent Advent, it is worth noting that not one of these passages makes this connexion, and some of them positively exclude it. The Thessalonians are told to be wakeful and sober, not as men keeping watch through the night for the coming of daylight, but because daylight has already arrived with the coming of Christ, and wakefulness and sobriety befit the perpetual daytime of his presence. In Ephesians the watchfulness is that required of the soldier on active service as a precaution against the activities of the devil (cp. 1 Pet. 5⁸). In the letter to Sardis the threatened coming of Christ is conditional and will happen only if the church fails to stay awake. The watchfulness which the church expected of its members had nothing to do with the Parousia. They knew that Christ would frequently come to them in times and in ways they did not expect, and that they must be alert to respond to his demands. (cp. Matt. 25³⁴⁻⁴⁵).

3. *a door for the word* means an opportunity for effective evangelism. It may be that Paul is asking them to *pray* for his release (cp. Philem. 22). On the other hand, even when he was at liberty, such doors did not open to him automatically (1 Cor. 16⁹; 2 Cor. 2¹²), and he did not consider imprisonment a serious interruption of his missionary work (Phil. 1¹²⁻¹³).

   On *the mystery of Christ*, see Eph. 1⁹; and on this as the cause of Paul's being *in prison*, see Eph. 3¹.

5. Cp. Eph. 5¹⁶. Christians are to have a sense of urgency, but it must not make them insensitive to public opinion: *outsiders* are not to be needlessly offended or antagonized by untimely criticisms of their way of life. The *speech* of Christians must give an attractive impression of

6. the faith they profess. *salt* was used both to preserve food and to make it palatable, and the participle *seasoned* shows that Paul had the second of these functions in mind. The greatest disservice that can be done to the gospel is to make it seem insipid. Moreover, *every one* is to be treated as an end in himself and not subjected to a stock harangue.

4: 7–18 *Messages and Greetings.*

7. *Tychicus* was a native of the province of Asia and had been chosen as one of the two delegates of the churches of that

province who accompanied Paul on his last visit to Jerusalem (Acts 20⁴), presumably as custodians of the money collected for the church there (Acts 24¹⁷; 1 Cor. 16¹; 2 Cor. 8–9; Rom. 15²⁵⁻⁶). There must have been many occasions when he acted as Paul's emissary (cp. 2 Tim. 4¹²; Tit. 3¹²). We think of Paul as a writer of letters, but his contacts with the churches must have been maintained largely by word of mouth through messengers.

8. *I have sent* is an epistolary aorist, looking at the action from the point of view of the reader. We should say, 'I am sending'. Tychicus was sent from Rome to Colossae *for this very purpose*, i.e. to carry news of Paul and to deliver his letter, but not for that purpose alone. He was the bearer of at least two, perhaps three, other letters: one to Philemon, one to Laodicea (v. 16), and the circular letter which we know as Ephesians (Eph. 6²¹). Paul must mean that he has made a special point of including Colossae in Tychicus's itinerary.

9. For the full story of Onesimus, see the letter to Philemon. This verse, however, contains the important information that he was *one of yourselves*. Since he became a Christian only on meeting Paul (Philem. 10, 16), and was therefore up to that time not yet a member of the Colossian church, this can only mean that he lived, with his master Philemon, in Colossae.

10. *Aristarchus* came from Thessalonica, but had worked with Paul for a time in Asia (Acts 19²⁹). He was another of the church delegates who accompanied Paul to Jerusalem (Acts 20⁴), and two years later we find him again with Paul on his voyage to Rome (Acts 27²). Paul calls him *my fellow prisoner*, but this does not mean that he was now or ever had been in prison with him. The word he uses means 'fellow prisoner-of-war (συναιχμάλωτος). It is an honorific title which he accords to a small group of friends who were Christ's captives like himself (Rom. 16⁷; Philem. 23; cp. 2 Cor. 2⁴), just as others were called fellow soldiers (Phil. 2²⁵; Philem. 2). It is, however, only fair to add that Eusebius thought the term quite appropriate to a literal imprisonment (*H. E.* II. xxii. 1).

Mark. Marcus was a very common name and may have been borne by more than one person of distinction in the early church. But there is a strong presumption that all the instances of the name in the New Testament refer to the same person. This Mark who is *the cousin of Barnabas* is readily identifiable with the John Mark of Acts 12¹², who accompanied Paul and Barnabas on their first missionary journey, and whose subsequent defection at Perga was the reason for the breaking up of the partnership (Acts 12²⁵; 13¹³; 15³⁷⁻⁹). This passage thus (cp. Philem. 24; 2 Tim. 4[11]) establishes a connexion between John Mark and Rome which makes it likely that he is also the Mark of 1 Pet. 5[13]. It is interesting that Mark should require to be identified by his relationship to *Barnabas*, as though Barnabas was a familiar figure to the churches of Asia (cp. 1 Cor. 9[6]). He was a native of Cyprus (Acts 4[36]), and it was to this island that he returned after parting with Paul. We hear no more of his movements, unless perhaps the incident of Gal. 2[11-13] belongs to a later date. We are left to guess by what means the Colossian church has *received instructions* about Mark. There must have been much more communication, even over large distances, than has left a direct trace in our records.

11. For the lack of support from Jewish Christians (*men of the circumcision*), in Rome, see Phil. 1[15-18]. From this verse we can deduce that Luke whose name appears at v. 14, was a Gentile.

12-13. On *Epaphras*, see 1[7]; and on the churches of the Lycus valley, see Introduction, pp. 157-160. E. F. Scott makes the interesting suggestion that the task at which Epaphras had *worked hard* was gathering financial help to repair the damage caused by the earthquake of A.D. 60.

15. *Nympha and the church in her house*. The manuscript evidence is fairly evenly balanced between this and the variant reading, 'Nymphas and the church in his house.' Lightfoot, followed by Moule, argues persuasively in favour of the masculine. Νυμφᾶν would be a normal accusative of a masculine contracted form Νυμφᾶς, while as a feminine it would be a Doric form hardly to be expected in Colossae. It is not clear whether the whole *church* of *Laodicea* met in this *house* or, if not, what was the relation between the house-church and the church as a whole. A similar problem is raised by the church meeting in Philemon's house.

16. It is odd that Paul should send greetings via Colossae to *Laodicea* when he was also writing to Laodicea. The problem is resolved if the letter from Laodicea was Ephesians, a circular letter without personal greetings.

17. *received* seems to imply that *the ministry* had been handed on to *Archippus* by someone else, perhaps Epaphras.

18. For Paul's own signature, cp. 1 Cor. 16[21]; Gal. 6[11]; 2 Thess. 3[17]; Philem. 19.

PHILEMON

INTRODUCTION

1. AUTHORSHIP.

Paul's letter to Philemon bears its own unique stamp of authenticity which few critics have ever wanted to question. Like Colossians, with which it is so intimately related, it was first attested by Marcion, who included it in his Pauline corpus, then by the Muratorian Canon. It was attributed to Paul by Origen (*Hom. in Jer.* xix), Tertullian (*Adv. Marc.* v. 42), and Eusebius (*H. E.* III. xxv). Jerome had to defend it against the attacks of those who in his day considered its theme to be beneath the dignity of an apostle. Today that argument could be used in reverse, since to our way of thinking the letter would surely not have been preserved at all without a strong tradition that it came from the hand of Paul.

2. OCCASION.

The letter is addressed to Philemon, Apphia, Archippus, and the church in your (sing.) house. It is a natural inference from this that the person addressed throughout in the second person singular is the first mentioned, that he is the owner of the slave Onesimus (v. 10), and that Apphia and Archippus are members of his household, his wife and son. Since Onesimus belongs to

Colossae (Col. 4⁹), it follows that his master is a resident of that town, apparently well-to-do, since he has a house large enough to be used as a meeting place and is well known for his benefactions (v. 7). Philemon had been converted by Paul (v. 9), and both he and his son had become Paul's colleagues in missionary work (v. 1), presumably during the three-year period which Paul spent in Ephesus (Acts 20³¹). Archippus now held some sort of office in the church (Col. 4¹⁷), possibly as a replacement for Epaphras during his absence in Rome.

We are not told how the slave Onesimus came to be in Rome, but it is safe to assume from Paul's appeal for him (v. 10) and the references to his past uselessness and wrongdoing (vv. 11, 18) that he was a runaway. The literature and law codes of the ancient world provide ample evidence that wherever there was slavery there were runaway slaves (e.g. 1 Sam. 25¹⁰). The penalties were severe, ranging from death (mandatory in the Code of Hammurabi) to flogging and chains. In Greece and Rome the commonest punishment was branding (Herod. VII. xxxv. 1; Arist. *Av.* 760; Juv. *Sat.* xiv. 24). The chances of successful escape were slight, though somewhat improved by the right of asylum in a religious sanctuary (Eur. *Suppl.* 267; Phil. *de Virt.* 124; cp. Deut. 23¹⁵⁻¹⁶). There were even some men who earned their living as slave-catchers (the Greek playwright Antiphanes wrote a comedy called *The Runaway-catcher*).

Onesimus had apparently robbed his master into the bargain (v. 18). Lightfoot deduces that the theft came first, and that Onesimus had run away to escape the consequences. But he may simply have 'packed up a thing or two' belonging to Philemon to provide for his journey, as the slave Geta proposes to do in Terence's *Phormio* (I. iv. 11–13). He had certainly not been a model servant, but we have no reason to think that he had been a dishonest one before his flight.

Rome might seem a long way from Colossae, yet its cosmopolitan populace offered better cover for the fugitive than anywhere else in the world. Half the population of the capital were slaves, the captives of many campaigns or the victims of kidnapping, piracy, sale of minors, and other forms of slave trade

(Sall. *Catil.* xxxvii. 5; Juv. *Sat.* iii. 62; Tac. *Ann.* xv. 44). We need not attempt to conjecture by what chance Onesimus in Rome fell in with Paul. All we know is that he was converted by him and became his very dear friend. For a time Paul was tempted to keep Onesimus with him to ease the burden of his imprisonment, and to write and tell Philemon that he had done this. But in the end a number of reasons made him decide otherwise. Two of these he mentions in his letter. No man ought to have generosity thrust upon him (v. 14). Divine Providence has been at work to ensure that Philemon's brief loss should be turned into permanent gain (v. 15). It is difficult, however, to believe that these were the only considerations that prompted him. A wrong had been done and a law broken, and restitution must be made. Legally a slave was his master's property, and only Philemon had the right to determine what should be done with him. Since the grim slave revolt of Spartacus in 73–71 B.C. Rome had suffered a neurosis about the growing numbers of her slaves (Tac. Ann. xiv. 45) and was suspicious of any laxity in controlling them. It would have been disastrous both for Paul and for the church if word had got about that he was harbouring a runaway slave.

Paul's letter to Philemon was written to accompany the returning slave and entrusted no doubt to Tychicus, the bearer of the other letter to Colossae (Col. 4[7]). It is an appeal for Onesimus, but we must not exaggerate its tone. There is not a hint that Paul is apprehensive of any of the more brutal forms of retribution. Philemon is a man of Christian character who can be trusted to behave with moderation and clemency. What he needs to be told is that Onesimus is now a Christian also, to be received home as a full member of the brotherhood, a reformed prodigal well able now to live up to his name, which means Profitable.

The comment has often been made that Paul does not ask Philemon to give Onesimus his freedom. 'The word "emancipation" seems to be trembling on his lips, and yet he does not once utter it' (Lightfoot). Some readers have detected an implicit request beneath the confident assertion that Philemon 'will do even more' than he has been asked (v. 21), and have argued that Philemon would not have preserved the letter unless he had acted on it. But the fact is that Paul leaves the matter wholly to Philemon's own judgment. There are, however, three observations to be made in this connexion.

(a) In his letter to the Colossians (3^{11}), as previously in Gal. 3^{28}, Paul had made an unequivocal declaration of principle: none of the causes of division or discrimination which were characteristic of the old world order are to have any place in the new humanity of Christ. Even in 1 Cor. 7^{17-24}, where he is warning the readers against a worldly and anxious preoccupation with status, he remarks in passing that a slave should take the chance of freedom if it is offered.

(b) It was one thing for Christians to behave in the home and in church as though the institution of slavery did not exist. It would have been quite another matter if, by a constant demand for legal emancipation, they had allowed Christianity to be identified in the public mind with the freeing of slaves. Ancient society was economically as dependent on slavery as modern society is on machinery, and anyone proposing its abolition could only be regarded as a seditious fanatic. The Christian liberty of which Paul was the outspoken champion certainly had its social consequences, but it existed only 'in Christ'. Where the Spirit of the Lord was, there and only there was liberty; and such liberty was not to be attained by any superficial changes in the structure of Graeco-Roman social and economic life.

(c) Emancipation could be an act of cruelty. Elderly slaves, for example, were sometimes given their freedom because they no longer earned their keep. In a world where slavery provided a large proportion of the labour force, even an able-bodied freeman might find it hard to make a living. The situation was particularly bad in Rome, where most of the free proletariat was on the dole, but to some degree the same conditions must have obtained also in the provinces. Onesimus might have had good reasons for preferring to resume his old position in Philemon's household, once he knew that he would be treated as a full member of the Christian family.

This then is the generally accepted view of the circumstances which called forth Paul's letter. A radically different theory has been advanced by J. Knox (*Philemon among the Letters of Paul*; see also his commentary on Philemon in *The Interpreter's Bible*). He has argued that the letter to Philemon is the 'letter from Laodicea' mentioned in Col. 4¹⁶, since both were written at the same time as Colossians, and it is unlikely that an important letter from Paul would have been lost. Philemon, then, must be resident in Laodicea, and Onesimus, who belongs to Colossae, must be slave to Archippus. The ministry which Archippus is to fulfil is the release of Onesimus in order that he may rejoin Paul to work as an evangelist. On to this theory of his own Knox was willing to graft the hypothesis of E. J. Goodspeed that Onesimus was the collector of the Pauline epistles, who wrote Ephesians as an introduction to them, and that he is to be identified with the Onesimus who was bishop of Ephesus when Ignatius wrote his letter to the church there in about A.D. 115 (see Introduction to Ephesians, pp. 25–27).

On critical examination this neat reconstruction falls apart. What is envisaged in Col. 4¹⁶ is the formal exchange of letters by churches in neighbouring towns. But the church addressed in this supposedly Laodicean letter must have been in Colossae, since it met in the house of Archippus, to whom *ex hypothesi* the letter is directed. It would be a very odd way of beginning a letter to place last in a list of three the name of the person for whom it is primarily intended. It is highly improbable that two of the three persons mentioned in connexion with a house church should actually have lived in another town. In fact, the only reason for associating Onesimus with Archippus rather than Philemon is Col. 4¹⁷, where Knox has given a most arbitrary interpretation to the phrase 'the ministry which you have received in the Lord.' For these reasons it is best to return to the traditional view.

Whether Philemon's slave was the Onesimus who subsequently became bishop of Ephesus we have no means of knowing. It is not impossible on grounds of age: if he was twenty when he ran away from Colossae, he would have been seventy-three in A.D. 115. On the other hand, Onesimus was a common name for a slave. What we can say with confidence is that it was Paul's advocacy which made it possible for a man with such a name to rise to a position of authority and leadership in the church.

ANALYSIS

1	**1–3**	Address.
2	**4–7**	Thanksgiving.
3	**8–21**	The Return of Onesimus.
4	**22–25**	Plans and Greetings.

COMMENTARY

1–3 *Address.*

The standard form of greeting which Paul addressed to churches needed only slight modification for use in a private letter. Formally the greeting is from Paul and Timothy to three members of a family and to the church which meets in their house. But once courtesy has been satisfied, the letter is from Paul to Philemon.

1. In a private letter reference to apostleship would be out of place, particularly as Paul has no intention of appealing to the authority of office (see v. 9). Yet *a prisoner for Christ Jesus* is itself a title of honour. The RSV translation obscures the double meaning of the Greek. Not only is Paul in a Roman prison for Christ's sake, he is also Christ's prisoner, and the metaphorical imprisonment is the cause of the literal (see Introduction, p. 1).

Philemon was a name with strong, though not exclusive, associations with Asia Minor. One of the most charming stories in Greek mythology was told of the Phrygian peasants, Philemon and Baucis, who entertained Zeus and Hermes unawares, and were suitably rewarded for their hospitality. Aristophanes refers to a Phrygian bird breeder of the same name; and a century after him there were two writers of comedies by the name of Philemon, father and son from Soli in Cilicia, who enjoyed great popularity in Athens. The name also occurs in inscriptions at Magnesia and Pergamum (see J. H. Moulton and G. Milligan, *The Vocabulary of the Greek Testament*, p. 670).

fellow worker seems to imply not only that he did the same work as Paul, but that at one time he had done so in Paul's company as his partner. As Paul had never visited Colossae (Col. 2¹), this must have been in Ephesus or its immediate neighbourhood.

2. *Apphia*, as Lightfoot has shown, was a peculiarly Phrygian name. Moulton and Milligan (p. 75) add further examples. *Archippus*, like Epaphroditus (Phil. 2²⁵), had in the past shared one of Paul's campaigns, and this no doubt had given him the qualifications for the ministry mentioned in Col. 4¹⁷. The pronoun in *your house* is singular and must refer back to Philemon. This has the effect of including Appia and Archippus in Philemon's household, probably his wife and son. On house churches, see Col. 4¹⁵.

3. Cp. Eph. 1²; Phil. 1². Col. 1² is curiously different.

4–7 *Thanksgiving*.

As in his letters to churches, so here Paul begins with thanksgiving. One reason why he was able to keep so many friendships in constant repair was that he took time to mention his friends individually in his prayers with gratitude for what each had contributed to the life and work of the church. Philemon has been an example to his fellow Christians and their benefactor, and this record encourages Paul to pray for his further growth in Christian insight, and gives him confidence that Philemon will accede to the request he is about to make.

4. *remember*. See note on Eph. 1¹⁶.

5. *I hear*. The present participle probably has an iterative sense: 'I keep hearing'. Col. 1³⁻⁴ suggests that Paul has been in regular communication with Colossae and does not rely only on the recent reports of Epaphras and Onesimus. It is worth noting that, whatever were Onesimus's reasons for leaving home, he seems to have had nothing but good to say to Paul about his master.

Paul does not elsewhere speak of *faith . . . towards . . . the saints* (cp. Eph. 1¹⁵; Col. 1⁴), and it is unlikely that he intends to do so here. Yet in view of the parallels πίστις must mean 'faith', not loyalty. The RSV has complicated the difficulty of the verse by taking the pronoun *your* with the first noun only, though its position in the sentence requires it to be taken with both *love* and *faith*. Lightfoot is probably right in his view that the dominant word in the verse is *love*, and that *faith* is mentioned almost parenthetically as its source.

6. This verse is full of problems. Literally translated it reads: 'in order that your sharing of the faith may become active in the recognition of every good that is in us toward Christ.' The phrase *and I pray* is not in the Greek, but has been inserted by the RSV to make it clear that the clause is syntactically dependent on v. 4, not on v. 5. But is Philemon himself the beneficiary of the prayer or the agent of benefit to others? The phrase which forms the subject of the clause is ambiguous. It can mean (a) 'the sharing of your faith (sc. with others)' (so RSV); or (b) 'your fellowship with us in the common faith' (so NEB). If we adopt (a), Paul is praying for the success of Philemon's pastoral and evangelistic work; if (b), his prayer is for the enrichment of Philemon's spiritual life. Again, does 'every good that is in us' mean 'all the blessings of our common life' (so RSV) or 'all the goodness within our attainment'? Moule has pointed out that, when Paul speaks of the good ($\tau\grave{o}$ $\dot{a}\gamma a\theta\acute{o}\nu$), he usually means something to be done rather than something to be possessed (e.g. v. 14; cp. Rom. 12^2; 13^3; 14^{16}; Gal. 6^{10}; Col. 1^{10}; 1 Thess. 5^{15}). Moreover, the word translated *knowledge* ($\dot{\epsilon}\pi\acute{\iota}\gamma\omega\sigma\iota s$) strictly means 'insight' or 'recognition' (see Col. 1^9). The prayer is, then, not for deeper appreciation of benefits to be enjoyed, but for deeper insight into good to be performed; and it is therefore certainly a prayer for Philemon himself: 'my prayer is that the faith you hold in common with us may express itself in growing insight into all the goodness open to us on the road leading to Christ.' Paul is preparing the way for the request that follows. Onesimus can safely be entrusted to Philemon's moral insight.

7. Paul identifies himself with his fellow Christians, even with those he has never met: *joy and comfort* given to them is also given to him (cp. Rom. 12$^{9-13}$; 2 Cor. 11^{29}). The perfect tense of the verb *refreshed* seems to point to some conspicuous act of generosity rather than to continual kindnesses. Scott makes the interesting conjecture that the occasion for it may have been the earthquake of A.D. 60 (see also Col. 4^{13}).

8–21 *The Return of Onesimus.*

The love for which Philemon is noted now becomes the ground of an appeal, though Paul points out that his rank as apostle and his situation as Christ's prisoner would have entitled him to put the request in the form of an order. The unsatisfactory slave, Onesimus, has been converted by Paul and has become his dear friend. Paul would have liked to keep him and is sure that Philemon would have agreed to let him stay. But generosity ought to be spontaneous, not forced, and Paul does not want to interfere with the workings of Providence. Philemon is to receive Onesimus not as a slave but as a fellow Christian, and give him the same welcome he would have given to Paul. In a solemn note of hand Paul undertakes to make restitution for the slave's peculations—unless of course Philemon is prepared to write them off against his own outstanding debt to Paul. Paul has made Onesimus true to his name ('Profitable'), and in exchange he wants some profit from the master, by seeing him do the right thing by his reformed slave; and Philemon does not need to be told what that is.

8. The phrase translated *I am bold enough* ($\pi\alpha\rho\rho\eta\sigma\acute{\iota}\alpha\nu\ \acute{\epsilon}\chi\omega\nu$) can connote either the freedom with which men speak or their right to speak freely. Here it is the right that is meant. Paul is not suggesting that it takes courage or effrontery to speak with authority to his friend, but that as an apostle he has the right to do so, a right he does not propose to invoke. Moffatt strikes the correct note: 'I would feel free to order you.'

9. Philemon is to be guided in doing the right thing by *love* alone, and *love* may be invited, but not compelled. The usual Greek for *ambassador* is $\pi\rho\epsilon\sigma\beta\epsilon\upsilon\tau\acute{\eta}s$, and all the manuscripts here have $\pi\rho\epsilon\sigma\beta\acute{\upsilon}\tau\eta s$, which properly means 'an old man'. There is, however, ample evidence from manuscripts of other works that the shorter spelling could do service for the longer. The RSV rendering is thus in order. But is it correct? We have to decide whether to take the parenthesis as the somewhat sentimental grounds for Paul's appeal ('I am writing not as an apostle but simply as the aged Paul and a prisoner into the bargain') or as a concessive clause ('though I am none other than Paul, Christ's ambassador and now also his prisoner'). The conclusive point in favour of the second interpretation is that for Paul to be Christ's *prisoner* is high rank, not cause for pity.

10. In the Greek the name *Onesimus* stands last in the verse. This is presumably the first news that Philemon has had of his slave since he ran away, and he might be expected to react to the mention of his name with annoyance, disgust, or contempt. With delicate tact Paul postpones the name until he has established the essential fact that *Onesimus* is now a Christian. The terms *child* and *father* may in this instance express a particularly close relationship, but this was Paul's normal way of referring to his converts (cp. 1 Cor. 4[15]; Gal. 4[19]). It was the fact that he had converted Onesimus during his *imprisonment*, while he was enduring the frustrations of ineffectiveness, that made him feel a special affection for him.

11. Paul's pun on the name tells us a little about the slave's past record. He must have been *useless* before Philemon was deprived of the use of him.

12. *my very heart.* The strength of Paul's affection for Onesimus and of his passionate regret at parting with him may be judged from the fact that at the time of writing he had a large circle of other friends at hand to relieve his imprisonment. Aristarchus, Mark, and Jesus Justus have been a comfort to him. Tychicus is on the point of leaving for Asia Minor, but Epaphras is still there, and so are Demas and his dear friend and doctor, Luke (v. 24; cp. Col. 4$^{7-14}$). Later, when he wrote Philippians, he had no companion but Timothy to whom he could entrust a special mission (Phil. 2^{20}), and yet, although he spoke appreciatively of Epaphroditus, he found it easier to say goodbye to him than he had done to Onesimus.

13–14. *I would have been glad . . . but I preferred.* The RSV misses the change of tense in these two verbs. The first is imperfect, the second aorist: 'I had it in mind . . . but I decided.' Paul is describing the debate which went on in his mind when he was trying to persuade himself that it was right to *keep* Onesimus. If Philemon had been in Rome, he would gladly have offered Paul any service he asked. Philemon was in Rome, in a manner of speaking, in the person of his slave, and would be happy to discharge his obligations by proxy. But Paul was too honest to be deceived by his own sophistry. However sure he might be of Philemon's attitude, to presume on his *goodness* would spoil everything. Philemon would do the generous thing, but everyone would know that he had had no choice. The bloom of grace and spontaneity would have been rubbed off the act.

15. Without in any way condoning Onesimus's misdemeanours, Paul suggests that Providence has arranged a temporary absence as a means to a permanent return. But Philemon could not have his slave *back for ever* if Paul prevented him from coming back at all. Thus Paul represents himself as loth to stand in the way of a divine plan. Knox's theory that Paul was asking for the release of Onesimus for missionary service is somewhat hard to square with this hint that Philemon would never have to part with him again.

16. Paul is not concerned with the legal status of the slave, since this is transcended in the new relationship which makes all Christians equal members in the one family of God. In the New Testament *brother* is almost a synonym for Christian. Paul assumes that his own affection for Onesimus must be exceeded by that of Philemon to whom he really belongs: *both in the flesh and in the Lord* means that Philemon will now find Onesimus intensely lovable, not merely in some spiritual fashion, because he is a Christian, but at the ordinary human level as well.

18. The sentence is hypothetical only in form. Paul knows very well that Onesimus has *wronged* his master and owes him a considerable sum of

money. He must have helped himself to at least enough to pay his way to Rome.

19. Paul dictated his letters to an amanuensis (see Rom. 16²²), and resorted to his own handwriting only for special assurances and greetings (see Col. 4¹⁸). It may be that his writing was too large and sprawling to be economical (Gal. 6¹¹). Here, to show how seriously he takes the matter of Onesimus's debt, he writes a holograph IOU, which would be legally binding, an example of the bond or promissory note which underlies the metaphor of Col. 2¹⁴. Yet, in the midst of this solemn surety, he cannot help putting himself in the place of Philemon, who had been converted by Paul and in this sense owed him his *own self*. Even when Onesimus's defalcations are charged to it, Paul's account with Philemon will not be overdrawn.

20. *I want some benefit*. Paul uses the verb from which the name Onesimus is derived. If Onesimus now lives up to his name and is a *benefit* to his master, Philemon must in fair exchange be a *benefit* to Paul. It is his treatment of Onesimus that will *refresh* Paul's *heart*.

21. The *obedience* Paul expects is not to himself (that he has forborne to ask), but to the gospel of love; *even more than I say* is the nearest he comes to hinting at emancipation.

22–25 *Plans and Greetings.*

His purpose accomplished, Paul brings the letter rapidly to a close with the customary greetings and blessing.

22. If this letter was written some considerable time before Philippians, Paul may have had greater confidence in his release than he shows in Phil. 2²⁴. But here too he may be simply making light of his own and his friends' fears.

23–24. *fellow prisoner*. See Col. 4¹⁰. The names all occur in the final greetings to the Colossians, the one omission being Jesus Justus. Perhaps he had left Rome in the brief interval between the writing of the two letters, or he may simply have been unknown to Philemon.

25. Cp. Phil. 4²³. After consistently addressing Philemon in the singular, Paul finally reverts to the plural *your*.

INDEX

Abbott, T. K., 24, 47, 55, 66, 157
Audet, J. P., 32
Austin, J. L., 66

Barrett, C. K., 69, 78
Barth, K., 108
Baur, F. C., 98
Beare, F. W., 43, 47, 55, 64, 66, 94, 104, 129, 141, 144, 150, 153, 169, 174
Best, E., 180
Bornkamm, G., 27
Bruce, F. F., 199
Burney, C. F., 175, 177

Caird, G. B., 28, 73, 90, 112
Carrington, P., 14, 26, 88
Chadwick, H., 11
Cook, A. B., 24
Cross, F. L., 32
Crouch, J. E., 88

Daube, D., 88
Deissmann, A., 106
Dibelius, M., 174, 200
Dodd, C. H., 26, 47, 104

Fairweather, E. R., 121
Findlay, J. A., 63
Frankel, Z., 162

Glover, T. R., 65, 129, 146, 169
Goodspeed, E. J., 13, 16, 18, 23, 25ff., 90, 140, 157, 217
Guthrie, D., 13, 24

Harrison, P. N., 13, 16f., 23, 28, 157
Higgins, A. J. B., 27
Holtzmann, H. J., 17, 23, 157
Hooker, M. D., 121

Johnson, M. D., 135
Johnston, G., 13

Käsemann, E., 174
Kilpatrick, G. D., 133

Kirby, J. C., 13, 25, 28, 73
Knox, J., 217, 222
Knox, W. L., 120

La Piana, G., 111
Lightfoot, J. B., 49, 99, 111, 116, 117, 120, 158, 162, 165, 168, 176f., 179f., 191, 196, 198, 200, 212, 214f., 219
Lohmeyer, E., 100ff., 122, 142, 174, 185, 191f.

Magie, D., 159
Masson, C., 13, 17, 23, 157, 174
Michael, J. H., 115, 152
Michaelis, W., 23
Mitton, C. L., 13, 18f., 23, 27, 99, 157
Moffatt, J., 13, 108, 116, 221
Moore, A. L., 107
Moule, C. F. D., 15, 120, 131, 168, 191, 207, 212, 220
Münderlein, G., 181

Norden, E., 174

Percy, E., 16, 36, 157

Ramsay, Sir W. M., 97, 159
Rathke, H., 12
Reitzenstein, R., 103
Robinson, J. A., 12, 36, 38, 44, 47, 49, 55f., 76f., 94
Robinson, J. A. T., 193

Schlier, H., 88
Scott, C. A. A., 193
Scott, E. F., 47, 73, 212, 220
Selwyn, E. G., 88, 116
Simpson, E. K., 56

Von Soden, H., 157

Westcott, B. F., 89

Zuntz, G., 10